Old too soon, smart too late

# Old too soon, smart too late

# KIERON DYER

## MY STORY

### with OLIVER HOLT

HEADLINE

*For Kie, Lexi, Kaden and Kody –*
*you are my everything.*

# CONTENTS

# FOREWORD BY CRAIG BELLAMY

As a player, I think I was as close to Kieron as anybody got. He is one of my best friends but he could be very guarded. Full of life one minute, then the next minute it's a struggle to get two words out of him. Some of the things he has written in this book cast some light on the reasons why.

I always had great respect for Kieron as a player and that makes it a lot easier to become friends. It's a good starting point. He might tell you that I always used to tell him he was shit when we were playing on opposite sides early in our career. Well, that may be true. But if I tell you how shit you are, you know I think you're damned good.

Kieron wasn't just good. We had a lot of top players when we were playing together at Newcastle and he was the best of all of us. He would have played at an even higher level had it not been for his injuries. I was blown away by his pace, and he had endurance too: a rare combination in a footballer.

Kieron got his head up so early when he was on the ball, or waiting to receive it, that he saw passes before other players did. He was an exceptionally bright footballer and an excellent passer of the ball, as well as a great provider of goals for others.

We have talked about going into management together, with him as my number two. I'm not sure it would work. I'm not saying we would be Dumb and Dumber but we would be Miserable and More Miserable. We can both get quite intense. I think I'd need someone to lighten the mood. And so would he.

Playing second fiddle to someone isn't in Kieron's nature and I think he will actually go on to be a great success as a coach or a manager, whatever he decides to do. One of the things I've always liked about him is his honesty. It shines through in everything he does and I know it always will.

# FOREWORD BY PETER TAYLOR

Kieron made an old man very happy when he asked me to write this foreword for him. I coached a lot of our most talented young players when I was the caretaker manager of the England team, and the boss of the England Under-21s, and when people ask me who was the best, I always mention Kieron.

He broke into the Under-21s very early for his age; at that time, everyone I knew in the game was raving about him. Everyone who had seen Kieron play told me that this was a lad who was destined for the very top. I think he believed that, too. He believed in his ability.

He had everything you could want in a midfielder. He would run all day, he was a fine short passer of the ball, his movement was terrific, and he could see things other players couldn't see. I knew he loved playing in central midfield and I had no hesitation playing him there for England. He was made for it.

One thing I always liked about Kieron was his confidence as a player.

He wanted to operate in central midfield but in the days when I coached him, he was brave enough to play anywhere I asked him. If I'd asked him to turn out at centre-forward, he would have made a success of that, too.

It is easy to play the 'what if' game, I know, but I am convinced that if Kieron had dedicated himself to the game properly a little earlier in his career and not suffered so much with injuries in what should have been his prime, he would have won more than 100 caps for England.

I think he would have played for Barcelona. I think we would have remembered him as an elite player rather than someone who fell just below that level. I think we would have been mentioning him now in the same breath as Steven Gerrard and Frank Lampard. Kieron really was that good.

## PROLOGUE: THE LOSS

When my playing career finally crawled to its tortured end and I agreed to appear on *I'm a Celebrity . . . Get Me Out of Here!* in the winter of 2015, some bookmakers offered odds on whether I would get injured in a bushtucker trial. Even I laughed at that.

Some people had decided I was best dismissed as a bit of a joke by then. In the dying years of my footballing life, I had been playing in fits and starts, desperately trying to rekindle the talent I still felt was within me. Every time I thought I was close, my body let me down.

I would play a game and then pull a hamstring in the next match, or tear a thigh muscle. I fought my way back and then it happened again. I lived in a state of almost constant embarrassment at my own frailty. In the common mind, I had become little more than a walking groin strain.

I was held up as an example of all that was wrong with modern football; a kid who had been given much too much, much too young and who was more interested in collecting his bulging pay packet and sitting with his feet up on a treatment table than playing the game the fans loved.

I was part of the first generation of English footballers who benefited from the wage explosion that came with that perfect storm of financial opportunity created by the release of the Taylor Report, the Bosman ruling and the formation of the Premier League, and the boom in English football they spawned.

Out of all of us, I was anointed football's 'King of Bling', the poster boy for the Baby Bentley Brigade. In the public mind, I was the epitome of the Golden Generation gone wrong.

More than Steven Gerrard, David Beckham or Paul Scholes, the leaders of England's gifted collection of footballers who populated the national side in the years either side of the turn of the century, I summed up our under-achievement. Forget the Golden Generation. I was seen as the face of a lost generation.

I was the perfect photofit symbol of wasted youth. And yes, there was a time when I, and people like me, felt so intoxicated by our new-found wealth and our rocketing fame that we behaved as if we were above the law and freed from the norms of socially acceptable behaviour that bound other people.

When it came to the scandals that provided the backdrop to that nagging feeling of lost opportunity for England in that period of near misses at major tournaments, of quarter-final defeats and penalty shootout failures, I had a record number of caps: I was always there.

I was there when the Ayia Napa sex tapes were filmed. I was at the Grosvenor House Hotel the night when the orgy that brought 'roasting' into the English language took place. I fought with my own Newcastle United teammate on the pitch at St James' Park; I was part of the high-stakes gambling ring that was a big feature of England get-togethers under

Sven-Göran Eriksson; and I was the dumb kid who crashed his brand-new Ferrari on a bridge crossing the Tyne and wrote it off.

I was closer than anyone to the great Sir Bobby Robson when he was Newcastle manager, but no one outside the club knew that, and I was typecast as the yob who let him down by refusing to play on the right wing before a crucial game against Middlesbrough.

I did let him down. I know that and I wish to God that I hadn't. There was context to what I did, but that context got lost in the idea that I had mocked the grand old man of the game, and when he was sacked soon afterwards, I was racked with guilt about it.

Some years later, I was at a pre-season game with West Ham in Malaysia when it was announced that he had died and I stood there during the minute's silence with tears streaming down my face.

Sir Bobby was the best man-manager I ever worked for, but he and I came together at a time when the great patriarchs of the English game were colliding head-on with the power of the new generation of million-aire players and their emboldened agents. The face of the game in this country was changing out of all recognition.

I wish I had known then what I know now. I wish I had had more perspective. I would like to have been a leader in the dressing room. I would like to have provided a voice that warned younger teammates against wasting some of the best playing days of their lives with a party lifestyle. But it's too late for that now.

Maybe it was the secret I dragged around with me that stopped me doing that, or maybe it was just youth. I won't ask for sympathy for kids like me whose paths are paved with gold by Premier League football clubs, but it is not an easy world in which to survive.

I came from a working-class area of Ipswich where prostitutes lingered on the corner at the end of our street, looking for business. One year, I was a kid living in poverty. A couple of years later, I was earning millions of pounds a year.

I wasn't the first who struggled to cope with making that adjustment and I wasn't the last. When I got money, I felt I wanted to make up for all the years I had none. I wanted to buy flash watches and flash cars. I wanted to buy them for my friends, too.

I came from poverty and I have no regrets about the way I spent my money. People can call it flash if they want, but that's not how I ever saw it. I had nothing and I was in a situation where I could have something. I could have dropped dead the next day. Why shouldn't I spend it? Why shouldn't I enjoy my life?

There was so much wealth in the game at that time. We are used to footballers' exorbitant salaries now but back at the end of the twentieth century, when I made my big move to Newcastle United, the levels of cash sloshing around were still intoxicating to us and a cause of suspicion and resentment for many fans.

In that climate, people just made up stories about the way players dealt with cash. I read an article once that stated as fact that I had burned a stack of £50 notes on a night out in Ipswich to show off about how rich I was.

That was someone's weird fantasy, but people still regurgitate it today as if it really happened. There was another story that when I was at Newcastle, I called myself '60 Klicks' because I was earning £60k a week. That was fantasy, too. I lost the plot a bit when I hit the big-time in Newcastle but never to that degree.

But I was there at the start of the gold rush. I was there when English footballers hit the jackpot. With the wages I was on, it felt like I was winning the lottery every week and I wanted to spend some of it and have some fun.

And I had fun. I dated pretty girls, I had a clandestine romance with Cheryl Tweedy from Girls Aloud, I went out every night of the week I could in Newcastle, when club rules allowed it. And in the best years of my career, I got the balance between hedonism and dedication horribly, horribly wrong.

By the time I started living my life more professionally – eating well, rarely going out, dedicating myself to the game – my legs were so full of metal and muscles that were vulnerable to pulls and tearing that I could not play at the same level consistently any more.

Alan Shearer nicknamed me 'Pinhead' during my years at Newcastle. He said I had the tiniest head he had ever seen. So whenever I headed the ball, Shearer would make a noise imitating the sound of air leaking from a ball to pretend I'd popped it. The name got shortened to 'Pin' and after a while everybody called me that. By the time my career was over and I had a collection of pins and screws holding my legs together, it felt especially apt.

When I was at West Ham and my leg was shattered by a tackle in a Carling Cup tie against Bristol Rovers, and the operation to repair it had not been a success, the co-chairman David Gold singled me out as an example of a player who was letting the club down because he was earning exorbitant wages and barely playing.

I laugh when I hear that sort of thing levelled at players now. Daniel Sturridge is the latest one who gets it. There always seems to be innuendo that he's faking it or, more commonly, that he can't really be bothered, or even more commonly, that he hasn't got the heart for the modern game.

Take it from me: that's garbage. I did everything I possibly could to stay fit. In the autumn of my career, when I was the first one in to the training ground every morning and the last one to leave, when I cherished every moment of my football life, I desperately wanted to stay clear of injury but my body couldn't do it.

I was embarrassed about the injuries I kept getting. I felt ashamed. It will be the same with Sturridge, just as I'm sure it was the same with Darren Anderton. Footballers don't want to be injured. They don't want to miss games. It's the last thing they want.

It always seems odd to me that players should be criticised for being injured. It's not their fault. I knew I was letting down the supporters and the managers whose jobs sometimes depended on whether I was going to be able to play for a sustained period of time or not.

There was at least one occasion when I tore a hamstring early in a match and played on until half-time. I was too embarrassed to come off. I was too embarrassed to put my hand up and signal to the bench that I couldn't carry on. Playing on was a kind of torture, but it was way better than the alternative.

I didn't want to hear that familiar groan from the crowd when they realised I was injured yet again. I couldn't bear to feel that mixture of pity and disdain you get from 50,000 people because you've failed to last a game again. And so I played on.

I got good at hiding injuries. Sometimes, I even played quite well with a torn hamstring. I'd make it through to half-time so that I didn't have to hear that collective groan and that ripple of polite applause that I dreaded more than anything and which became the soundtrack to the dog days of my career.

When it came to an end and I gave up the struggle to get fit and stay fit, I signed up for the jungle. I did it mainly because my kids wanted me to do it and I wanted to make them proud. And, yes, I did break down in the rainforest a couple of times, just not in the way the bookmakers had been anticipating.

I cried in the camp. Maybe it was partly the hunger and partly the tensions that come with being confined in a small group for a couple of weeks, but however famished I might have been, that was something I would never have done a few years earlier. The secret I carried with me always stopped me doing that.

It was only at the end of my career at QPR, when Joey Barton introduced me to the late Peter Kay, who had set up the Sporting Chance clinic, that I finally felt able to talk about what had happened and turn away from being the closed, suspicious, distrusting person I had been for all my adult life to that point.

Until those counselling sessions with Peter, I had always pushed people away. If someone new joined a group of friends I was with on a night out, I wouldn't speak to them. I wouldn't trust anyone, because I had made that mistake before and it had cost me.

I was especially tough on my oldest son, because I saw that he was a sensitive, slightly vulnerable kid in the same way I had once been. The poor kid couldn't understand why I was treating him so harshly. I was trying to do it for his own good. It was my way of trying to toughen him up so that I could protect him. I've explained to him now why I acted the way I did, but I wish I could get those years of his childhood back.

I've told my family about my secret now. My sister rushed upstairs to be sick when I started going through it. But at least they know why I sometimes behaved the way I did. I've told my close friends, too. Eventually, I even told my dad.

I can add all that to the list of things I wish I'd done earlier. I know I must have been a nightmare to be around a lot of the time. Uncommunicative, sullen and insular, I shut myself away and shut myself down.

That's the way I was then. I was younger and I still had my secret. I was always quick when I played. I always felt that once I started to run, no one would catch me. But it was only when I let that secret go that I felt free.

# THE MACHETE

Every Sunday, my dad and a big group of his mates used to play football in Christchurch Park. It's a lovely open space, right near the centre of Ipswich, and they'd converge there, often after a big night out at the Caribbean Club, and have a game. If I wasn't playing a match somewhere myself, I'd go down to watch. The events of one particular Sunday, when I was 12 or 13, have stuck with me.

My dad's name is Leroy Charlesworth Dyer. Everybody calls him Charlie. He was well known around Ipswich in those days. People knew not to mess with Charlie Dyer. If I ever got into a row with somebody when I was a teenager and it looked like things might turn nasty, I just mentioned my dad's name. That was always the end of the argument. No one wanted to know after that.

My dad is from Antigua originally. He came over on a boat when he was eight. He wasn't with my mum when I was born. It was an on-off relationship. They got back together when my brother, Mario, and my sister,

Kirsha, were born. Then they separated again. Mario died in childbirth and my sister and I were brought up by my mum.

She worked at Tooks Bakery. That's been demolished now. She also had loads of other jobs to make sure we had what we needed. She works at Tesco now, even though I've told her she doesn't need to. I've told her she can have what she wants, but what she wants is to keep working and be the way she's always been.

My dad didn't have a job. When he lived with us, he'd get up around midday or early afternoon. He got money from the social, or some hustle out on the streets or at the pool table. I might try it on with my mum, but my dad just had to cut his eye at me and I knew to shut up. He never laid a hand on me all his life. He was never strict in that kind of way.

He was one of the tough men. It was Charlie Dyer and Jason Dozzell's brother, Tony Swallow: they were the two. People used to say the name 'Charlie Dyer' around town as a way of intimidating others. The two men struck fear into people.

I used to go up to the Caribbean Club on Woodbridge Road when I was a bit older and I was a footballer, and slam some dominoes down with the older generation. That was their life really. Every day, they were in the Caribbean Club playing dominoes and most nights they would have a Blues, like a West Indian rave. Typically, a Blues would start about 2am and finish seven or eight hours later.

Everyone would go up there and smoke their spliffs and play dominoes. Downstairs, there was a pool table and loads of tables with mats and the dominoes. Upstairs, there were massive speakers that were as tall as the ceilings for when they had their Blues later on.

Sometimes, my dad would be on the door for a Blues. The promoters loved him because he would never let anyone in free. It didn't matter if it was his best mate. He had been given strict instructions and he abided by them. Whoever you are, he is making you pay.

I knew he would have made somebody pay if I told him my secret, too. He would have stabbed the man who did it to me in the heart. He would have killed him within an hour of me telling him about it. Then he would have been in jail for the rest of his life, and I would have had that on my conscience, too. So I never told him. Not for 25 years. Not until a few months ago.

I'd seen the way he could be. I'd seen him that afternoon at Christchurch Park. One of the other things about my dad: he was one hell of a bad loser. He hated losing. He was incredibly competitive, even if it was a kickabout on a patch of grass with a group of blokes who were probably still hung-over or a bit spacey from the night before. It didn't matter to my dad.

I got my sporty genes from my dad. He was very quick. When we had the parents' 100m race at school, he would win it by about 40m. He seemed to be pretty chilled a lot of the time, but when he was playing sport or competing at something, a switch got flicked.

That Sunday in the park, one of his mates, a fella called Dodi, lit up a cigarette during the game. Dodi was on my dad's team and my dad's team was losing. I could see that my dad was starting to get wound up. He told Dodi to put the cigarette out and Dodi told him to shut up.

My dad just went for him and there was a big melee and the rest of the men got in between them and separated them and tried to calm things down. I was watching from 20 or 30 yards away. After a while, I heard my dad say: 'You wait there,' to Dodi. Then he started marching back towards his car in the car park.

Dad got to the car and opened the boot. Everyone was watching him by now. He rummaged around in the boot. He had a big Head holdall in there and he was looking in that. He pulled out a machete. Don't ask me why he had a machete in the boot. Anyway, he pulled it out, closed the boot, turned around and marched towards Dodi.

Dodi realised what was happening fairly quickly. He knew what my dad was like. He knew by then that he had crossed a line. So Dodi started running. Not just running, but sprinting. He was running for his life and my dad was running after him. My dad was faster than him, and Dodi knew my dad was faster than him.

My dad was nearly on him when Dodi saw a teenager on a push bike. He'd found his saviour. He caught up with him and threw him off the bike and jumped on it himself. He was pedalling furiously. My dad was so close to him, but not quite close enough, and eventually Dodi managed to put a bit of distance between them. My dad realised he wasn't going to catch him on the bike and he slowed down and stopped.

I guess I got my speed from my dad. And maybe my love of football, too. It probably helped that I grew up at 19 Dillwyn Street, a house in the middle of a red-brick terrace that stands a few hundred yards from Portman Road. Before they built the flats on the corner, I could see the Ipswich Town sign on the side of the stand.

When I started playing for the club as a teenager, I often walked home with the fans after matches. It wasn't a particularly nice part of town: at night, prostitutes loitered on the corner of Dillwyn Street and Handford Road. We were in the heart of the red light district where several prostitutes became the victims of a serial killer in 2006.

There was a network of relatives around the place that helped to look after me sometimes when my mum was working. In fact, my family was bigger than I realised. I knew I had an elder sister Joanne from a previous relationship of my dad's, but one afternoon I'd come home from school and was watching cartoons in the front room when there was a knock at the door.

I opened it and there was a black man standing there. He asked if my mum was in. I told him she was upstairs, doing some chores. He nodded. 'I'm your brother, Mark,' he said. That was news to me. I didn't know I had an older brother, but it turned out he was another kid from one of my dad's previous liaisons. I acted all blasé about it and went back to watching cartoons.

I did know that I had a younger brother. I was born in December 1978 at Heath Road Hospital in Ipswich and my brother, Mario, was born there in February 1986. My mum, whose name is Jackie, had a normal pregnancy, as far as I know, and there had not been any hint of problems. I was taken round to my auntie Theresa's when my mum went into labour.

But when my dad took me up to the hospital the day after Mario was born, instead of me dashing up to meet him, we pulled up in the car outside and my dad broke the news to me. 'Kieron, your brother passed away last night,' he blurted out.

I didn't really know what to say. I have heard a lot of stories about how the death of a younger sibling can affect an older child very badly. He sees the grief around him and it makes him never want to experience that grief again, and so it affects his ability to form strong relationships with his own kids in later life and with those around him.

That wasn't really the case with me. Maybe it was because I never knew Mario. He was never around and so, to me, it didn't feel as if he had been taken away. I never got a chance to get to know him, so I didn't miss him. I was told he lived for a couple of minutes after he was born and that was it. My parents were heartbroken.

When I got up to the ward where my mum was, she put on a brave face. I could see she was devastated, but she didn't want to upset me and she gave me a big hug and we chatted about other things. I realise now what a monumental effort it must have been for her to appear cheerful for my sake.

I guess that's another of the reasons why it didn't damage me too much. It's not something that ever leaves you, though. When I went on *I'm a Celebrity . . . Get Me Out of Here!* in 2015, I donated my fee to the Jude Brady Foundation, which is a charity that tries to raise awareness of stillbirth and neonatal death.

I got to know Jude's dad, Peter, after we were introduced by DJ Spoony, a mutual friend. I became a patron of the charity, which Peter founded with his wife Lynn after Jude died at birth in 2006. To be able to help them a little bit was one of the reasons I went on the show.

A year after Mario died, my sister Kirsha was born and that helped to ease my mum's pain, I think. I wasn't always close to my sister and there was a long period when we didn't speak or see each other, which is something I still regret.

Kirsha got in with the wrong crowd in Ipswich. I was playing for New-castle by then but my friend, Milo, told me she had a London boyfriend and was getting involved with the wrong people. Not long after that, she was driving a car that I had given her as a present and the police pulled it over, drugs were found in the car and she was given a suspended sentence.

Then a few months later, I got a call from Milo saying that she had fallen in with another bad crowd. I rang up my mum and told her to tell my sister that she needed to sort herself out. My sister denied it all. It's difficult to rein a kid in. They don't listen to you and I suppose I wasn't exactly an example of someone who was living his life right.

Two weeks after that, she got pulled over again. The guy she was with told her to put the drugs in her bra and, like a clown, she did it. So the police searched him and he had nothing on him and then they found the drugs on her. She said the lad had told her to do it and he denied it. They found his fingerprints on the drugs as well so they knew he was lying, but she went to court, and this time they threw the book at her.

So, in 2008 Kirsha was jailed for six years for being part of a conspiracy to supply crack cocaine and heroin. She was 20 when she was jailed and I didn't go to visit her in prison. I was angry because of the pain she caused my mum. It nearly broke my mum. Her hair started falling out with the stress. I was so hurt and mad that it made me turn away from my sister.

Kirsha was sent to Peterborough Prison first of all, then later in her sentence she was moved to somewhere in Kent where the regime was a bit easier. I didn't want to see her. Like I say, I still regret that. I'm incredibly proud of her for the way she has turned her life around now. She works in finance and she lives at home with my mum, which is the way my mum likes it.

I don't think my dad was ever in trouble with the law, despite that episode I witnessed in Christchurch Park. The Caribbean Club has shut down now and so his friends tend to congregate round at his house. You can't smoke in the clubs now anyway, so every weekend they're up at his place, playing dominoes and doing their thing.

That generation of West Indian men, they call my dad Moses. That is his nickname in the Ipswich community. I guess he has mellowed a little bit now. He seems to be regarded with a lot of respect among his friends and associates.

My mum still works at Tesco in town where she does the till and all sorts of things. She's on the early shift and gets into work at 6am. She enjoys it. She likes being self-sufficient and has always worked for a living, and I guess she sees no reason to stop now.

When I give her gifts, she doesn't want to take them and asks me to take them back. She's stubborn. She was embarrassed when I bought her a new house in a nice area on the other side of town. She didn't want to leave Dillwyn Street but eventually, after about 18 months and a lot of persuading, she came round to the idea.

I'll never forget how hard she grafted when I was a kid. She worked so much that we were spoiled. I loved football from quite an early age and she always made sure I had the latest trainers and the best boots. Right from the start, she always supported everything I did in the game.

I was first spotted when I was 10, playing for my primary school. One of my friends was a lad called Paul King, and his dad, Alvin, was a reporter for the *Ipswich Star*. He saw me playing for the school and told Ipswich Town that they ought to send a scout to watch me.

That was the start, really. I was drawn into the Ipswich youth system and quickly identified as a player of promise, even though everyone always seemed to worry that I was too small and too slight. From that point on, we got complimentary tickets for Ipswich home games.

I didn't use them that much but then, when Ipswich were promoted at the end of the 1991–92 season, I became a regular. It wasn't so much that I was a fan of Ipswich back then but that promotion meant that Ipswich became founder members of the Premier League.

I liked Chris Kiwomya, Paul Goddard and Jason Dozzell, but I was desperate to see the Premier League's big stars up close. It was my first glimpse of the football big-time.

## THE POETS' ESTATE

I went round to the house where it happened recently. I had to tell my nan about it. It was just her and my dad. They were the last two left. The last two that I hadn't been able to tell. The last two in my family who didn't know about the secret I'd kept hidden for so long.

I looked around at the area as I drove up there. The streets on the Whitton Estate are mostly named after literary figures like Homer, Coleridge, Kipling. Sometimes, it's labelled the Poets' Estate but there isn't much else poetic about it. Thackeray Road is where I was abused. The name still strikes dread into me.

It was raining as I approached the street where my nan lived. A catering van stood outside one house with a giant pair of rosy red lips painted on the side. 'Lip Smackers', the sign said. In another driveway, there was a Mister Softee ice-cream van abandoned for the winter.

It's strange that: there aren't many things more miserable than an ice-cream van that is locked up and deserted and a long way from sunshine.

All the smiling and all the laughter gone. All the excited faces gone. All the magic and the fun gone. Just a van, looking ugly and sad in the rain.

I stood outside my nan's for a minute or two, leaning on the side of my car, staring at that semi-detached house and looking at the outside wall of the front room on the ground floor. Some Christmas decorations flapped in the wind outside a house across the road even though Christmas was long gone. I knocked on the door, went in and told her what had happened.

My mum worked the Friday night shift at Tooks Bakery on the Old Norwich Road when I was a kid. So every Friday evening, I went up to my nan's on Thackeray Road after school, stayed the night with her and went home on the Saturday morning.

My nan had separated from my granddad but she didn't live alone. She shared the house with her brother, my great-uncle Kenny, and with her son, Kieron, who we all called Dooey. Dooey had a girlfriend called Rachel around that time, when I was 11 or 12, and the two of them were inseparable.

Maybe these days, when everyone seems so attuned to the dangers of abuse, particularly within families, the alarm bells would have been ringing about Kenny. It wasn't just that he was a single man in his fifties, who had never had a partner and was still living with his sister. There was more to it.

I know now that there had been complaints about him in the past. Somebody had even told one of my relatives to make sure Kenny stayed away from an area called the Grove, a green space near the estate where kids played and hung out after school. He had been spending so much time there, he was unnerving people.

I didn't know any of that then. Kenny was part of my family. He was my great-uncle. It never occurred to me not to trust him. It never occurred to me that I ought to feel wary around him. It never occurred to me that this man was going to blight my life.

I had this thing about denim jeans when I was a kid. I loved the feel of them, and often I'd fall asleep on my mum's lap or my nan's lap when they were wearing them. This particular Friday night, Kenny was wearing jeans and I fell asleep on his lap while I was watching television.

Then I woke up. I woke up but I was scared to open my eyes. Kenny had slipped his hand down my trousers while I was asleep and now he was fondling me. I froze. I was petrified. I didn't know what to do. Kenny must have sensed that I'd woken up, because he started shushing me and trying to reassure me.

'Let me finish what I'm doing,' he said. 'Let me finish and I'll buy you loads of chocolate tomorrow.'

He pulled my trousers all the way down to my ankles and he kept saying that same phrase over and over again: 'Let me finish, let me finish.' I knew he was doing something terribly wrong, but I was frozen. I couldn't move. I couldn't speak. I couldn't do anything. 'Let me finish what I'm doing,' he said again, like he was in some sort of trance.

Then he bent his head down into my lap and started trying to perform oral sex on me. I was still terrified. This was my great-uncle. It was my nan's brother. I knew how fond my nan was of him. I was still frozen. You know when you have one of those nightmares when you can't scream? It was like that.

Eventually, I managed to push him away. I told him to leave me alone. He'd pulled my trousers down and I pulled them back up and backed away from him.

'Don't tell anyone,' he said. 'This is our secret.'

I went out of the room into the hall and there was a telephone there on a table. My mum's number was 2145760. I rang it. I wanted to tell her everything that had just happened. He was still in the living room. He was talking urgently to me in stage whispers.

'You can't tell anyone,' he said. 'You can't tell anyone.'

I heard my mum's number start to ring and then she picked up and I heard her voice at the other end of the line. At that moment, Kenny came out of the front room and stood staring at me. He put his finger to his lips. My mum asked if I was OK and I just asked her if she could come and get me in the morning. She said she would.

I put the phone down. Kenny walked back into the living room. I ran upstairs and went straight into my Uncle Dooey's room and burst into tears. He and Rachel asked what was wrong and I told them Kenny had been touching me.

They tried to console me. 'I promise this will never happen again,' Dooey said. He said I didn't need to tell anyone what had happened. I think that was probably because he was worried that my dad would kill Kenny if he found out. He was right about that. He would have killed him.

With perfect hindsight, people may speculate now that Dooey did the wrong thing by advising me to keep quiet, but I don't agree with them. He was just a kid himself and I feel sorry for him, actually, because he was dragged into the whole affair through no fault of his own. I think he was put into an impossible situation by what had happened to me, and by the secrets and lies within our family. He knew that if the truth came out, it would rip the family apart. I have no doubt he just did what he thought was best.

I did what Dooey said. I did what Kenny said. I didn't tell anyone. I bottled it up. It was my secret. I didn't tell my dad, I didn't tell my mum and I didn't tell my nan. I tried to live life as if nothing had happened. The reality was, that just wasn't possible.

I still went round to my nan's regularly, for a start. I hadn't told my mum so she didn't think to stop me. She didn't know what he had done to me. When I got to my nan's, Kenny was always there. Of course he was always there. He lived there.

I did everything I could to stay as far away from him as possible.

I tried never, ever to be alone with him. But to get out of that house through the back door, you had to walk through the kitchen and when Kenny knew I was going out, he often lingered there.

I would see him and my heart would sink, but he didn't care. He seemed to have become emboldened by what had happened. He probably felt empowered by the fact it was obvious I hadn't told anyone. There hadn't been any repercussions, so he was free to carry on.

As I walked through the kitchen, he'd try to feel me up. He'd try to grab my backside or my crotch. He'd shout and leer. 'Wey-hey,' he'd go as I tried to get past him and he made a lunge at me. I hated it. I really hated it. Any time it looked like I might be alone with him, I was petrified.

So that was how life went on. Every time I had to go and stay at my nan's, I dreaded it. I found it hard to sleep at night wherever I was. I used to creep into my mum's bed and lie at the foot of it because I got night terrors. That was still happening when I was 15. I found it hard to be by myself at night. I worried that Kenny would come back when I was defenceless.

I got a reputation in the family for being a bit of a sissy. They found out I slept in mum's bed sometimes and I got teased for it. If they'd known the truth, it would have been different. But apart from Dooey and Rachel, and Kenny, no one else knew the truth.

I found myself wondering if there were other victims. I found out that one of my relatives came back to my nan's once and gave Kenny a vicious beating. The rest of the family were horrified and dragged him away. It was put down to a drunken assault, but it was more than that. That relative has said since that Kenny had tried to assault him, too.

There is another member of my family who had some behavioural difficulties. He had problems with his speech and stuff like that. I know he stayed at my nan's quite a lot, too. My guess is that Kenny was a sexual predator. It wasn't just me. There must have been others.

I watched with a feeling of dread when so many footballers revealed recently that they had been the victims of sexual abuse when they were playing for their clubs. Their abusers were football coaches, mostly. I was lucky in that way, at least. I never had a problem in football. I was a victim of the most common form of abuser: a family member.

I didn't really sleep properly for two years after it happened. Two years. Two years of thinking about it all the time. Two years of lying awake in bed. Two years of being terrified of what the night might bring. I couldn't get it out of my head, no matter how hard I tried. That was just the start, too. He altered the way I was. He made me suspicious and untrusting. He changed my nature.

Kenny died when I was 21. I went to his funeral. If I hadn't gone, people would have asked why. I sat there at the service, next to all my cousins and they all had tissues. They were crying for him. They were crying for that bastard.

Someone offered me a tissue and I snapped. 'No thanks,' I said, 'I'm not shedding any tears for that prick My nan came up to me and hugged me and said: 'What am I going to do without him?' I felt so sorry for her, but I thought: 'Why are you crying for this c***?' I hated him.

I kept it all bottled up for a long time. I told a couple more people about what had happened. I mentioned it to my cousin, Emma, who I was really close to, and to my best friend, Neville. But that was it.

It was only when Joey Barton joined me at QPR in 2011 and said that anybody who wanted to could go and have a chat with Peter Kay, the counsellor from the Sporting Chance clinic who had done so much to turn Joey's life around, that things changed.

I started talking to him and I said I didn't really know why I was there. I guess that's what a lot of people who want to break free of something start off by saying.

My mum and my ex-partner, the mother of three of my children, had told me they thought I might be depressed because of the string of injuries I'd suffered and the way they had wrecked my career. I told Peter Kay I didn't think I was depressed, but I talked about my mannerisms and my stubbornness and the way I acted around some of my loved ones.

Peter said it sounded to him as if there was something more to it. He asked if I was telling him everything. I thought there was no way I was telling a stranger what happened to me as a kid, but in the end I broke down and the secret I'd kept for 20 years came spilling out.

It was an incredible relief. It allowed me to try and fix the way I was a little bit, too.

The way I was then, when I used to think people were disrespecting me even for the slightest thing, I would say 'f*** you' to show them that they could not take advantage of me.

I developed that 'f*** you' attitude because I didn't have it when I was a kid, alone in that room with Kenny, and I paid a heavy price for not having it. Kenny took advantage of the trusting boy that I once was.

Then there was the way I was around my older son, Kie. My younger son, Kaden, was a bit of a rebel and hard as nails, and I gave him an easy ride. But Kie was a sensitive kid, a bit like I had been, and I sometimes made him suffer for that.

I could be tough with him. I saw so much vulnerability in him, particularly when he was the same age as when I was abused. Every time he showed any weakness or vulnerability, I snapped at him. Deep in my psyche, I was so scared that someone was going to take advantage of him the way they had taken advantage of me, and I wanted him to man up so that could never happen.

Peter Kay made me see all that. I was so stubborn that I was falling out with friends over nothing. If I thought someone disrespected me, I wouldn't speak to them for six months. It happened with my mum, my sister, my best mates, Nev and Leechie. All over petty things. All because I couldn't show vulnerability or weakness. Deep down, it was because someone had taken advantage of me before and I was determined it would never, ever happen again.

Maybe that's why sometimes people talked about the negative body language I had. My nature and mannerisms changed. Maybe that's why, throughout my career, fans said they didn't think I was trying when, actually, I was the one who was running the furthest and trying the hardest. Maybe I was just giving out hostile vibes, even to my own family. Maybe some of the time, I was just acting like a fool.

Here's another thing: I never made eye contact with people when I was talking to them. I always looked away. I looked down or I looked past a person when we were having a conversation. Again, I think that was a trust issue and it was the fact that I felt ashamed of what had happened to me.

I hate that Kenny made me feel like that. How could the man make me feel ashamed when it was him who abused me? And yet he did make me feel ashamed. He did damage me. And his actions ruled my life for 20 years.

My family and a lot of my friends always used to remark about what a grumpy sod I was. They'd laugh about my mood swings. They didn't know what I was dealing with, but when I look back now, I can't really blame them. They just saw the effect, not the cause.

One of my regrets is that my relationship with my cousin, Tiffany, suffered. When we were kids, we were so close we were like brother and sister, but Kenny was like a father-figure to her and she idolised him. I resented and hated her for that and so we drifted apart. We speak now but we have never been as close as we were then. She hadn't done anything wrong but our friendship became another causalty of what Kenny did to me.

Sometimes, when I was having a conversation with someone, I'd just switch off. I'd just stop listening. Understandably, a lot of people found that rude and thought I was making it blindingly obvious that I wasn't interested in what they were saying to me.

But for all those years after what Kenny did to me, it was just a device I'd learned. I'd taught myself how to stop thinking about the abuse. I'd taught myself how to switch my brain off, how to anaesthetise myself, how to try to dull the pain and the shame.

I've improved in a lot of ways in the last few years, but unfortunately, I can't switch that device off. The self-protection mechanism still kicks in. It's like I'm listening but I'm not hearing anything that's being said.

Sometimes, even now, my wife will get to the end of a sentence and say: 'You didn't hear a word I said, did you?' I'll try and bluff it out and she'll ask me to repeat what she said. And then I have to admit defeat.

I did find it very hard to trust anybody. I was OK with people I knew and whom I had spent time with and grown to like. I could be the life and soul of the party then. But if somebody new came into the group, I'd be the last to talk to them and help integrate them. I'd always be watchful.

I was so withdrawn. I never let strangers in. Even people close to me, on some days they couldn't get a sentence out of me. When I was with the mums of my children, I would never give 100 per cent. I always kept something back. When you have trusted someone in your family and they have abused your trust, it damages you. I wasn't the first to find that out.

If friends brought strangers round, I would just go out of the room. People must have thought I was rude, but I would never trust anyone I didn't know. Something that happened to me so early in my life had a destructive effect on me all the way through to my thirties.

I did feel liberated after I had spoken to Peter, though. He said I had to sit down with people close to me and tell them what had happened and explain why I had been behaving that way. I rang Neville and his girlfriend and told them. Every time I told the story, I was inconsolable.

Then it was my ex's parents and her sister. It got a bit easier each time, but I was always in bits by the end. I still well up now when I talk about it.

I suppose the hardest thing was when I called my family together and told them. We all went round to my auntie Carol's: me, my cousin Emma, my auntie Theresa, my mum, my sister and my cousin Letty. When I told them, it was as if pieces of a jigsaw were fitting together. Suddenly, things they had seen and discounted took on a different hue. There were lots of tears. My sister had to run upstairs to the toilet to be sick.

When I think about that day I told them, I wonder how they feel today. They must feel some guilt that they left me and their children alone with that monster. Maybe my aunties feel relieved because, for the most part, they had daughters and he only seemed interested in boys. So they got away with it. They got away without any abuse.

That man has haunted my life for all these years and now all my relatives know what he did. I don't blame them one bit for what happened to me. None of them. It has never crossed my mind to do that. But I wonder if Kenny will now be haunting their lives, too.

For me, it was all a massive relief when I started telling people about it. It was liberating to unburden myself of the secret. It made me feel better about myself, too. When I was acting like an idiot, I thought that was just me. I thought I was a fool. I thought I was a mean, nasty fool.

But now I understood the reasons why I had been acting the way that I had. I knew that snapping at Kie was wrong, and when Peter helped me come to terms with why I had been doing it, it gave me the peace to change the way I behaved.

Kenny blighted 20 years of my life. He took a part of my youth. He affected my relationships and my friendships. His death didn't change that. It was only when I met Peter Kay that I took my life back. I don't even feel that bitter about it any more. I'm just glad that that secret didn't stay hidden for ever.

# THE HARD SCHOOL

## 3

I joined the Ipswich Town youth system when I was 10 and for my first three or four years at the club, I was probably regarded as its best prospect. There were a lot of good players coming through, though. Tes Bramble was in the year below me and he was exceptional. His brother, Titus, followed soon after him. Darren Bent came after that.

When I was 14, everyone else had a growth spurt. Mine never happened. So I went from being the top man every week to playing against the powerful kids that seemed to populate the youth teams of the London clubs and never getting a kick. That was hard to take.

I was lucky that there were people in charge at Ipswich like Tony Dable, the youth development officer, and the academy director, Bryan Klug. They could see how much technical ability I had in training and five-a-sides. Nobody could live with me in those games, but in proper matches I didn't have the power in my legs.

I couldn't get away from anyone and I was being pushed off the ball, but they could see my potential and they kept playing me in the teams. When I was 15, and John Lyall was the first-team manager, Tony Dable told me I would be guaranteed a two-year YTS spot at the club when the time came, which was a huge relief.

We didn't get anything in writing but it seemed clear that Tony had had a conversation with John Lyall and that they had given him the go-ahead to tell me the news. It didn't do an awful lot for my commitment to my school work, but it did take the pressure off me at a time when I was worrying about my size.

Then things went awry, as they have a habit of doing at football clubs. Ipswich were struggling near the bottom of the Premier League and John Lyall resigned. In November 1994, George Burley was appointed boss. He sacked Tony Dable, and so suddenly the verbal agreement I had that I would be given a YTS place counted for nothing.

When it came to the selection day for the awarding of the YTS places, I sat there waiting outside the office belonging to Paul Goddard, the youth-team manager. It soon became apparent the kids who were being given YTS places were the lads who were physically big. They were already playing in the youth team and I was nowhere near the youth team.

I went in for my meeting and they said they had told George Burley that I should be given a YTS place but that he wanted to make his own mind up. I was told nothing was certain and that the decision had been taken to give me a month's trial in the youth team. I didn't think I was ready for the youth team. I thought that was the end of everything. I was devastated. I felt very bitter towards Burley.

The next three youth-team games were Arsenal at home, Chelsea away and Peterborough at home. I had the game of my life against Arsenal, where I played in centre-midfield but Burley didn't see it. I am eternally grateful to Richard Naylor, who was playing alongside me. I was about 5ft tall and weighed six stone. Richard couldn't have been more different, at 6ft 3 and about fifteen stone. He was the hardest lad in the youth team.

I started against Chelsea, too. Burley showed up this time. I played the first 25 minutes and then they brought me off. I feared the worst, but Burley said he had seen enough just in that short time and he wanted to welcome me to the club. That was a huge moment for me. It was the first time I really started to believe I might have a future as a professional footballer.

After that, my last year at school was a waste of time. I went through the motions. I wasn't a bad kid at school, although I suppose I would say that. I was just cheeky. I tested teachers to see how far I could push them. But I wasn't into the academic side of things. Science, in particular, was just an hour of me looking out of the window.

When I started as a first-year YTS at Ipswich, my stature was still an issue. I was still too small. I was given a programme of weights to do and I started getting stronger. And I could run and run and run. In training with the other lads, I used to be miles and miles out in front.

People called me busy for doing that. They thought I was showing off for the coaches. I thought they were jealous. I didn't realise until I got towards the end of my career, and I saw all these busy youth-team players striding out in front, how I must have looked to the senior players. I laughed then at the way I once was.

You might find it hard to believe now but I was totally dedicated to being a professional footballer back then. Because of what happened with my great-uncle Kenny, I was very guarded and I only had three very close mates, Milo Hodge, James Leech and Neville Jackson.

They were my friends throughout my youth and they are my friends now. It was always very hard for me to welcome a stranger into our group, and so the four of us were a tight-knit little posse. I was fortunate that none of them ever smoked or did drugs, so I never had temptation put in my path.

When we came back for pre-season, we did a strength test on legs and biceps and I registered in the top three in the 18-strong youth-team squad. I'd come on a lot. I set myself a target of getting into the youth team but as that 1995–96 season progressed, I was picked more and more frequently for the reserves as well.

I played in several different positions and the first year went really well, except that I blamed myself for our exit from the FA Youth Cup. We'd got to the quarter-finals, where we played Wimbledon at Plough Lane. We were 2–1 up late in the game when I got caught on the ball. I desperately tried to rectify the mistake and chased back but brought the guy down for a penalty. They equalised, the match was drawn 2–2 and Wimbledon won the replay.

It was hard work being an apprentice in those days. It was a far cry from the cosseted existence in warm changing rooms that apprentices enjoy now. Sometimes, it seems they have it so good in the youth set-up at some clubs that it takes the hunger away from them to progress any further. They have the lifestyle way before they make it to the first team.

They are not allowed to clean the boots of the first-team players any more. They don't have to clean the changing rooms or sweep the steps of the stands as the players of my generation did. There is good and bad in that. I think they have it too easy now but, equally, there was much that my generation endured that I would not wish upon them and which is better off out of the game.

On a typical day, I would get into the club at 8am and get home about 6pm. I spent the whole day at the club. I was lucky, because I only lived a few hundred yards from Portman Road. It wasn't like I had a long journey to get in. I didn't have to live in digs like some of the other lads.

It seemed to me that I always got the worst jobs. Six of us would get assigned to doing the home changing rooms and making sure the bath was clean, six would do the away changing room, while a couple of others would be allotted the physio's room and the corridors.

I had to come in and make sure all the youth-team and first-team footballs were pumped up and clean. Then I had to get all the equipment – bibs, balls, cones and discs – to the youth-team and first-team pitches. After training, I had to collect it and bring it back in.

I was also assigned the manager's room, which was a cavernous office, and to make sure that was clean. So George Burley would be running his finger along his desk like some sort of old-school headmaster, checking for dust.

I was on £45-a-week YTS money in those days. I lived at home, but I got £60 digs money as well. My mum let me keep most of it, so I was on about £80 a week. I was lucky in one respect, too: I cleaned Gus Uhlenbeek's boots and he was a good tipper. At Christmas, Gus gave me £200, which I was over the moon about. That seemed like a fortune in those days.

When I started my second-year YTS, my goal was to play in the first team that season. I was in the England Under-18s with Michael Owen, Michael Bridges and Rio Ferdinand and they were all playing for Premier League clubs. Just being in their company on international breaks made me more confident when I went back to Ipswich. I started to believe I could make the step up, if I ever got the chance.

It was around that time that I came across Craig Bellamy for the first time. Craig became my closest friend in football, but he was a motormouth even when he was in the Norwich youth team. He used to strut around the pitch, saying that everyone else was crap. Every time I played against him, I wanted to knock him out.

Later on, when I had broken into the Ipswich first team, Craig and I were both involved in the Ipswich–Norwich derby. I started and he was on the bench. He finally got on for the last five minutes, and as he was waiting to run on to the pitch, I happened to be standing by the touchline.

He glared over at me and said: 'You're shit.' He said it with proper disdain, too. I thought: 'Hang on a minute, I started this game, I've played 20 or 30 times for the first team already and you're coming off the bench and you're calling me shit?'

That kind of dynamic continued even when I moved on from Ipswich. The next time we came up against each other, I was at Newcastle and he was at Coventry City. I had one of the games of my life, scored a wonder goal, and we won 3–1.

As I was celebrating my goal – I'd run from the halfway line, beaten a couple of players and slotted it past the goalkeeper – Craig was standing on the centre spot, waiting to take the restart. He was looking at me, shaking his head. 'You're just a lucky prick,' he said.

I had started getting in the first-team squad quite a lot under Burley, and the truth was that even though it had been my goal at the start of that season, I hated it. There was a lot of master-and-servant rubbish going on.

The younger lads travelled on the coach to away games but had to fetch lunch from the microwave for the established first-team players. We were on our feet most of the time, taking the senior players tea and drinks. On a four-hour round trip, we'd get to sit down for perhaps half an hour.

I'm not asking you to get the violins out but it wasn't exactly great preparation for a game. When we got to the stadium, more often than not we'd be told we weren't even on the bench anyway. I suppose I should have been grateful, but I would rather have been playing for the reserves.

It was a hard school back then. No one was going to make it easy for you. But I was 17 and I was quick and full of running, and when I did well in one particular training session and ran rings around one of the senior players, some of the other experienced lads started making fun of him. I soon wished that they hadn't.

He was a big player at the club, and was one of the major influences in the dressing room. He didn't like being made to look a fool. So after the training session, I went into the first-team changing room to help some of the YTS lads finish their chores so we could get away early and he came in.

He strode over to the centre of the room, naked apart from his slip. I thought there was something odd about the way he was standing, and then I saw that he had started straining. I wondered what the hell was happening. I thought maybe he was about to collapse.

Then piss started dribbling down his leg and he took a big dump in his slip. He took it off and splattered excrement all over the floor. He pointed at me. 'Clean that up, you little shit,' he said. I thought: 'F***ing hell.' That put me in my place. That's how the school was. Put the young lad back down.

After that, any time he came near me, I let him tackle me. If you did that to a youth player today, you'd probably get sacked. I don't imagine it would go down too well with the members of Manchester City's Tunnel Club, for instance, if they were staring down into the changing room and they saw that kind of thing. It might put them off their prawn sandwiches.

Times have changed. I got on well enough with him, but I had made him look foolish and he wasn't having it. It was a tough environment then. Whenever they said I'd be training with the first team, I'd think 'here we go'. I understand why he thought I needed to be brought down a peg or two, but at the same time, I was just playing football. I wasn't trying to humiliate him. I was just playing my normal game.

I also understand why some people mourn the loss of that hierarchical system at football clubs and the idea that young players were somehow taught respect by being treated like that. It appeals to the idea that footballers today are spoilt kids surrounded by yes-men, paper tigers who disintegrate at the first hint of adversity.

I am involved with the Ipswich youth academy and there have been a couple of occasions where I have been about to criticise a lad for something, and I have been warned not to, in case I shatter their confidence because they are so sensitive.

I think back to the abuse I used to get from people like Ian Marshall. Just brutal. It made you feel this big. It was all: 'You c***, what the f*** are you doing here, get me a cup of tea now.'

I believe kids should still do jobs, but I can see why they keep academies away from the first-team players, because the kids wouldn't survive. Things have gone to the other extreme. They are too protected. They are wrapped up in cotton wool.

What happens when they get into the first team at 17 and they cost the team a game with a mistake? They are going to get slaughtered in the dressing room. They are not going to know what's hit them. They will end up crying in the corner somewhere.

But there's a line. If young players are taught to behave like animals by senior professionals, if those are the kinds of actions that are tolerated and encouraged by the system at the time, then why is it any surprise to anyone when young players indulge in excesses of their own?

That's the contradiction. Disciplinarians are advocates of the old school but they fail to see that the kind of example that some of them set has an effect. Not long after that, I was on an England Under-20 trip in Malaysia when things got wild, but I wasn't particularly surprised. It was probably just an extension of what the players on that tour had witnessed at their clubs.

A few days before Christmas that season, most of the youth players were allowed to go home to see their families, but because I lived locally I had to come in and do my duties as normal. I trained well on Christmas Day and then went into the boot room to start cleaning 15 pairs of boots.

I was on my second or third pair when George Burley came in. 'Don't do that,' he said. 'Go home and get plenty of rest.' I was buzzing. We had a game at home to Crystal Palace on Boxing Day and suddenly I thought I might actually have a chance not just of making my debut but also of starting the game.

We were doing OK in what was called Division One in those days. It was the second tier of the game and we had some good players. Richard Wright played in goal, we had James Scowcroft up front and Geraint Williams and Danny Sonner in midfield. We were one of the better teams in the division, and the club had ambitions of making it back to the Premier League that year.

As it turned out, Paul Mason recovered from an injury that Burley had thought would keep him out, so I was on the bench. But a few minutes from the end, on 26 December 1996, I was told to get changed and I ran on to make my professional debut.

I did a bit of a dribble, played someone in for a chance and generally hurtled around like a mad thing until the final whistle went. I walked back home after the game, but I felt a bit different this time. I was a player now. I felt a surge of pride about having played for my home-town club and that pride has never left me.

I made my first start for Ipswich in early January, when I was picked in the side to travel to the City Ground for the FA Cup third round tie against Nottingham Forest. I got the first lucky break of my professional career that day, too, when Burley told us where we were playing.

I had been a bit worried, I have to admit, that I would be playing right-midfield. It wasn't because I felt, as I did later in my career, that it meant I would be banished to the periphery and exiled from the heart of things. It was lot more simple than that. It was because Stuart Pearce was playing left-back for Forest.

I didn't particularly fancy playing against a man with his reputation that early in my career. The guy would have snapped me in half. So when Burley told me I was playing left-midfield, it gave me a huge lift straight-away. We were well beaten, but I had decent game. Bryan Klug came to watch and told me I was our best player, which gave me another boost.

We went on a great run after that. We won six of our first nine league games in 1997 and we didn't lose a game until 15 March, when we were beaten by Bolton Wanderers. Then we won five of our last six matches without conceding a goal and drew the other.

We finished fourth in the end, six points off the second automatic promotion spot, which was secured by Barnsley, but still right in the mix. A few months after the start of my career, I found myself involved in a Division One play-off semi-final against Sheffield United, who had finished fifth, a point behind us.

Burley took me aside before the match and told me I was going to start instead of Paul Mason. Mason wasn't a great defender and Burley knew that I would run all day and block up one side. It was a cautious choice by him, but I wasn't complaining. I played the whole 90 minutes and we drew 1–1. We were confident we'd get through.

The day of the second leg, Burley pulled me into his office and told me that he was recalling Mason. I expected that and I understood it. I didn't have any problems with the selection. We were leading 2–1 with 13 minutes to go but Andy Walker equalised for them to make it 2–2 on the night and the match went into extra-time.

We couldn't force another goal and they won on the away-goals rule.

I was absolutely gutted, not just because we'd missed out on a shot at promotion, but because winning that match would have meant I might have played at Wembley in the final against Crystal Palace.

It was tantalising but it couldn't spoil the excitement I was feeling. My career was just starting. Anything seemed possible.

# 4

## THE BAG

I had a full summer ahead of me in 1997. I wasn't going to get an awful lot of rest, but I didn't want any rest. All I wanted was to play. As soon as we lost the play-off semi-final to Sheffield United, I went straight into hospital to have my tonsils out and then, after a couple of days of recuperation, I joined up with the England squad that was heading out to the Under-20 World Cup in Malaysia.

I had been in or around England youth teams for a few years by then. When I was a kid, it was still called England Schoolboys and they competed with the Under-16 teams of the other Home Nations for a trophy called the Victory Shield every summer. England pulled out of it in 2015, but the rest still contest it. I didn't quite make it into the team.

I got close, though. When I played for my school, I was selected for South Suffolk Schoolboys, and then there were trials for the full Suffolk side and I was successful in those. The Suffolk manager selected his best two players to send to the South of England side and I made that, too. I was down to the last 50, but I didn't make the cut for England Schoolboys.

I was only about 5ft tall when I was 15, and one of the coaches told me and my parents that my size had counted against me. I was disappointed, but I wasn't bitter. I had no complaints. In fact, I thought it was an honour to be considered among the top 50 kids in the country. I wasn't discouraged. It made me want to work even harder.

When I started to get into the first-team squad at Ipswich, I made it through into the England ranks soon enough. I was fortunate that Russell Osman, who was an Ipswich Town legend, was the England Under-18s assistant manager and he came to watch me when we played Bristol City in the FA Youth Cup.

Paul Goddard didn't mention to me that Russell would be there because he didn't want to put me under any pressure, but after the game, Russell took me aside and told me I would be selected for the next England Under-18 game, which was against Scotland at Gigg Lane in February 1997.

When I joined up with that squad, I met Michael Owen for the first time and realised just how ridiculously talented he was. Sometimes, it feels to me now that Michael is damned with faint praise because his career petered out, but he was one of the best players I have ever seen when he was in his teens and early twenties. I was in awe of him.

It was a good squad. Michael was special but people thought John Curtis was the golden boy. He played in central defence at that time and every club wanted to sign him. He ended up going to Manchester United. It never quite worked for him there but he still had a decent career, even if it never hit the heights many thought it would when he was a teenager.

That was my first taste of England representative duty and we beat Scotland 4–1. It was at that game when David Manasseh from Stellar, the football agents, approached my mum and dad and asked them if their son was playing in the game. He asked them if he could come and meet me in Ipswich.

When they told me, I was against it initially because George Burley had drummed it into me that Ipswich was a family club and that there was no need for us to dirty our hands with agents. He said we had no use for an agent because the club would look after us. But my dad said he thought we should hear David out, and so I agreed to meet him.

David came round to our house. He was talking to me about the help he and his partner at Stellar, Jonathan Barnett, could give me and I started to switch off. As I have said, I got quite good at doing that. I didn't really hear much of what he was saying until he mentioned the words 'adidas factory'. My ears pricked up then.

He said that he could get me a boot deal. Not only that but he could organise it for me and my mates to go up to the adidas factory near Stockport and fill my car up with trainers. I didn't need to hear any more after that. I basically said: 'Where do I sign?'

I signed a contract with him and it was probably the best move I ever made. Agents get plenty of criticism, but a lot of that criticism is lazy. It makes me laugh when agents and players are labelled as greedy. No one ever aims that at the clubs. Clubs are businesses run by cold, hard businessmen. They will take a player for everything they can if you let them.

Players aren't negotiators. They aren't businessmen. They are working-class kids who have grafted hard and made sacrifices to get a chance to be a professional footballer. Even if they make it, they won't have a long career, so when they sign a deal, it needs to be the best one they can get.

Sure, Gary Neville never had an agent but he was a sharp kid and his dad was the commercial manager at Bury. His dad had a head for business and he helped Gary and his brother, Phil, when they came to negotiate their deals with Manchester United.

Every player needs independent advice, no matter what Burley and Ipswich chairman David Sheepshanks may have told me. Clubs want to pay players as little as possible. That's how businesses work. A player needs an agent. I got lucky because Stellar are the best agents you can have, and I came to trust David so implicitly that he became one of my best friends.

A couple of months after the Scotland game, I played for the England Under-18s again, this time in a qualifier against Portugal, again at Gigg Lane. We won that 2–1, but I couldn't play in the return leg because I was involved in the play-off semi-final against Sheffield United with Ipswich.

I had been told by then that I was going to be selected for the tournament in Malaysia, which was back then called the Fifa World Youth Championships. I was devastated when Ipswich didn't make it through to the play-off final at Wembley but it did mean that I could go to Malaysia, and I was excited about the strength of the squad we had.

There were some good players in the group we took out to the tournament. Michael Owen was the headline act and a few national newspaper journalists came out to cover our matches just on the strength of the fact that Michael, who had already burst into the Liverpool first team by then, was going to be involved.

Jamie Carragher was in the party, too. He played in central midfield in those days. He was neat and tidy and he had a great football brain. He was one of those players who had so much football intelligence that he looked like he had played about 400 first-team games.

Jason Euell was in the squad, too. Jody Morris, who had broken into the Chelsea side, was one of the leading influences and Danny Murphy, who was just about to seal his move from Crewe Alexandra to Liverpool, was already a fine player. John Curtis was probably more highly rated than any of them.

It is strange to look at that squad list now and see how some players made it and some didn't. It seems so random sometimes. Matthew Upson had a fine career but Jason Crowe, who was a highly regarded defender at Arsenal at the time, never quite became the player so many people expected him to be.

You could probably say the same for Curtis and the Leeds forward, Paul Shepherd. Sometimes it comes down to mental strength, and other times it just comes down to the opportunities you are given at the club where you're playing. But there is real poignancy about looking down lists like that and seeing some whose dreams came true and some whose dreams were broken.

The manager of the England Under-20 team was a guy called Ted Powell. He was a nice bloke. A kind bloke. He was like a lot of the guys who ran the FA youth teams at that time. He reminded me a bit of a schoolteacher. He wasn't necessarily a coaching genius, but he wanted to think the best of you.

I didn't know any of this at the time, but after the tournament I looked up his background. He'd been a top-class amateur player in the 1960s and 1970s, he'd played wing-half for Sutton United and Wycombe, managed both clubs and had won the Under-18 European Championship with England in 1993. He wasn't Johan Cruyff but he wasn't a slouch, either.

The trip to the Far East didn't start off particularly well. We flew out to Singapore to play a couple of warm-up games but soon after we arrived, Nigel Quashie, who was one of our best players, had to fly home. For a lot of us, it was our first time away and Nigel was hit badly by a combination of jet lag and homesickness. He was on the plane back before the tournament began.

When we got to Malaysia, we were based in the southern city of Johor Bahru, where we were to play all of our three group games against Ivory Coast, UAE and Mexico. The hotel was fine, but we were cooped up for most of the day and there was nothing to do. It was very boring.

I know that sort of complaint from young footballers drives a lot of people mad. They say 'read a book' or 'watch a movie' or 'go and experience some of the local culture'. That's all very well, but we weren't encouraged to leave the hotel and we weren't really interested in the local culture anyway.

I'm sorry but that's true. We were kids. We wanted to play football, not tour a local market or visit sites of historical interest. The FA did their best but it was a relief when the games started.

Some of the players struggled with the humidity in the opening game against Ivory Coast, even though it was an evening kick-off. I was a fit lad so it wasn't really a problem for me, but there were stories about some of the boys losing half a stone in weight during that match.

It took Michael Owen all of six minutes to score his first goal of the tournament, and even though Ivory Coast equalised midway through the first half, Paul Shepherd got the winner 20 minutes from time. We had thought that Ivory Coast might smash us in the heat, so it was a tremendous boost to come through it with a victory.

I played left-back in that match and again in the next game against the UAE. We coasted through that, but I did get a glimpse of Michael's lust for goals. We were already 2–0 up when we got a penalty five minutes after half-time. Danny Murphy had scored the first two and he wanted to take it to get his hat-trick. Michael let him in the end, but he was in a real huff about it.

I think he realised that it would look bad if he didn't give it up. He scored himself two minutes later anyway to make it 4–0, and we got another after an hour with an own goal. Michael scored again in the final group game against Mexico to give us a 1–0 win. We had three wins out of three, which set us up with a last 16 tie against Argentina.

There were 17,000 people at the Larkin Stadium that evening in Johor Bahru, but we struggled to match Argentina's quality. They had Juan Román Riquelme and Pablo Aimar in their team and they were too good for us. Riquelme and Aimar put them two-up in the first half, and even though Carra got one back for us early in the second half, we couldn't get an equaliser.

So we went out of the tournament to Argentina, just as the senior team were knocked out by them a year later at the World Cup in France. They deserved to beat us in Malaysia, but their victory raised a couple of questions that still haven't been properly answered by English football 20 years later.

Argentina had Riquelme, Aimar and Esteban Cambiasso in their team, who were already becoming established players for their clubs and world-class talents. Some of our best players, such as Rio Ferdinand, Emile Heskey and Richard Wright, didn't even travel to Malaysia because their clubs were reluctant to release them and the FA didn't want to rock the boat.

We had been very well behaved on the trip up until then. We had been for one night out, with the permission of Ted Powell, but it wasn't a particularly heavy evening. We were all back when we said we'd be back. I was rooming with John Curtis, though, and it was noticeable that both he and Michael decided they'd stay in rather than let their hair down a bit. Michael knew what it took even then.

But on the night after we lost to Argentina, things got messy. Really messy. We all headed for the hotel bar and stayed in there. Journalists who were there have told me stories about some escapades that went on, but I didn't witness them myself so I can't verify them.

I do know that at one stage someone decided it would be funny if we all took a shit in a plastic bag and went to hang it on Ted Powell's bedroom door. Don't ask me why we thought that would be amusing or acceptable in any way, but we did. In that climate, at that age, after a few drinks, it seemed like the funniest idea in the world.

Maybe it was something to do with the culture that existed at a lot of clubs in those days, which I've already described. At Ipswich, it was a senior pro taking a shit in the middle of the dressing room floor and ordering me to clean it up. But there were versions of him at most clubs in those days.

The rest of the young lads in that England Under-20s squad in Malaysia would have had the same experiences I had when they were apprentices. So what they did that night in Malaysia was wrong, but it was also learned behaviour. They were copying established professionals they looked up to. It was the way our culture was in English football back then.

So the plastic bag was passed round from player to player. One by one, someone would disappear with it into the toilet and then emerge and give it to another player. Not everyone did it. I didn't, but I'm not taking any credit for it. I didn't dump in the bag, because I didn't need a dump. Others obviously answered the call.

When everyone who wanted to take a turn had completed their task, one of the players took the bag up to Ted Powell's room and hung it on his door. It wasn't because we didn't like him. It wasn't because there had been any resentment building in the squad. There was nothing like that. Again, we just thought it would be funny.

If you want an example of what's wrong with English football, you've got it right there. If you want to know why we haven't won a major tournament since 1966, just refer to that evening in Malaysia when a group of young England players thought it was a good idea to hang a bag of their own shit on their manager's bedroom door.

A lot of our failings are there in that image of that bag of shit. Think of everything it shows: a lack of respect, a lack of decency, a lack of professionalism, a lack of seriousness, a lack of intelligence, a lack of responsibility, and a football culture that's shot to pieces.

Can you imagine Riquelme or Aimar taking part in something like that? No, you can't. It's not the way their players are brought up, but it was the way we had been brought up. We were doing that to the manager of an England team. It doesn't bear thinking about.

We make fun of authority, we don't respect it. We laugh at authority, we don't learn from it. And when we want to establish supremacy or superiority or make each other laugh, we smear shit on dressing room floors or hang it on hotel room doors.

No one ever said anything about that bag of shit. Ted Powell never mentioned it. There was never any inquest into who had done it or where it had come from. I don't know to this day whether one of the other lads thought better of it and rushed back up to the room to remove the bag before Ted Powell found it. Maybe he found it and chose not to say anything; or maybe a hotel employee found it and took it away.

I got back to my room that night and threw up all over it because I was so drunk. Paul Goddard, who was the assistant manager, had to come round the next morning and drag me out of bed because we were all on an early flight. That must have been nice for him. I had a real stinger of a hangover. I made the flight, but it was a long journey home.

I look back on that episode now and wonder if it was our culture that was holding us back. We didn't see what we'd done as primitive or bestial, so what does that say about our mindset? It says we were used to it. It says we didn't see it as particularly odd or sick. It says we were caught in a vicious circle.

The mindset, generally, could be summed up in two words: f*** it.

We acted the way we did without considering the consequences. And at some point, inevitably, that mindset is going to bleed into performance. Lack of responsibility, lack of respect, lack of independent thinking: it's all there in the failures that have haunted us for so long.

A few months later, there was another controversy when five players – Frank Lampard, Ben Thatcher, Rio Ferdinand, Jamie Carragher and Danny Murphy – were banned from attending the Italy–England World Cup qualifier in Rome after doing something that displeased Peter Taylor, the Under-21s manager, after our match against the Italians in Rieti.

One of the lads thought he had got away with it and was bouncing up and down at the back of the bus, when Taylor marched up and hauled him off as well. The media had a field day with that, but I was never quite sure what they were supposed to have done wrong.

Perhaps it's no coincidence that now the culture's finally changing in English football and apprentices aren't humiliated any more, and the influx of foreign players has altered the atmosphere in our dressing rooms, we've finally won something.

In June 2017, after a gap of 20 years since our trip to Malaysia, the England boys flew out to the East again and won the Under-20 World Cup in South Korea. A few months after that, England's Under-17s won their age-group World Cup in India. It's taken a while but maybe we are finally putting the culture in place that will give us the foundation to become a power in the game again.

# 5

## THE G-MEN

I was excited about being back in Ipswich for the start of the 1997–98 season. It's funny when I think about it now at the end of my career, with everything I know about injuries and pressure and football politics and all the things that can get in the way of you enjoying the game, but at that point those things hadn't crossed my mind.

All I cared about that pre-season was playing football. I loved the game and I was still pinching myself that things were going so well. People talk about the fearlessness of youth and I definitely had that. Things were going beautifully and it didn't occur to me that it would ever be any different. I felt like my football career was going to be one long upward curve.

My experiences in Malaysia had probably exaggerated that feeling. Playing with Premier League stars and holding my own alongside them had done wonders for my confidence, and I thought I could make a big contribution to Ipswich that season by helping the club to go one better than the play-offs and win automatic promotion to the top flight.

I got my first taste of the machinations that can take place in the game soon after the season had started. The club was starting to realise that I could be a decent prospect, and I think they might have had the first hints of interest from other clubs, so I was called into George Burley's office and offered a new contract.

I was embarrassed to tell Burley I had an agent. I listened to him telling me there was no signing-on fee but that the money that they were willing to pay me was the most a kid my age had ever been offered by the club.

He said it was the best they could do and that Ipswich was a family club and that things were tight and there was no more money available. This was still a negotiation and, maybe naively, I believed him. So I shook his hand and walked out of the office.

When I got home, I told my mum the club had offered me a new five-year deal and she asked whether I had mentioned it to David Manasseh. I said I hadn't and so she told me I had to ring him before I signed anything.

Mum got Jonathan Barnett on the phone and he told me not to sign the contract and not to listen to Ipswich. I didn't really want Stellar to get involved at that point. I didn't want to rock the boat.

Jonathan rang up George to say he was my agent and negotiated the deal for me. Hey presto, I was given a much higher wage of about £900 a week and a signing-on fee that was somewhere in the region of £100k. So George Burley had told me it was the best they could do and they could not possibly do more, and then it all changed when an agent rang them.

That was a lesson for me. Burley was fuming with me because I had shaken his hand, but I wasn't too bothered because he had said there was nothing else he could do and that wasn't true.

I was pleased about the money, but it also opened my eyes for the first time to the way employers can act in football. There is so much bullshit with clubs. The public and the press tend to paint players' agents as the enemy, but that's way too simplistic.

There may well be the odd unscrupulous agent, but there are certainly a decent number of unscrupulous clubs, too. Clubs will try to pay players as little as they possibly can. That's just business. And players need to make sure they get the best deal they possibly can. That's business, too. The reality is that a club will try and exploit a player if it can. If you have a good agent, they'll stop that happening.

After I had made my first-team debut, I had been put on a contract worth £300 a week and an extra £500 for every first-team match I played in. By then, I was usually either on the bench or in the team, so that was £800 a week. There was a £300 win bonus, too, so suddenly I could be on more than £1,000 a week some weeks.

That kind of money is a shock to the system when you come from a lower-class family. My mum raised me on her own. We never went abroad for a holiday. I didn't have a passport until I was 15. I didn't go without but, yes, I would class us as poor. So when I got money, I wanted to indulge. I wanted to indulge myself and I wanted to indulge my friends.

Soon after I signed that first contract, I drove down to the Lakeside shopping centre in Essex and bought myself a Gucci watch. I measured wealth and attainment in symbols for a long time. Later, it would be a Ferrari.

In the late 1990s, Gucci made a watch with a big 'G' emblazoned on it. Some people would probably say that 'G' stood for gaudy, but I loved it. It cost £900 and it felt amazing to be able to afford that. A few months later, at Christmas, I bought three of my best friends the 'G' watch, too.

I was still living at home with my mum. I gave her money to help pay the bills, but I didn't really have any other outgoings. So I went to Lakeside every other weekend and bought watches. I bought watches and jewellery for my dad. It just felt good being able to give things to people who wouldn't otherwise have been able to afford them.

All through my career, I never tired of the feeling of doing that. I took 20 of us to Barbados once and 15 to Dubai, all of us in business class. I was in a position to do that and it gave me a lot of pleasure, so why not?

There is no better feeling than seeing people, who are usually at the back of the plane, finally getting on the beds in business class and watching them press all the buttons and the beds are up and down and they're saying: 'Oh my God.' Things like that give me such a buzz. It's because I know how they feel. It's because that's how I felt when I first got to sit there.

Sure, people called me the 'King of Bling' later in my career, but that's OK. I wouldn't change that. I would have still bought my expensive watches. My childhood had been poor and I wanted to catch up. Why couldn't I enjoy myself? Why couldn't I treat myself?

Sometimes, it seems that the public and the press hate the idea that footballers have money to spend. It feels like they still can't quite get their heads around the fact that kids from poor backgrounds suddenly have more money than them and they resent it. I think that's where a lot of the criticism of modern players comes from. It comes from jealousy and the idea that footballers have managed to bypass the class system.

The class system is still strong in our country and it's still difficult for some people to see footballers moving into nice areas that have previously been the preserve of old money. When footballers spend money on beautiful houses, they are vulgar. When lawyers spend money on beautiful houses, they are tasteful.

When I was young, the explosion in players' wages was just starting to happen and I rode the wave. That first contract at Ipswich that Jonathan Barnett negotiated for me was my first indication of the power that players had. I hadn't grasped then just how much the pendulum was swinging towards us. With every year that passed, it became more and more apparent that players called the shots now.

Burley had had a good summer in the transfer market. He had signed the striker David Johnson from Bury, Matt Holland from Bournemouth, Mark Venus from Wolves, and Jamie Clapham from Spurs. We had lost players, too, but I thought we would be stronger than the season before.

That wasn't immediately apparent in the results. We made an indifferent start and, in fact, we were mid-table for the first half of the season. Burley brought Jason Dozzell back in on a short-term contract for a quick fix later in the campaign, after he was released by Spurs, but that turned sour fairly quickly.

Jason had been my hero as a player. He had broken into the first team at Ipswich while he was still at school and he had come round to my house once because his mum used to live round the corner.

Jason made a great initial impact when he rejoined the club. We played Manchester United at Portman Road in the League Cup in the autumn and beat them 2–0 and Jason was brilliant. But then we played at Charlton shortly afterwards and Jason was struggling with a virus and had to come off.

He was spotted out in Ipswich that night and a few of the fans made a song and dance about how he shouldn't have been out if he had a virus. There was a suggestion that Burley and David Sheepshanks thought Jason was a bad influence on me. Whatever the reason, when Jason's short-term contract came to an end, the club chose not to renew it.

Burley could be difficult. It wasn't all sweetness and light between me and him. I suppose it rarely is when managers and players are involved. I'll always be grateful to him for giving me my debut and having the faith to play me regularly, but he didn't develop me.

Quite rightly, Burley gets praise for having brought young players through during his managerial career, and he did that with Theo Walcott, Alex Oxlade-Chamberlain and Gareth Bale when he was in charge at Southampton. In my case, he got the credit for developing me and that was wrong. It was Bryan Klug and Paul Goddard who deserved the credit for that.

Burley was under a bit of pressure after our mediocre start to the 1997–98 season and he decided to change things around a bit by adding Bryan Hamilton to the coaching staff, who had just left the Northern Ireland job after they had failed to qualify for the 1998 World Cup.

Bryan's arrival helped to spark a change in our fortunes and, in the second half of the season, we went on a brilliant run. We won 16 of our last 20 league games. In that run, which began with a victory at the Hawthorns against West Brom at the end of January 1998, we only lost once.

I'd started the season at right-back but in the run-up to that game at West Brom, Bryan Hamilton urged Burley to play me alongside Matt Holland in the centre of midfield because he thought I was being wasted at full-back and he wanted to see me higher up the pitch.

The problem was that our club captain, Geraint Williams, played in that position and Burley didn't really want to drop him. I felt awkward about it, too, because Williams had been brilliant to me while I was coming through. He always encouraged me and helped me during games and looked after me. He was a fantastic pro.

In the end, Burley made the decision and told Williams he was leaving him out for the West Brom game. I was worried that he might be bitter towards me but if he was, he hid it extremely well. He was exactly the same. In fact, if anything he was even more encouraging than he had been before.

It takes a big man to act like that in a football team. There are all sorts of undercurrents of machismo going on and it is easy to feel humiliated and resentful if you are left out for someone else. He had played more than 200 times for Ipswich and now he was being omitted for some snotty kid.

Geraint Williams could easily have made things difficult for me because that was effectively the end of his Ipswich career. He never really regained his place in the side and he left that summer to join Colchester United. But he never displayed a moment's bitterness towards me. I'll always love him for that.

I thrived in centre-midfield and everything seemed to click. Holland was a good box-to-box player, I liked to get on the ball and we complemented each other well. Our bad start to the season cost us the chance of competing with Nottingham Forest or Middlesbrough for the automatic promotion spots, but we made the play-offs comfortably and went into our semi-final with Charlton Athletic with real momentum.

I was confident we were going to go up this time, and I was so sure we would beat Charlton that I had begun to think about playing the final at Wembley before we had even started the semi-final. We had beaten Charlton comfortably at home during our great run a couple of months earlier and I was complacent. I was about to get my come uppance.

Everything fell apart for us in the play-offs. We were at home in the first leg but we were nervous and hesitant and we went 1–0 down after 12 minutes when Jamie Clapham turned a cross from Keith Jones that was meant for Mark Bright into his own goal.

It was a bit of a shock to the system. I'd been telling myself we just had to show up to win the game, and now we were up against it. I couldn't get into the game either. Keith Jones man-marked me and barely gave me a kick. Nobody's ever done a job on me the way Jones did. He followed me everywhere. He was like a rash. I was no help to the team at all.

We put them under a reasonable amount of pressure for much of the game and we thought the tide might have turned our way when Danny Mills was sent off in the second half, but we couldn't get past their defence and we went to The Valley the following Wednesday facing a one-goal deficit.

Of course, we still harboured hopes of making a comeback but it never really looked like happening. Shaun Newton put them 1–0 up ten minutes before half-time and that was it. Jones did another job on me and I couldn't shake him. It was incredibly frustrating. It was an empty, empty feeling when the final whistle went.

I vowed to myself then that I would never go into a game feeling complacent again. I'd really believed we were going to go up that season by winning the play-offs. We were on an amazing run and we were better than Charlton. I knew we were. But we didn't play like we were better than them. We thought it was just going to happen automatically.

I didn't watch the play-off final between Charlton and Sunderland, but it turned into one of the greatest games there has ever been at Wembley. It ended in a 4–4 draw after extra-time and Sunderland won the penalty shootout 7–6. I told myself if I'd approached the semi-final like a proper professional, that could have been us. I was the only Ipswich player who made it into the PFA team of the year that season. It was a consolation but not much of one.

## THE IMAGINARY CIGAR

I was desperate to win promotion for Ipswich in the 1998–99 season and not just because we had come so heartbreakingly close in successive campaigns. There was another reason, too: I began to sense early on in the season that it might be my last for my home-town team.

We were up near the top of the table almost from the beginning this time. We started with three goalless draws and a defeat to Sunderland but after that we only lost twice in the next 14 matches, and it felt as if this was going to be our year to go straight up.

I was getting a lot of attention from the media and from other clubs by then. The other lads made fun of me, because every time we played on Sky they gave me the man of the match award.

There were scouts from Premier League clubs at every Ipswich game, mainly watching our keeper Richard Wright and me. At one game, we were told there was a representative from every single top-flight club in the stand to run the rule over us.

At the beginning of 1999, I was even called into the full England squad by Glenn Hoddle for a friendly match against France, the world champions, but a few days after the announcement, Hoddle was sacked for making comments about the disabled and Howard Wilkinson took charge in his place.

I think Wilkinson had designs on getting the job full time and so he wanted to put a strong side out. I was told that Hoddle was going to start me that night, but Wilkinson didn't even put me on the bench and I watched the game from the stands. I was disappointed, but it was still an incredible honour for me to be named in the squad. It made me even more determined to get another chance.

On 2 March, we played Watford at home and Micah Hyde and I both went for the ball early in the game. I got there just ahead of him and nicked the ball away and he smashed me. There was nothing malicious about it. I was just too quick for him. I was in a reasonable amount of pain, but I thought I might be able to run it off.

A few minutes later, I got the ball on the edge of the box and curled in a shot that went under the keeper for our first goal. I celebrated but when everyone was jumping on me, I could still feel that there was something wrong with my leg. Soon after that, I got the ball again, went to twist away and heard a crack.

I was carried off on a stretcher and when I got to the hospital, they did an X-ray and said I had broken my fibula. It wasn't a bad break, and the fibula isn't a weight-bearing bone so it could have been worse. The prognosis was that I would be out for six weeks.

We were second in the league when I broke my leg and we won five of the next six games to strengthen our position. Sunderland were away and clear at the top and we had edged just ahead of Bradford, who were managed by Paul Jewell at the time, in the battle for second.

When I came back, four or five games from the end of the season, we still had the advantage over Bradford. In my first game back, I felt a long way off the pace and I kept getting caught on the ball. The team started to tie up a little bit. We lost at Bolton in the middle of April and then beat Stockport County. We still had our fate in our own hands when we played Crewe Alexandra at home on 24 April.

We really should have beaten Crewe. They weren't a very good side but they were in a desperate battle of their own, against relegation, and we were struggling with nerves. I got caught in midfield during the game and Crewe capitalised on my mistake and scored. We lost the game 2–1 and Bradford moved into second place. There were two games left.

I felt responsible for the defeat to Crewe and I went to see our assistant manager, John Gorman, and said I felt I should be left out for the next game, against Birmingham City at St Andrews. He said the only way I was going to get sharp was by playing matches. We lost against Birmingham, too.

The last game of the season, we had Sheffield United at home and Bradford went to Wolves. We had to win and hope that Bradford drew or lost. We did our bit, at least, with a 4–1 victory in which I scored the first goal. Finally, I felt like I was sharp again.

But as the minutes ticked down, we knew that Bradford were winning at Molineux. They were 3–2 up in the dying seconds when Wolves hit the woodwork and Jewell looked into a television camera and puffed on an imaginary cigar to show he wasn't feeling the nerves.

People in the crowd at Portman Road were getting updates from Wolves and we heard a big commotion when Wolves hit the post and assumed Wolves had got an equaliser. When the final whistle went in our game, I thought we were up. I thought I was a local lad who was about to be playing in the Premier League for his home-town club.

It was about a minute later when we were told that Bradford had held on and we were in the play-offs. I broke down in tears on the pitch when we were doing the lap of honour. The only consolation was that I felt sharp again and confident I could put it all right in the play-offs.

We finished third so we played the sixth-place team, Bolton Wanderers, who had finished ten points behind us in the table, in the play-off semi-finals. We played the first leg at the Reebok Stadium and lost 1–0 to a late goal from Michael Johansen.

In the second leg, we played a 4–4–2 with me on the right of midfield, Bobby Petta on the left and Jim Magilton and Matt Holland in the middle. Matt put us ahead with a terrific strike after 14 minutes, Bob Taylor equalised to put them back ahead on aggregate and then I scored early in the second half to bring us back level again.

Away goals only counted double after extra-time, so we were starting to think about an extra 30 minutes when Per Frandsen equalised for them on the night six minutes from time, a goal which put them ahead on aggregate. In the last minute, I scored with a header from outside the box to make it all-square again.

We should have had the momentum with us going into extra-time after scoring so late, but we had a lot of old legs in that side. Tony Mowbray was a fantastic player and a great bloke but he was right at the end of his career by then and Taylor scored again to put them 4–3 up on aggregate after 96 minutes.

That meant we needed two goals to go through. Matt Holland got one back four minutes from the end to make it 4–3 to us on the night and 4–4 on aggregate. We tried desperately to get the goal we needed but we just couldn't find it from anywhere and we went out on away goals.

There were no tears this time. I just sat on the pitch feeling stunned. We had given it everything, but it wasn't quite enough. It was a cruel way to see your hopes dashed again. Three years in succession we had got to the play-offs and three years in succession we had fallen at the first hurdle without ever making it to Wembley. It was a bitter disappointment.

The supporters were brilliant. They gave us a standing ovation and I took off my boots, tied them together, walked over to the North Stand and threw them and my shirt into the crowd.

I would have stayed if we had gone up. No question. But now I thought it might have been my last game for Ipswich. Because we were still going to be in the second tier, Ipswich might have to listen to big offers for me if any came in.

All sorts of thoughts rushed through my head as I walked around Portman Road that evening, applauding the fans. Even though we came up short, if this was goodbye, it was quite a way to say it, scoring two goals and being part of a team performance that made me very proud.

A couple of days later, I had a meeting with George Burley and David Sheepshanks. Jonathan Barnett met me half an hour before I was due to see them and asked me what I wanted to do and whether I wanted to leave.

My head was still spinning. There had been talk that Arsenal and Leeds were interested in signing me, and Jonathan said I should tell Burley and Sheepshanks that if a Premier League club came in for me, I wanted to be given permission to speak to them.

The meeting was fine. Burley was reasonable enough. He said that if nothing materialised in the way of offers that were acceptable to Ipswich and I started the new season still at Portman Road, then he wanted to be sure that I would give my all. I assured him I would. That was a no-brainer.

That summer, I was on holiday with friends in Ayia Napa, a resort in Cyprus, and I got a voice mail from Ruud Gullit, who was the manager of Newcastle at the time, telling me that they were interested in signing me and they would like to talk.

Harry Redknapp, who was the West Ham boss then, called me, too, and said they wanted me. He pointed out that I had loads of friends at the club like Rio Ferdinand, Frank Lampard and Trevor Sinclair and that it would be easy for me to fit in straightaway.

I started pre-season at Ipswich and Burley called me into his office and said they had had lots of bids but none of them had met their valuation of what I was worth. He told me to keep my head down and remember that I was still an Ipswich player and might remain so.

Soon after that, someone came to see me one day after training and said Burley wanted to see me in his office. I went in and he said they had accepted a bid. I thought he was going to say that it was from Leeds. In fact, I was hoping he was going to say it was from Leeds.

David O'Leary had come to watch me play three times and I knew they had bid for me. They were doing well and buying good young players. They seemed to be building for the future and Jonathan Woodgate was a close pal of mine. I had my heart set on joining them.

But Burley told me the bid they had accepted was from Newcastle. He said I had to drive to Stansted to meet my agent there and fly to Newcastle for talks. So I met David Manasseh at the airport and he said the personal terms had already been agreed. I was excited but I felt a tinge of sadness, too, because I had been hoping that Leeds might intervene at the last moment.

Perhaps there was also a bit of sadness that that was the end for me at Ipswich. I knew there was no turning back now. The club had accepted an offer for me and, one way or another, I was on my way.

There is not too much sentiment in football these days, but Ipswich is my home-town club, I grew up across the street from Portman Road and I was attached to the place. There were a lot of good people there who had been important to me and to whom I owed an awful lot.

It burned a little bit when they finally got promoted at the end of that season without me. But with the money they got for me, they were able to buy Marcus Stewart, John McGreal, Jermaine Wright and a few others and still make a profit. If I'd stayed, they wouldn't have had the money to buy them and we might have missed out again.

One of the regrets I have is that I never played for Ipswich in the Premier League, but I could at least take a bit of pride in the fact that they got promoted. I celebrated it as happily as everyone else in Ipswich.

I knew that I gave everything in the time I was there and I helped to provide them with the means to invest in new players after I had left. It was hard to leave, but it was the right thing for everybody.

I tried to leave in the right way, too. I never asked for a transfer, for a start. When they sold me, according to the terms of my contract, I believed that I was due a signing fee. Even though Ipswich sold me for £6.5 million, they didn't agree. They insisted I had instigated the move and consequently believed I wasn't entitled to the money. I wasn't too bothered about the money, but it was the principle that annoyed me.

We had to go to an FA tribunal and things got very heated. They seemed to be disgusted with my behaviour. If looks could kill during that hearing, I would have been a dead man. I won the case but Burley and Sheepshanks made it clear that they were unhappy with the ruling and lodged an appeal.

After they had lodged the appeal, Jonathan Barnett called me. He told me that Sheepshanks had made an offer to settle it all. He told him that I should accept only half of what I was due and nothing more, and if I didn't accept I would not be welcome at Portman Road. They said I wouldn't be allowed to watch a game or set foot in the training ground.

I was surprised. I had been at the club since I was 10 years old. They had just sold me for £6.5 million,. They had built a new team off the back of me. Now they were threatening to turn me into a pariah at the club.

I was more than surprised, actually. I was flabbergasted. I thought it was sad. But I accepted their terms because Ipswich meant a lot to me and I figured life was too short.

Burley was weird with me for a long time over my move. I didn't get it.

It wasn't his money. They accepted the offer for me. They didn't have to sell me. It wasn't as if I was threatening to go on strike or anything.

As far as the transfer went, it turned out Newcastle had outbid everyone else. When I got to Stansted that day, I didn't have long to decide whether I wanted to join them or not. The flight was boarding. I thought about it. I knew it was a fantastic club with a great tradition and brilliant, passionate fans.

It was a chance to play with a legend like Alan Shearer, Gullit was the manager, and the increase in salary was mind-boggling. They were offering me £16k a week. I was 20 years old. I looked at David Manasseh and said: 'Let's do it.'

## THE SUICIDE NOTE

Things moved quickly. I got on the flight to the North East and when we landed, Freddie Fletcher, the Newcastle chief executive, met us on the tarmac and drove me straight to a clinic so I could do a medical. I passed the medical, signed my contract and then got another plane to Holland so I could meet up with the squad and manager Ruud Gullit.

Gullit was complimentary the first time I met him. He had arrived in Newcastle a year earlier, promising to deliver 'sexy football'. He had a reputation for not signing English players. He told me he didn't sign English players because they drank too much beer but that he had done his homework on me and he knew I didn't drink. He obviously hadn't done his homework very well.

Gullit has never had a great reputation as a coach but I loved him straightaway. I thought he was a brilliant coach. His sessions were so good. They were lively and innovative and clever. And he was thorough, too. He would go through every position in the team and tell you your job.

I think the reason he struggled as a manager was that he had been such a good player himself that he couldn't understand why some players couldn't do what he wanted them to do. That's the reason a lot of top players don't make the transition to management successfully.

At Newcastle, he wanted his centre-halves to be spray cans, pinging long passes left and right. During one training session, he asked Nikos Dabizas to drill the ball out to me on the right, missing out the full-back, but Dabizas was either hitting it way over my head or too far to my left or too far to my right and Gullit started getting annoyed.

So he demonstrated the skill himself. He drilled the ball to me with his right foot and it was inch perfect. Then he repeated it with his left foot and it was inch perfect. He couldn't get his head round the fact that we weren't as good as him. When he joined in training, he was still the best player on the pitch.

I think that was the problem that Glenn Hoddle had when he was the England manager. With him, it came across as arrogance. There was the famous time when he was said to have humiliated David Beckham and Paul Scholes during the 1998 World Cup because he was trying to teach them a set piece and they couldn't master it.

Players like Gullit and Hoddle and Gianfranco Zola went to clubs as the manager but they still had better technical skills than the players they were coaching. When I was at West Ham and we were struggling against relegation, a couple of us begged Zola to register as a player because we knew he could still have made a big impact in the Premier League.

Gullit signed a slew of other new players the summer I arrived. Alain Goma and Elena Marcelino arrived at a combined cost of more than £10 million to try to improve the defence. Franck Dumas and the goalkeeper, John Karelse, were brought in, too. The club already had players like Shearer, Gary Speed, Rob Lee and Nolberto Solano on the books, but as soon as I got back from Holland, it was impossible not to sense the tension around the club.

Rob Lee, who was Shearer's best mate, and Stuart Pearce, both relics of the Kenny Dalglish era that preceded Gullit's reign, were training with the reserves, away from the first-team squad. Lee hadn't even been given a squad number.

It was clear to me straightaway that Gullit was engaged in a battle of wills with the senior players, including Shearer. He knew that Shearer was too powerful to treat the way he was treating Lee and Pearce, but he seemed to make little pretence of the fact that he was tolerating him reluctantly.

A few days after the Holland trip, we went up to Scotland for preseason games against Livingston and Dundee United, and Gullit made a speech at one of the team meetings. What struck me immediately was that when he talked about how he wanted his team to play and how he saw the season unfolding, he never mentioned Shearer.

It didn't bother me, particularly. In fact, in some ways, I loved it. Gullit was putting all the emphasis on youth and the new signings rather than the old guard. But Shearer was a legend on Tyneside. He was the club captain. He was still a fantastic striker. It all seemed odd.

Alan clearly wasn't happy with the situation, and the atmosphere at the club didn't get any better when the season began. In fact, it deteriorated. In the opening league game against Aston Villa, the first Premier League game of my career, Alan was sent off for the first time in his career.

Alan was shown a second yellow card 20 minutes from the end for a foul on Ian Taylor, and five minutes after that, Julian Joachim scored the winner for Villa. I came off the bench in the second half when Marcelino was injured and played well enough.

It wasn't quite the match I was expecting for my debut, but it was a taste of the constant controversy that was to pepper my Newcastle career. I soon began wondering what I had got myself into.

We followed up that opening-day defeat by losing to Tottenham at White Hart Lane in midweek and then getting battered by Southampton at The Dell. By then, some journalists were writing that Gullit was already on the verge of the sack, and a 3–3 draw with Wimbledon at St James' Park did nothing to ease the pressure on him.

It was obvious that the next game, an evening kick-off against Newcastle's fierce local rivals, Sunderland, on Wednesday 25 August, would be pivotal in deciding whether Gullit survived in the job and whether he would be allowed to take the club forward in the direction he wanted to. If we had won that game, I believe he would have stayed and Shearer would have been sold to Leeds.

The schism between Gullit and Shearer became even more obvious in the days leading up to the Tyne–Wear derby. On the eve of the game, we had a match in training between the team that would be starting against Sunderland and the lads who had been left out.

The first team played the training match in their kit. The ones who had been left out were handed bibs. I was waiting for things to start and I saw John Carver, Gullit's assistant, start handing out the bibs. He gave one to Duncan Ferguson and then he gave one to Alan. I found it hard to believe.

Shearer had been suspended since his sending off on the opening day, but he was available again now. The fact that he wasn't given a bib meant he wasn't playing against Sunderland. He was the England captain, he was a Newcastle legend and Gullit hadn't even pulled him aside before training to tell him he wasn't going to recall him.

Give Shearer his due: he took the bib and put it on. I could tell he was hurt but I was impressed with his professionalism. Sure, you might say that he didn't have any choice and that's what any footballer ought to do, and if that is the manager's decision, a player has to obey it.

There is some truth in that, but Alan wasn't just any player and there are ways of doing something like that. I don't think Gullit was interested in being diplomatic, though. It felt as if he wanted to bring things to a head. If so, he was going the right way about it.

If I was the England captain and I'd been dropped for a huge derby game and the Newcastle manager hadn't pulled me aside to tell me the reason I wasn't playing, I would have spat my dummy, but Alan didn't do that. He was grim-faced, but he got on with it. Maybe he could see what was coming.

So in this practice game, there was me, who'd only just arrived at the club, playing number 10 for the first team and Paul Robinson, a 20-year-old kid who'd only made one start for Newcastle, alone up front. And in the reserves, the forwards were Alan Shearer and Duncan Ferguson.

Funnily enough, the second XI absolutely battered us. Alan scored two, Dunc scored three and we lost 5–1. But Gullit stuck with it. The same team started against Sunderland: Paul Robinson in attack with Silvio Marić, another bit-part player, behind him and Shearer and Ferguson on the bench.

I thought Alan deserved all the credit in the world for the dignity with which he handled that situation. It has always stuck with me how he just got on with his job. He probably thought that with that team, there was no way in the world that we were going to beat Sunderland and he decided to ride the whole thing out.

I could also understand Gullit's logic, though. The season had started badly and his job was on the line. He and Shearer were at odds with each other and he probably didn't trust him when the chips were down. I understand that logic, but I don't think Gullit went about it the right way.

Even if he was suspicious of Alan, even if he wasn't sure about him in the long term, he should have realised that Shearer was a Geordie through and through and that there was no way he wouldn't give everything for Newcastle in a match against Sunderland.

When the team sheets were released to the press and they saw that Gullit had left Shearer out, the media said it was a suicide note, but even though Sunderland started well, I put us ahead with my first goal for the club midway through the first half when Robinson played me in and I lifted the ball over Thomas Sorensen.

We were playing well and in control, but then it started to rain. I know that sounds like an excuse, but it felt more like fate to me. It wasn't just a bit of drizzle. It was a monsoon. It was a filthy night. I noticed that some of the press guys got so wet that they fled for the press room to watch the game inside before their computers blew up. It turned the match into a bit of a lottery.

Sunderland dealt with it better than us. Gullit brought Duncan off the bench, but Niall Quinn equalised with a glancing header midway through the second half and the Newcastle fans grew increasingly angry. They started chanting Shearer's name and demanding that he should be brought on.

Gullit brought him off the bench with 17 minutes to go. Then, two minutes later, Kevin Phillips scored to put Sunderland ahead. The playing conditions were farcical by now. The rain was still falling. The ball kept getting stuck in the puddles that had formed on the pitch.

Everyone was aware of the significance of the game and it felt as if we were playing through some sort of apocalypse. The gods were angry because Shearer had started on the bench.

Nobby Solano missed a great chance to equalise late on and Kevin Ball hit his own crossbar with a misplaced backpass but we couldn't get back on level terms, and when the final whistle went it was met by a howling siren of boos from the crowd.

At his post-match press conference, Gullit pointed out that we were leading when Duncan and Alan were both on the bench. It wasn't very subtle and they were both furious. Duncan said he was going to go and confront Gullit in the morning. Alan told him he would have to get in line. The situation at the club seemed to be spiralling out of control.

I got into training early the next morning. I was living in a suite in the Gosforth Park Hotel at the time and existing on room service, so I usually got to the training ground before a lot of the other lads and had some breakfast. That morning, Alan pulled up in his car as I arrived. He said he had come in to give Gullit a piece of his mind. Duncan was already there.

Neither of them got to see Gullit in the end. He went to see the chairman Freddy Shepherd that morning and resigned. At a press conference later, he blamed intrusions into his private life for his exit. 'I know there are still a lot of people who want me to stay, and there are a lot of people who want me to go,' he said, 'but I think that the moment has come to resign.'

He also addressed the elephant in the room, which was his relationship with Alan and the fact he believed he was being judged on his reputation rather than his performances. 'As everybody knows, I don't think that Alan did his best when I was coach here,' he said. 'Therefore, if he didn't play well, then I had to substitute him.'

I was gutted for Gullit. He had signed me, after all, and he was the reason why I had started the season so well. He had faith in me and I responded to that. I also respected him for what he was trying to do and for the player he had once been and the skills he still had.

Even though we had started the season badly, our performances were way, way better than our results. We threw away leads in practically every game. We battered Villa in the opening game of the season and we could have beaten Spurs and Southampton, too. But we didn't.

Our weaknesses at the back and the fact that Gullit was trying to change the old guard at the club and move them on created a toxic situation for him. If we had been winning, he would have got his way and Alan would have left. But his position was weakened because of the results, and when we lost to Sunderland even I could see there was no way back for him.

Steve Clarke, who had arrived at St James' Park as part of Gullit's backroom team, was appointed caretaker manager. I'm sure that was an honour for him but it was also a poisoned chalice, particularly as his first game in charge was away at Manchester United, who had just won the Treble.

He let it be known he was going to restore Rob Lee, Alan and Dunc to the side. I had been given Rob Lee's number 7 shirt because he had been ostracised by Gullit and I offered to let him have it back when he was brought back into the fold. It turned out the rules didn't permit it, but I think he appreciated the gesture. He took it back the next season instead.

Other stuff didn't proceed quite so harmoniously. We had a training session the day before the game and we were working on set pieces. Steve Clarke said to Dunc that he was supposed to have been marking Niall Quinn during the Sunderland game and that it was his fault Quinn had scored the equaliser.

Dunc was a scary man. Don't get me wrong, he was kind-hearted at the bottom of it all. He was always generous to the youth-team kids with tips at Christmas and stuff like that. I loved him as a bloke and as a player, but he was physically intimidating and he had a temper. He kind of froze and stared at Steve when he said what he said about not marking Quinn.

'You what?' Dunc said.

He had a ball in his hand and steam was coming out of his ears. Steve Clarke stuck to his guns and repeated what he had said. It takes a brave man to do that.

Dunc tossed the ball up in the air and leathered it at Steve as hard as he could. It hit him. Not in the head, but it did hit him. Steve Clarke went red, but he carried on with the session. Dunc was still picked in the team. We lost 5–1.

That was actually relatively tame for Dunc. Later that season, we were playing in a five-a-side in training. Fortunately, I was on Dunc's team. They were always properly competitive matches and we were losing this one. Alessandro Pistone was on our side, too, and he kept making mistakes and Dunc screamed at him to pull his finger out.

'F*** off, Dunc,' Pistone said.

The game went on, but Dunc stopped dead. He stood stock still, his eyes not moving off Pistone, as Pistone continued to play. Pistone ran around, oblivious, and soon afterwards, the whistle went and training finished. Some people went off to do warm-downs or practise their finishing and I went into the treatment room with Pistone and Derek Wright, the physio, for a massage.

I was sitting on the massage couch when the doors swung open. It was Dunc. He pointed at Pistone.

'You told me to f*** off, yeah?' he said.

Pistone looked at him, bewildered.

'Outside now,' Dunc said.

'What?' Pistone said, starting to look scared.

'Outside now,' Dunc repeated. 'You and me.'

'What? What?' Pistone said, panic spreading all over his face.

'Don't make me ask you again,' Dunc said, 'or I will come over there and drag you outside.'

By this time, tears were streaming down Pistone's face and he was jabbering. You may remember that when some Newcastle players handed out Christmas presents to their teammates the December before I arrived at the club, Pistone was given a sheep's heart, the idea being that he didn't possess one of his own.

'Dunc, Dunc, Dunc,' Pistone said.

'Outside now,' Dunc shouted at him.

I was trying not to laugh. I could see the rage in Dunc's eyes and Pistone started pleading with him. There was no way he was going to set foot outside that room. I think he was so scared, he might not have been able to walk by that stage.

'I will tell you this once,' Dunc said. 'If you ever tell me to f*** off again, ever, I will crack your skull.'

Dunc turned and walked out of the door. Pistone was a wreck. He was inconsolable. I sat there and thought: 'I will never, ever mess with that man.'

A week after Gullit resigned, it was announced that Bobby Robson was taking over as Newcastle boss. I was thrilled. He was an Ipswich legend, having managed them for 13 years between 1969 and 1982, and someone I had ingrained respect for. He was always someone I had looked up to, right from the time when I was a kid.

In fact, this was his first club job in England since he left Ipswich to become England manager in 1982. He had taken England to the World Cup semi-finals in 1990 and managed some of the biggest clubs in Europe since then, including PSV Eindhoven, FC Porto and Barcelona. And, of course, he was a Geordie through and through. He had been born and brought up in the area. His dad had worked down the pits. He was fond of saying that he bled black and white.

I was away with England when the news broke that he had been appointed as Gullit's successor. I had seen him at Ipswich games now and again and I had spoken to him once before, after an England Under-21 game in Rieti in 1997 when he was at Barcelona.

I was in the tunnel after the game and he came up and shook my hand. He told me he was there to watch Francesco Totti playing for the Italy Under-21s but that I'd been the best player on the pitch. He told me he'd take me to the Nou Camp one day. I dined out on that with my friends for a long time.

He asked me where I lived in Ipswich and talked about his house on Constitution Hill, which was the best road in town. I've got a house near there now and I think of him every time I drive up it. It seemed like a good omen for me when he got the Newcastle job.

I was preparing to make my full England debut against Luxembourg when Sir Bobby got the job. It happened that Sir Bobby was the guest of honour at Wembley that day. He came down the line of players before the game, shaking hands, and when he got to me, he paused. 'Stay fit, son,' he said. 'I can't wait to work with you.'

## THE FEAR

I loved my England debut. It was beautiful. It was one of the best moments of my career. I knew it would be. We were playing Luxembourg and so even though it was my first appearance, there wasn't much pressure. It was 4 September 1999. I went out there in the glorious sunshine of that late summer and, for 45 minutes, I played like a dream. Most of the rest of my England career, the sun went in.

The way I looked at it before the game, Luxembourg were a poor side. They probably had the quality of a third-tier team in English football. So I knew I really ought to be able to shine against a nation like that, playing in Wembley's wide-open spaces with my pace. And that was how it worked out.

Kevin Keegan, who had been given the England manager's job after Glenn Hoddle was fired for making remarks about the disabled, was one of those rare things: an England manager who picked players on form. Even though I probably wasn't his first choice to start when the squad joined up, I was flying in training and he recognised that. When the team was named the day before the game, I was in the starting line-up at right-back. It went Nigel Martyn, Martin Keown, Tony Adams, Stuart Pearce, Ray Parlour, David Beckham, David Batty, Steve McManaman, Alan Shearer, Robbie Fowler.

And Kieron Dyer. Kieron Dyer, from Ipswich, in the full England team. Playing in a European Championship qualifying match. Playing in the same team as David Beckham, Stuart Pearce and Tony Adams. Adams was amazing in the dressing room before the game, motivating everyone, getting in your face. He made the hairs on the back of my neck stand up.

'If this is what he's like before a game against Luxembourg,' I thought to myself, 'what's he like when we've got a big match?' I guess that's what made him the player he was. Even then, when he was a veteran, when he'd seen it all, every match was hugely important to him.

I was absolutely buzzing. Playing right-back was fine by me. I'd played there plenty of times for Ipswich. I knew I could do a job there. Anyway, I didn't really care. I was 20 years old and I was going to be playing for England. It had been my dream to play for my country, just as it is the dream of every kid who loves the game.

When the game started, I felt as if I could run for ever. I tore up and down the right wing, and after 11 minutes I set off on a mazy dribble that only ended when I was brought down in the box. Shearer sent the goal-keeper the wrong way and smashed the penalty into the back of the net.

Shearer scored another midway through the half and then set up our third goal for McManaman. A couple of minutes after that, I overlapped down the right, ran on to a pass from McManaman, skipped past a challenge and pulled the ball back for Alan to score. It was his first international hat-trick and we were 4–0 up after half an hour.

McManaman made it 5–0 two minutes before half-time, but by then I had begun suffering from what I thought was cramp, although it turned out later it was something called compartment syndrome, which would eventually need an operation.

I didn't know that then. I just thought the exertions of the day and all the exuberance I had been feeling had got to me. I had been rushing around like a dervish for 45 minutes. I had to have treatment at one point and when I got back up and waited on the touchline to go back on, the whole of Wembley started singing *'there's only one Kieron Dyer'*. It doesn't get much better than that.

And you know what? It didn't get any better than that. That was the high point of my England career. It sounds glib, but it's true. That 45 minutes was probably the only time in my appearances with the national team that I played with no fear. I played with joy and with abandon and the crowd loved me and we smashed the opposition. It was a perfect snapshot of the way playing for your country should be.

After that, it was never quite the same. Sometimes, I was injured. Sometimes I was left out. Even when I was picked, a lot of the time I played with the wrong mindset. Most of all, I was worried about making mistakes. That's the England player's disease. We're all scared in an England shirt. It's one of the main reasons we never achieve what we're supposed to achieve.

Sure, some players are more scared than others. I sat next to a player on the bench at an England game once – and this was a player who had played for Liverpool and other leading Premier League clubs – and it was a game when the fans were giving the lads a bit of stick. This player turned to me and said: 'I hope I don't get on today.'

Too often, that was what it was like with England. That is what it is still like. Too many players are afraid to make a mistake, because they know that when they have an England shirt on, they will get battered by the media and by the fans if they don't do well.

So they do the easy thing. They try to hide. I did it. You get the ball and you take the easy option. You don't do the brave thing. You don't try to make something happen. You don't try the clever pass because you're worried that it's a risk and the crowd will get on your back or the press boys will give you a three in their marks out of 10.

So you do not try to stand out. You do not try to alter the game. You try to disappear. You try to make damn sure you do not do anything wrong and you limit your ambition to that. And when you limit your ambition to that, you become average.

Look at the way that Raheem Sterling has been treated as an England player. He is one of the most talented individuals we have, and yet there have been times during his international career when he has been made a scapegoat for the team's failings.

He was probably our best player at the 2014 World Cup – although I accept that's not saying an awful lot – but at Euro 2016, everyone seemed to decide it was his fault that Roy Hodgson's team was stinking the place out and everybody started talking about his attitude and hinting that he didn't care.

Really? But that kind of thing is typical. It's also cyclical. It happens every time, after, or during, every major tournament. It even happened to John Barnes, who was one of the greatest England players. There was a time when he was booed relentlessly, too. It's hard to believe when you think about it now, but it happened.

At Euro 2016, it was Sterling. At Germany 2006, it was Ashley Cole who got it in the neck. Remember when Sterling got back from France 2016 and the story appeared about him taking his friends round a new house and showing them how lavish it was?

It was all presented in a manner meant to suggest that Sterling had shrugged off the disappointment of losing at the Euros, because he never really cared in the first place. It turned out that it was a house he had bought for his mum. But if it wasn't him who got the grief, it would have been someone else.

So is it really any surprise to anyone that when players play for England, they tend to go into their shell? They don't play with the same freedom they show with their clubs. They don't express themselves. They're not the same players. It's not hooliganism that's the English disease any more. It's fear. It's the fear we play with.

It's not just fringe players that it affects. It's not just players like me, who won more than 30 caps, or the lad who played for Liverpool that I mentioned earlier. I played in England's game against Andorra in Barcelona in March 2007 and I saw what the pressure of playing for England could do to the greatest players.

Players like John Terry and Rio Ferdinand, world-class players, elite centre-halves, could barely play a five-yard pass in that match because of the pressure they felt. The atmosphere in the Olympic Stadium that day was poisonous. We were being vilified by our own fans. The fear of getting a bad result against Andorra and the humiliation that would follow crippled a lot of us.

I was sitting on the bench in the first half, watching it. It was brutal. I've never seen anything like it. Some of the squad, who were in the stand, had to move out of their seats because they were getting so much abuse. It was 0–0 at half-time and the jeering from the stands when the lads came off was deafening. And this, just to be clear, was from our own fans.

I came on in the second half for Micah Richards, but I had it easy, really. Steven Gerrard had put us ahead a few minutes earlier and things had calmed down a bit. I was also playing just off the striker, who was Jermain Defoe by then, and that was a position I loved. We won 3–0 in the end, but I'll never forget how much hatred there was towards the team that day.

It seems to come with the territory when you play for England. Our fans and our media exist in a state of habitual disappointment. We still hark back to 1966 and that World Cup win. We always talk about under-achievement. We talk about how the players don't care and how far behind the rest we are.

I'm not sure that the facts bear that out. It's a convenient narrative, but it's lazy, too. When I was in the squad, we had players like Paul Scholes, JT, Rio, Sol Campbell, Gary Neville, Frank Lampard, Steven Gerrard, Wayne Rooney, Ashley Cole, all world-class players, and we were just dismissed as failures for England.

We were dismissed as the Baby Bentley Generation. People damned us by calling us the Golden Generation and then snorting with derision at the self-regard of that label, given that we were a group of players who won nothing for their country.

When people say we under-achieved, I sometimes scratch my head. In the 2002 World Cup, we lost to Brazil and they had Rivaldo, Ronaldinho and Ronaldo up front, which has a claim to be the best front line in the history of international football.

They had Roberto Carlos and Cafu, who were probably the best full-backs ever. Edmilson was one of the best holding midfield players at the time, as was Gilberto Silva. And Lucio was a monster at the back. Yet people say we under-achieved by losing to them in the quarter-finals.

I don't think we under-achieved. We were a very good side and we were beaten by an even better side. When people say we didn't reach our potential in that tournament, sometimes you just have to hold your hands up and say we met a brilliant team.

Two years later, at Euro 2004, we lost on penalties to Portugal. If we had won that shootout, if Wayne Rooney hadn't been injured, I think we would have won the tournament. Anyway, because we lost on penalties, we were branded failures and under-achievers again.

It's a very fine line. Everyone says how the England team that got to the semi-finals at Euro '96 was so successful, but that team was outplayed by Spain in the quarter-finals and we only beat them on penalties. At the Euros in 2004 and again at the 2006 World Cup, we lost on penalties in the quarters and we were failures. Perception is a strange thing.

I watch Sterling playing for England now and I feel sorry for him; it's the same with Alex Oxlade-Chamberlain. I sat in a bar to watch one of England's qualifiers for the 2018 World Cup and Sterling was being battered by everyone in there. And then people wonder why the players sometimes give the impression they don't enjoy playing for England.

Gareth Southgate knows what a big problem the fear that comes with playing for England is. He spoke about it less than an hour after England had qualified for the 2018 World Cup. He said it was the single biggest challenge he had to face in trying to get the team to perform at the highest level.

I don't see the situation getting better any time soon. If anything, the success of the Premier League seems to have increased expectations that we should be winning tournaments. People sometimes don't seem able to compute the fact that just because a league that is stocked with brilliant foreign players is strong, it doesn't mean our national team will be strong, too.

It often works in the opposite way. If only 30 per cent of the players in the Premier League are English, then the England manager has a small group to work with. His job his getting harder, but expectations are getting higher. And when expectations aren't met, disillusion sets in and players get singled out and fear grows.

I was blissfully unaware of that dynamic when I began my England career against Luxembourg. When we were 5–0 up at half-time, I thought it was easy, this England lark. Keegan decided to substitute me at the interval because of the cramping sensations I was having, but I was still as high as a kite.

We won the game 6–0 in the end after Michael Owen came on as a sub and bent a beauty into the corner from 25 yards. In the banqueting halls, where players meet up with friends and relatives afterwards, they were all telling me that the goals dried up as soon as I went off and that pumped up my ego even more.

I got a more realistic taste of what playing for England was like a few days later when we played Poland in Warsaw. We were a long way adrift of Sweden at the top of the group and we needed to draw against Poland just to squeeze into the play-offs.

Gary Neville started at right-back this time and I came on for Steve McManaman with about 20 minutes to go with the scores still goalless. I was pleased that Keegan trusted me in such an important game and we saw the match out to seal the runners-up spot in Group 5.

We had a friendly against Belgium at the Stadium of Light later that autumn and I felt like that was a big chance for me. Keegan tried out a new system with three centre-backs and me as right wing-back and Steve Guppy as left wing-back. I was absolutely terrible.

We won 2–1 but I got done for their goal and got dragged early in the second half. The performance improved considerably after I went off, which is never ideal. Sir Bobby Robson was the guest pundit in the Sky studio and the presenter, Richard Keys, mentioned that it had been a long game for me. Sir Bobby said I was too good to be playing wing-back, which made me feel a bit better.

I missed the play-offs against Scotland because I'd had a calf operation. We squeezed through to the finals of Euro 2000, which were taking place in Belgium and Holland at the end of that season, but I felt that my absence in those games and my performance against Belgium had damaged my chances of making the final squad.

I started a friendly against Argentina at Wembley in late February and got hooked after an hour again in a game that we drew 0–0. The next month, I was put back down to the Under-21s to try to help them qualify for their European Championships that summer by beating Yugoslavia in a play-off in Barcelona.

I was happy to play. I always enjoyed playing for the Under-21s, and it wasn't exactly as if I was alone in being asked to help out. It must have been one of the strongest Under-21 teams we ever put out. Jamie Carragher, Rio Ferdinand, Frank Lampard, Steven Gerrard and Emile Heskey were all in it, too, and we beat the Yugoslavs 3–0.

But when it came to the crunch for the senior squad, I just had a feeling I was going to miss out. It was the end of my first season in the Premier League and I was starting to run out of steam.

My form for Newcastle was indifferent, and even though I made the last 30 as Keegan whittled down his selection, I didn't make the bench in a Wembley friendly against Brazil at the end of May and I felt the writing was probably on the wall.

We had one final friendly, against Ukraine, on the evening of 31 May and we knew that that afternoon, Keegan was going to tell the players who he was leaving out of the final squad that they hadn't made it.

We were staying at Burnham Beeches, the hotel in Buckinghamshire where the England squad always used to stay in the 1980s and 1990s when we trained nearby at Bisham Abbey. I was in a room next to Rio Ferdinand.

Some time in mid-afternoon, I heard Keegan knock on Rio's door, so I knew he was getting bombed. A few minutes later, I heard Rio's door close and then Keegan's footsteps in the corridor. They got closer and closer to my room. I knew what was coming. Then he knocked on the door.

He was fine. He told me he was leaving me out and then he said: 'You know what, I still don't know what your best position is.' Everyone had always told me that my versatility was a positive, but that made me feel like it was a negative. Anyway, I took it OK. In fact, I took it so well, he asked me if I'd be a substitute for the Ukraine game that night. I came on for the last nine minutes.

Did it hurt not making the Euros? Of course it hurt. But the blow wasn't as hard as it might have been because I expected it. If you think you're nailed-on to get in and you don't, that must be very difficult.

I played against Ukraine and then I decided it was time to move on. I had a free summer to look forward to, after all.

## THE HOLIDAY

When Kevin Keegan broke the news to me that he had decided to leave me out of the squad for the Euros, I didn't waste time making alternative arrangements for the summer of 2000. Rio Ferdinand and I flew to New York at the beginning of June and went on a shopping spree. Then we decided we would head for Premier-League-on-Sea, otherwise known as Ayia Napa.

The first lads' holiday I had ever been on was in 1996 when I went to Magaluf, in Majorca, with about ten of the Ipswich youth team. None of us were on professional contracts so we were earning £47.50 a week. No one knew who we were, we stayed in some dump that was infested with cockroaches and we had a great time.

The following season, I had broken into the first team and when I went to the Under-20 World Cup in Malaysia, in the summer of 1997, Jody Morris and Jason Euell, who were also in the squad, said that Ayia Napa in Cyprus was the place to go and that we should all head there.

I took their advice and I loved it. It was miles better than Magaluf.

The music was better, everything was better. It was when garage music was at its height and I loved garage. The first two years I went, I was an Ipswich player and no one really recognised me. When I went with Rio in the summer of 2000, it was different.

Suddenly, I was a Premier League player and an England player and everyone wanted a piece of me. I would find that claustrophobic now, but back then I loved it. I got off on it. It was a real buzz. We were young boys with no ties and I loved the idea that everybody was craving my company.

I didn't care why. I didn't think about the reasons why they wanted to have a drink with me or come back to my room. I was a kid. I was having a good time. I was friends with DJ Spoony, who was big in that scene. It was a time of excess and I didn't know how to deal with it.

It didn't occur to me that I was being large or irresponsible or ruining things for other people. I had money and fame and I was drunk on both. It went to my head. None of it looks great when you look back on it in black and white, but I was young. It was part of growing up. I don't regret that.

When I got to Ayia Napa in that summer of 2000, it felt like every Premier League player who hadn't made it to the Euros was there. Aside from me and Rio, there was Michael Duberry, Jody Morris, Frank Lampard, Robbie Keane, Jonathan Woodgate, Emile Heskey, Andy Myers, Paolo Vernazza, Ashley Cole and Titus Bramble – and that was just the group I hung around with.

There were so many of us that one afternoon, we decided we'd have an 11-a-side on the beach. It was like a Premier League game and the whole beach stopped to watch. A crowd gathered round us and we were all showing off and messing about. It was the Premier League's first overseas game, when the idea was still just a twinkle in chief executive Richard Scudamore's eye.

Rio brought some friends with him on that trip, too, and they were in charge of the group camcorder. There were no smartphones in those days, obviously, and so one or another of Rio's pals used the camcorder as the record of the trip. They filmed anything and everything on it.

It was a holiday where all sense of restraint was absent. On that trip, more than at any other time, I think there was a general feeling among the footballers there that we could do anything we wanted. We didn't have to play by the rules that other members of society abided by and so we cut loose.

It was a dangerous feeling. You behaved badly and nobody told you not to. Everybody wanted us in their bar or their club and so we were indulged whatever we did, however we dressed, however we behaved. When you're a young footballer, a millionaire overnight, no one ever seems to say 'no'.

We'd roll into a nightclub straight off the beach, sweaty and sandy and dirty, just in a vest and shorts, and they'd let us straight in. People on the door just moved aside and 12 or 15 footballers strolled straight in. I suppose they wanted to be associated with us; they thought it brought their place kudos and that it might become known as the place to go.

So Jonathan Woodgate and I would be throwing pints of beer at each other in a packed bar in our beach gear, while other people would be trying to have a drink in their smart clothes, getting drenched by our booze. Woody and I drank WKD alcopops a lot of the time: we said it stood for Woody and Kieron Dyer.

We were kids whose egos were out of control. We were kids who were discovering that in the age of celebrity, some people would do almost anything to be with you. I was not unnerved by that. I was intoxicated by it.

When we saw how big we were over there, when we realised the level of fame suddenly attached to being a Premier League footballer, we thought we were above the law and nothing and no one was going to stop us from having a good time.

I was a young, single man and I had girls throwing themselves at me. Any of the players who were there in Ayia Napa that summer could have slept with three girls each day if they wanted to. The amount we drunk, it was carnage, absolute carnage. What were we drinking? What *weren't* we drinking?

I say I was young and single and that is how I thought of myself at the time. But it wasn't really true. The real truth is that I was a kid who had no idea of his responsibilities and was too immature to accept them. I thought of myself as single, but the reality was I was about to become a father.

I had an on-off girlfriend in Ipswich and we had split up when I joined Newcastle. But when I visited Ipswich during the season, we hooked up again and she became pregnant. We split up again soon after that, but when I went to Ayia Napa, she was seven months pregnant. Our first child, Kie, was born on 4 August.

I look back on it now and see a young man out playing the field while a woman was pregnant with my child and it's terrible. I cringe when I think about it. It must have been terrible for her and her family when all the headlines broke about my behaviour out there. At the time, that didn't really occur to me. I didn't pay much heed to the way I was behaving.

I'm sure a lot of people think like that when they get older. We look back on the way we behaved when we were younger and we wonder what we were thinking that we could be so wrapped up in ourselves and so ignorant of the feelings of others.

I played the field in Ayia Napa. I wasn't as prolific as some of the other lads, but I'm not looking for any credit for that: if I didn't score with as many girls, the main reason was that I was too pissed a lot of the time. I was so wasted one night, I even slept through one of England's matches at the Euros.

Our favourite game in Ayia Napa was actually more like an endurance test. We called it '24 Hours'. Typically, we'd all meet at a hut on the beach in late morning. We'd gather round and somebody would lay down the rules. If it was midday, somebody would say: 'Right, the time starts now. We are not allowed to go to sleep until midday tomorrow.' So the game would be underway and the 24 Hours would begin.

We would lie in the sun, drinking and laughing and messing around. Maybe we'd play a game like 'Rock, Paper, Scissors' and whoever lost would have to pay a penalty. Inevitably, the penalty – we called it a punishment – involved drinking large quantities of alcohol.

It was a long stretch of beach, and every 50 metres there was a big rubbish bin where holidaymakers could dump their cans of beer and their crisp packets. The lads put a shot of tequila on a bin. In fact, they put a shot of tequila on every single bin for 500 metres – so ten bins and ten shots of tequila.

The punishment entailed a sprint from the beach hut down the beach to the first bin, then gulp down the shot, and sprint back to the beach hut. Then sprint to the second bin, down the shot, and sprint back to the beach hut, and so on. Run, drink, run, repeat.

I'm not the biggest drinker, so by the time I got to the third or fourth bin, I was starting to feel it. Once, I tried to hurdle a sun-lounger on the way back to the hut, hit the top of it and went sprawling face down in the sand. *Uh-oh, you're in trouble,* the lads sang. That meant I had to do more shots.

There we were in 30 degrees heat, the sun beating down, sprinting up and down a public beach, necking shots and having a laugh. After our first day there, there were some pictures of us enjoying ourselves printed in one of the papers back home. The headline said we were animals. But you know what? It was the end of the season, we thought we were invincible and we didn't give a shit.

When the sun went down, we left the beach and headed for the bars and clubs. Some of them were grouped around the main square. Most of them closed at 3am or 4am, but there was one called River Reggae that stayed open until 7am. So we would head for that. The sun was up again by the time we left.

There were still five hours to fill before the end of 24 Hours so after we left River Reggae, we headed for an off licence to stock up on beers or alcopops and take them down to the beach. You weren't allowed to fall asleep. Michael Duberry and Andy Myers were the senior players and Andy was as hard as nails, so what he said was the law.

Sometimes, we'd take girls down to the beach and play drinking games. If someone couldn't down a beer in one or do a shot or whatever, they had to do a forfeit. That might involve them lifting up their top or trying to stop the traffic for 20 seconds by doing something, which would usually be ... lifting up their top.

We knew there were cameras around and we knew that reporters from the *Sun* were following us. We didn't care. They printed one picture of me on the back of a moped with Rio. That was astonishingly tame compared to the rest of the stuff we got up to, but it got me in trouble because my contract said something about not riding on motorbikes.

It's crazy really, when you think about it after all this time has elapsed. If I was there now and I knew that there were newspaper reporters there and we were being watched, I would get on the next flight home. Being called 'animals' in the press ought to have curbed our enthusiasm, but we just carried on and on and on.

That time has passed now in football. Most current-day players are more discerning. They are more discreet. They have got used to earning millions and they know where to go and where they can party without being so closely scrutinised. They separate themselves from the public now. They have to. When we were young, we went out just like everyone else.

Now, I think most top footballers would be more likely to go to a bar in Marbella, Miami Beach or Las Vegas and have a glass of Sauvignon Blanc or a bottle of Pol Roget than get wasted with the masses in Ayia Napa or Malia.

That period when the twentieth century ended was a moment where footballers were still coming to terms with the fact that their wealth set them apart. Before it, English footballers didn't have that level of popstar celebrity or disposable income.

After it, the popularity of camera phones and the advent of Facebook and Twitter meant that players simply couldn't get away with behaving like that any more. That trip to Ayia Napa was football's height of excess.

I took a couple of girls back to my hotel room when we were there. One night, I was having sex when one of Rio's pals came into the room and started filming us on the group camcorder that had all the footage of the holiday on it. He'd been down to reception to get a key for my room and had sneaked in. I hadn't set it up and it wasn't done with my consent.

When we realised someone else was in the room, I jumped off the girl and told the guy to get lost. It was completely wrong. The girl was mortified, obviously. I apologised profusely to her and made sure I took her back down to reception where she got a taxi and went back to her hotel. It wasn't my finest hour, but I saw her by the beach the next day and we had a chat and all was forgotten.

There was another night when Rio and Frank and a couple of others took a couple of girls back to their room. On that occasion, the girls knew there was a camera filming them and they were up for it. They were all filmed having sex in the room.

I'm certainly not trying to portray myself as an innocent party. I was having a good time. In the cold light of day, my actions didn't show a lot of respect to the woman involved. But I wasn't complicit in secretly filming her, which is what I was later accused of. Nor did Frank and Rio secretly film anyone. Whatever you think of our behaviour collectively, no one was tricked into anything they didn't want to do.

The thing was, that camcorder was always around. Every morning, when we met up at the beach hut, we'd all look at the footage from the night before. It was usually people dancing, chatting up girls, being stupid. In every bar, you see a funnel being poured down someone's neck and women dancing with their skirts up around their waists. That's the way it was in Ayia Napa.

There were other people around, hangers-on, people on the periphery, friends of friends who weren't really friends at all, and they knew there was lively stuff on that tape. And one day, whoever was in charge of the camcorder at the time was attacked. He was targeted. He had got on his moped and he was followed and somebody put a knife to his throat and said 'give us the camera'. He handed it over. 'Make sure you don't f***ing tell Rio,' the guy said.

I flew home from Ayia Napa none the wiser about the theft of the camcorder and got back to Ipswich on a Friday lunchtime. I met up with some of my friends and we went on an all-day session. In the evening, we went to a club in town called Hollywood and one of my mates got into an argument. I jumped in, thinking I was the king of something or other, and the guy smashed me in the eye.

His friends piled in and my friends piled in and the doormen marched me away and took me into a back room. They said my eye was in a bad way. I went to hospital and the next morning I had to have tests to check whether my vision had been permanently damaged. That sobered me up pretty quickly.

I stayed at my mum's whenever I visited Ipswich and while I was at the hospital, she phoned and said the press were outside the house. I thought: 'Bloody hell, they found out about that fight quickly.' I went home, cut through a back alley and jumped over the back wall so I could get in without being seen.

They were there all day Saturday and they said they wouldn't leave without a quote. They said they were from the *News of the World*. My mum told them I was in Newcastle, but they weren't having it and they stuck around. They finally disappeared late on the Saturday night.

On Sunday morning, I asked my mum to get me a paper from the newsagent. I wanted to see what they had said about the fight. I was still in bed when she got back. She had a face like thunder. She had a copy of the *News of the World* and she threw it at me. 'You're an embarrassment,' she said.

I stared at the front page and suddenly everything became clear. Those reporters weren't interested in my fight. They probably didn't even know about it. The paper had got footage of some of the sex sessions in Ayia Napa, including the excerpt where the guy sneaked into my room. We were castigated for what we had done.

I would never deny that the way I behaved wasn't exactly ideal. I wasn't proud of it. But because all the footage was on the same camcorder, the incidents were all grouped together to make it look as though they happened at the same time or, at least, on the same night.

But the night Frank and Rio got the girls back to their room, I wasn't there. And the night the girl came back to my room, they weren't there. I was accused of secretly filming the sex I'd had with the girl in my room,

even though I'd had nothing to do with that. You might think the distinc-
tion is irrelevant, but I would never have done that. I was embarrassed
and angry when the guy came into the room.

But we were all grouped together. 'England Stars in Video Sex Shame',
the headline said, or something like that. It was spun that the girls had
been duped into being filmed when actually, in the case of the girls who
got together with Frank and Rio, it had been done with their consent.
That detail got lost in the torrent of criticism that came our way.

To make things worse, the *News of the World* contacted my agent and
said they were going to run a story that I'd had a party at my house in
Newcastle and that I'd been taking drugs at it. The story wasn't true. In
fact, it was total bullshit.

I have never had a party with any drugs. I am so anti-drugs. I have
never even taken a drag of a cigarette. When I speak to people who have
taken cocaine, they say the first hit of the drug is so good, it can never
be replicated so you are always chasing that. The idea of how easy it
would be to get addicted scares the hell out of me.

The *News of the World* offered a deal. They said they wouldn't run
the story if they could have an exclusive interview with me about Ayia
Napa. I told Jonathan Barnett they could run the story, as far as I was
concerned. I didn't quite see the logic of doing a deal to buy off a story
that was a complete load of bollocks.

But Jonathan said that my reputation was in the gutter as it was and
that this might finish me. He said it might kill my career if club executives
thought I had a drugs problem. I saw the sense of that, but I was being
blackmailed by the paper, basically. I didn't want another heap of bad
publicity so I agreed to the interview.

The reporter they sent round asked me how many girls I had slept with
on the holiday and I said I didn't know. They turned that into a headline

that made it sound as if I had been with half of Ayia Napa. 'I Was So Drunk I Don't Know How Many Girls I Slept With', was the headline. That's the way the media works. They always get their way.

Maybe I deserved what was coming to me. I don't know. Did I treat women badly? I never hit a woman or physically abused a woman, but maybe that doesn't fully answer the question. Did I disrespect girls because once I got what I wanted, I'd be done with them? Yes, I may have been guilty of that.

When I got back from Ayia Napa, a lot of my friends tried to console me about the criticism that was being aimed at me by telling me I hadn't behaved any differently to thousands of British lads who went on holiday to Cyprus, the Costa Brava and some of the Greek islands.

For a while, of course, I told myself that my friends were right. It was what I wanted to believe. We all want to protect ourselves from the sanctimony of others. But the truth is that just because a lot of other people are doing it, that doesn't make it right.

I've thought about that a lot in the last few months when there has been so much focus on sexual harassment in all parts of our culture. Maybe what happened in Ayia Napa doesn't fit neatly into that category, because what went on between me and the girls who my mates and I hooked up with was consensual – but I'd be stupid to say it didn't raise questions about our behaviour.

British men seem to go on those holidays with an expectation that women will behave in a certain way, and if a woman doesn't behave in that way, you look for another woman who will. It's not just British lads who behave like that on holiday, but it is mainly British lads.

I don't think the way we behaved in Ayia Napa was necessarily a comment on English footballers, although it was probably exacerbated by the amount of money we earned. Sure, we felt a degree of entitlement, but, for some reason, the majority of British lads on holiday feel a degree of entitlement when it comes to women.

It's part of our culture. Sometimes, we don't like to shine a light on it, but it's still there. Footballers now may have found a way of being more discreet than we were back then when one century bled into another, but men's behaviour towards women in those resorts hasn't changed.

I was part of that culture and now I'm not. In the end, I wised up. I grew up. Look at my life now and the most important influences on it are strong women. My wife, who has brought me so much happiness; my mum, who has given me so much love and who has always believed in hard work; Zoe, the mother of my daughter, who is the most determined person I know; my auntie Theresa, my cousin Emma, my auntie Carol and my sister, Kirsha, who has turned her life around.

It would be easy to say that Ayia Napa was just a moment in time, but I don't think it was. Ayia Napa, and places like it, are still there and kids who don't know any better are still doing what I was doing nearly 20 years ago.

## THE BEST

# 10

Sir Bobby Robson was not the best tactician I ever played for. He was, by and large, a 4–4–2 man. There was nothing particularly innovative about the way his teams played, nor was there anything special about his training sessions. He didn't take training a lot of the time, often leaving that to Steve Clarke or John Carver.

But let me tell you why the man was a genius and why I loved him and why I loved playing for him. Let me tell you a story that might explain a little bit how, beyond some of the bluster he liked to convey, he was the greatest, smartest, most astute manager that I ever played for.

Midway through his first full season in charge of Newcastle United, a week before Christmas of 2000, we played Bradford City at St James' Park in a league game. We weren't in a great run of form. The previous week, we had been battered 5–0 at Arsenal. A couple of weeks before that, we had lost at home to Sunderland.

So there was a bit of tension around the place and the fans were restless and getting on our backs a little. Gary Speed scored a terrific goal in the first half, but it wasn't a great opening 45 minutes. Bradford were poor and we weren't much better. None of us excelled and there was a bit of grumbling from the supporters when the half-time whistle blew.

When we got into the dressing room at half-time, Mick Wadsworth, who had arrived at the club in the summer as Sir Bobby's assistant manager, started having a go at Christian Bassedas, in particular, and singling him out for his poor performance. I listened to this and I couldn't believe what I was hearing.

I didn't really rate Wadsworth. He had spent his coaching career in the lower leagues and I couldn't see that he brought that much to the club. The fans didn't rate him, either. They thought he was out of his depth and I think they were probably right.

On that occasion, I just thought it was wrong that he was picking on Bassedas. Bassedas wasn't a kid but he had been brought over from Velez Sarsfield in Argentina in the summer and he hadn't really settled and the fans were giving him stick a lot of the time. He was an easy target for Wadsworth.

I looked around the dressing room and thought there were other people Wadsworth should have been having a go at. Alan Shearer had had a really poor first half, but Wadsworth didn't say a word to him. He kept having a pop at Bassedas. He was ripping him to pieces.

I felt he had a habit of targeting players who he knew wouldn't have a go back at him. He often had a go at the younger ones like Lomana LuaLua and Shola Ameobi, who were just starting out on their careers and didn't have the confidence to stand up for themselves.

I told Wadsworth I thought he was out of order for singling out Bassedas. 'Why are you picking on him?' I said. 'Al's been shit. Why don't you say something to him? Is there any chance of you slaughtering one of the senior players?'

I told him I thought he was a coward. I told him I saw him always picking on Shola and LuaLua and that I'd have more respect for him if he just once had a go at a senior player like Speedo or Al. I was starting to lose it. I could feel myself about to go.

Maybe it all ran a bit deep with me. Somewhere in my psyche, I think it went back to being abused by Kenny. I didn't like it when I saw vulnerable people being picked on, especially when the strong ones were left alone.

But Wadsworth lost his rag when I stuck up for Bassedas. He went mad. 'How dare you speak to me like that,' he shouted. 'I'm the coach here. Listen to what I'm saying.'

He was shouting and yelling and I started shouting back at him. Then Sir Bobby joined in and had a go at me, too. He defended Wadsworth. He told me that I had no right to have a go at Mick and that I ought to have a bit more respect. I'd lost it totally by then. I started crying.

I said I wasn't going to go out for the second half. I wanted to go home. I started to get changed and walked over to the showers and turned them on. Speedo came over and tried to calm me down. He told me to go back to my peg and get my boots back on. I told him I'd had enough and that I wasn't going back out.

Then Sir Bobby came over. I thought he was going to give me a rocket and tell me how childish I was being. And I was ready for another row. Nothing was going to change my mind now.

But Sir Bobby didn't have a go at me at all. 'Son,' he said. 'What you said in there was absolutely right. I couldn't say that in there, because I can't undermine any of my staff. I have got to back their authority in front of you. But you were right to stick up for Bassedas and say what you said about the other lads. I admire you for that, son. You're a real leader.'

It wasn't what I was expecting at all. I started to feel a bit calmer. 'Come on, son,' he said. 'Let's go back into the changing rooms. I need you out there for the second half. You had a brilliant first 45. You were the best player on the park. But I need you out there so we make sure we get the three points.'

I could feel all the anger ebbing away now. I thought that as long as Sir Bobby understood why I'd said what I'd said then it didn't matter about Wadsworth. He wasn't important. I knew now that Sir Bobby was on my side, anyway. I walked back over to my peg, got my kit back on and did up my boots.

I went out there in the second half and played my heart out, feeling ten feet tall because of what Sir Bobby had said to me and the way he said he liked the fact that I'd spoken out. Twenty minutes from the end, I scored what turned out to be the winner as the game finished 2–1.

When I got home, I thought a little bit about what had happened and the way Sir Bobby had handled the situation. He had basically turned a one-man dressing room revolt into a masterpiece of man-management. He had turned something that could have been a crisis into a triumph.

I was happy because the manager had come and spoken to me and said I was right to do what I had done. And Mick Wadsworth was happy because Sir Bobby had stood up for him in front of the players and legitimised his authority by slapping down the player who was challenging him.

Sir Bobby was a genius like that. He made everybody feel good about themselves, and that is the greatest gift a manager can bequeath. He was a magician. He could do it with me time after time and he could do it with other players, too, that were beyond the reach of other managers.

That was one of the strange things about the way his relationship with the younger players at Newcastle was regarded. There seems to be this idea out there that players like me and Craig Bellamy had no respect for him and that we mocked him because of his age, but actually, the opposite was the case.

In our different ways, Craig and I revered him. We had the utmost respect for him. In Craig's autobiography, he said that he felt, if anything, I was too close to Sir Bobby and that Sir Bobby treated me as his favourite. 'Because they were so comfortable with each other,' Craig wrote in *GoodFella*, 'they would have disagreements in front of everybody that others misinterpreted as serious differences.'

There was a lot of talk about the brats, but Sir Bobby knew how to put us in our place. There was a lot of garbage talked about how he lost the dressing room in his later years at the club, but that was lazy. He never lost the dressing room.

There was one game where we were leading at half-time and Sir Bobby brought Craig off early in the second half because he thought the game was won and he wanted to save Craig's legs for a bigger match that was coming up the following week.

We won the game 3–0 but when we got back to the changing room, Craig was cursing and raving about how he had done all the running and how everyone else had profited from his efforts, and how he was always the first one to be hooked but everybody else judged him on his goals.

Sir Bobby grew exasperated by this, and in the end, he said: 'Will you shut up.' Craig never knowingly shut up about anything and he kept jabbering away about the injustice that had been done to him and finally Sir Bobby snapped. 'I'll squash you, son,' he said, 'like an ant.'

Craig looked a bit taken aback but after a brief pause, he started complaining again.

'Who are you?' Sir Bobby said. 'Ronaldo, Romario, Stoichkov, Hagi, Guardiola, Luis Enrique, Gascoigne: these are the people I deal with. And who are you?'

The changing room went quiet. Even Craig went quiet. And then Craig looked over at me. 'He's got a point, hasn't he,' he said.

We could be a volatile bunch at Newcastle. Groups of over-entitled young men often are. But Sir Bobby had the measure of us. Sometimes, he defused issues before they blew up. Sometimes, he had to deal with the aftermath of an incident and calm things down. He dealt with both scenarios in an expert fashion.

In March 2004, for instance, Craig and Sir Bobby's assistant, John Carver, had a public falling out at Newcastle Airport as we were preparing to fly out to a Uefa Cup fourth round second-leg match against Real Mallorca. It had started over some stupid prank where Craig had left his car in JC's parking spot at the training ground and escalated from there.

It ended up with Craig chucking a chair at JC, which led to a wrestling match on the floor in a part of the departure lounge that had been cordoned off for us. Sir Bobby was giving a press conference on the other side of some screens and all the media boys could hear pandemonium coming from our area. Sir Bobby came storming in and told everyone to get on the plane while he dealt with Craig.

By now, Craig was saying he wasn't getting on the plane and that JC had disrespected him and that he was missing his wife and it was turning into one hell of a mess. Sir Bobby gave John Carver a proper bollocking and asked him what he had been thinking and sent him off towards the plane as well. Then he put his arm around Craig. 'Walk with me, son,' he said.

Sir Bobby started talking to him about his kids and his missus and how things were at home and if his kids were doing OK at school, and Craig said he felt he had to answer the questions even though he didn't feel like saying a word. The next thing he knew, he was sitting down in his seat on the plane.

After the departure of Ruud Gullit, Newcastle felt like a whole different place with Sir Bobby in charge. Rob Lee was reintegrated and Sir Bobby called a swift halt to the idea of trying to freeze Alan Shearer out of the team.

Sir Bobby made everybody feel at ease. More than that, he made everybody feel good about themselves. When Craig signed at the start of the 2001–02 season, he always said that with the amount of compliments Sir Bobby paid him, he would go out on to the pitch at St James' Park believing he was bigger and stronger than Didier Drogba.

If I ever progress to being a coach or a manager, I'll remember that. I'll remember that sometimes, important though tactics are, we can get too obsessed with systems and shape. The most important thing is that a manager can make his players believe in themselves and their ability. That's a manager's best weapon.

In my case, when Sir Bobby came in, he knew that I liked to play centrally. The problem was that we had Gary Speed playing in central midfield, and now that he had rehabilitated Rob Lee, there wasn't any room for me to play there, too, because there was no question of Sir Bobby switching from 4–4–2. So one afternoon after training, he called me into his office.

He sat me down and started speaking. He said he wanted me to play on the left side of midfield and my spirits sank. I had my heart set on playing in the centre of midfield. I thought that was where my talents were best utilised. I wanted to be at the centre of the action, not reliant on someone else to feed me the ball on the flanks.

It was a recurring theme throughout my career. I always wanted to play in the centre, and most of the managers I played for seemed to find a way of playing me wide. I suppose they saw my pace and thought that was where I was best. But I had a horror of being marginalised. I didn't want to be dependent on someone who either didn't have the ability or the inclination to get me the ball. I wanted to be controlling things.

'Look, son,' Sir Bobby said, 'I know you are our best player in the centre. You are miles better than Gary Speed and Rob Lee, but I need them there because they are experienced lads. They can't do what you can do for me on the left. They haven't got your kind of ability.

So straightaway, he had told me how great I was. I could feel the resentment draining out of me.

'I want you to play on the left but I don't want you to play on the left, if you know what I mean,' Sir Bobby said. 'I just want you to start on the left. You go where you want. Those two will do all your donkey work for you, because you are better than them.'

I came out of his office grinning from ear to ear, because he had just told me I was the best midfielder at the club. He had turned a negative into a positive. I know he probably told Gary Speed that he was our best player, too, but that didn't matter to me at the time.

I saw Jermaine Jenas going into his office once with a face like thunder after Sir Bobby had dropped him. JJ wanted to have it out with him but I saw him when he came out, too, and he had a big grin on his face. Sir Bobby had told him he was our best player as well. He said he had just been giving him a little break because it was an easy game.

He was a clever man. Even the stuff about him mixing up players' names — I was convinced that was an act a lot of the time. There were funny stories about it, of course. When Shola Ameobi joined up with the England Under-21s on one occasion, Howard Wilkinson asked him what his nickname was. Shola said he didn't have a nickname.

'Well, what does Bobby Robson call you?' Wilkinson asked him.

'Carl Cort,' Shola said.

There were grains of truth in those stories. He called Bryan Robson 'Bobby' apparently. 'No,' Bryan Robson said, 'you're Bobby.' He called Gary Speed 'Sheedy' a lot of the time. He called me Kevin. I might be wrong, but I think he knew what he was doing. Maybe sometimes he forgot names, but he also used the appearance of confusion to defuse tension.

If there was tension or unrest in a team meeting and he got a name wrong, everyone would laugh and suddenly the tension would be gone, the angst would dissipate and we would be talking about the things that mattered.

I heard some people talk about him as if he was an idiot sometimes and that angered me. He was a great manager. He had managed at some of the leading clubs in the world and he had led England to what is still their best performance in a World Cup since 1966 when he took them to the semi-finals in Germany in 1990.

You don't get to achieve that and you don't get to manage a club of Newcastle's size into your seventies if you are not a very bright and savvy manager. He was a kind man, but he could also be a ruthless man. He was a gentle man, but he could also be a tough man.

You don't get to the top in a game like football and stay there for as long as Sir Bobby stayed there without having a range of qualities. So I get bored of people patronising his memory and pretending he was some kind of saint. He wasn't that but he was a great, great man, and it was my privilege to work with him at a wonderful club for five years and to watch and to learn.

# 11

## THE GANGSTER

Sir Bobby Robson knew how to make an entrance. In his first home game in charge of Newcastle United, the club he had always loved, we beat Sheffield Wednesday 8–0 at St James' Park on 19 September 1999. Alan Shearer, liberated from the yoke of Gullit, scored five times. I got our fifth, a minute after half-time. It was quite a day.

'It's only three points,' Shearer told the press after the game, 'but the new manager has given the team a real lift during his two weeks in charge. He has put in a hell of a lot of work. He understands people, he's got everybody playing with a smile on their face.'

It was a great start for Sir Bobby. He was 66 and this was to be his last job in the game. It was a fine way to announce his arrival, and before long we were climbing the table and moving steadily away from all thoughts of relegation danger.

I loved being in Newcastle. I'd just made my England debut and attracted a few decent reviews for my 45 minutes against Luxembourg, and now I was playing well in a Premier League side where suddenly there was a whole load of new optimism.

I did have one major off-the-field alarm, which was my first real glimpse of how things could get out of a hand in a football-obsessed city like Newcastle. I guess I had started to get a name for myself as someone who had a few flings here and there, and one day Alan Shearer pulled me aside at the training ground at Chester-le-Street.

He said his dad had heard a rumour that I had got a local gangster's daughter pregnant and that the guy was looking to teach me a serious lesson and do me some real damage. I told Alan it was rubbish but it didn't do a lot for my peace of mind.

I was sure it couldn't be true. I wasn't that wild that I didn't know who I was sleeping with. I hadn't had any one-night stands that I couldn't account for. I was sure that I was in the clear.

The next day, Freddy Shepherd phoned me. He told me the same story with the same leading characters: a gangster's daughter, an unwanted pregnancy and the threat of a gory punishment. Now I was starting to get seriously worried. I began to wonder if there was something I'd forgotten.

Ten minutes later, the police called me. They said they were concerned for my safety and that they were going to station an officer outside my house and install some surveillance equipment so that they could monitor any movement near it.

I was in bits by now. There was a guy called Lawrence, who used to do a lot of driving for the players and knew everybody in Newcastle, and I asked him to find out what he could. There was another guy, Pugga, a big fella who owned the Black Bull pub opposite St James' Park, and I asked him the same thing.

That evening, my phone rang and it was a withheld number. I don't usually answer a call when it says that, but I was so alarmed by now that this time I pressed the green button. It was the father in question on the other end of the line. My heart fell into my stomach.

The guy couldn't have been nicer. He said he had heard the rumours, too, and he had asked his daughter about them. He said his daughter had told him that she had never even seen me, let alone slept with me.

He said he was sorry for any anxiety that I might have been caused. Before he rang off, he said that if I ever had anything I needed sorting out, I should give him a ring.

I felt incredibly relieved. The next week, I was in a bar on the Quayside and some girl started tapping me on the shoulder while I was trying to buy a drink. I turned round and I was about to tell her to get lost when she introduced herself and pointed to her tummy and did an 'I'm pregnant' gesture. It was the guy's daughter. I bought her a bottle of champagne.

On the pitch, it was an unremarkable season in the league. We finished safely in mid-table, in 11th place. We did get to the FA Cup semi-final against Chelsea but we lost 2–1 and it was an opportunity missed. It was a close game and I had a brilliant chance in the dying seconds that the Chelsea keeper, Ed de Goey, somehow managed to save.

If we had won that game, I think we would have won the final, which was the last one to be played at the old Wembley before it was demolished. Chelsea beat Aston Villa in the final and I think we would have done, too. It wasn't to be the last time we came up just short in my spell at Newcastle.

The next season wasn't great. I suppose you could call it a consolidation season. We were never in trouble and we were never contending, neither in the league nor in any of the cup competitions. We bought Carl Cort but he struggled with the pressure of his £7 million price tag, and Shearer was injured for half the season. We finished 11th again.

I'd played well in that season, though, and my name was being linked with a lot of clubs. I knew for sure that there was interest again from Leeds United because Jonathan Woodgate had told me.

Things started to get serious and one evening in the close season, I went over to Woody's house and met with one of the Leeds officials. It's called being tapped up and that's how it happens. While I was at the house, I was told that David O'Leary, the Leeds manager, really admired me as a player.

A story was planted in the papers saying that I was worried about a lack of ambition at Newcastle and that Leeds were keen to sign me. A fee of £25 million was mentioned. Freddy Shepherd read it and called me into his office at St James' Park for a meeting with him and Sir Bobby.

Freddy was raging. He asked if the story was true. I said I'd like to know if there was interest from Leeds. That was true. Leeds had reached the semi-finals of the Champions League that season and it still seemed then that they were a team going places, whereas at Newcastle we were mired in mid-table. I was quite keen on the idea of moving there.

Freddy didn't see it that way. He made it clear he wouldn't entertain the idea of me leaving, whatever the price. He got more and more angry. He picked up the phone in his office and said: 'We're bigger than Leeds. I'm going to ring Ridsdale [the Leeds chairman] now and ask him what the hell he's thinking.'

While he was talking, he started smacking the phone on the desk-top until he smashed it. I thought it might be hard for him to ring Ridsdale with it now. I looked across at Sir Bobby and he winked at me. Whatever I thought about the idea of a move to Leeds, I liked Freddy's passion for the club.

A few weeks later, just before we played 1860 Munich in the semi-finals of the Intertoto Cup in late July, I broke down with an injury that ruled me out for a few months, and that was the last I heard of the interest from Leeds. The way things turned out at both clubs, it was a lucky escape.

The 2001–02 season was a different story. Sir Bobby bought Craig Bellamy from Coventry City for £6 million in the summer and paid £9.5 million to bring in the left-winger, Laurent Robert, from PSG. He bolstered the defence with Sylvain Distin and, in the January transfer window, after we had made a good start to the season, he improved the squad from a position of strength by paying Nottingham Forest £5 million for Jermaine Jenas.

We started the season well. We got to the Intertoto Cup final and even though we lost to Troyes, that run gave us momentum that we took into the season. We went the first four league games unbeaten, a run that included a tempestuous 4–3 victory over Manchester United that ended with Roy Keane being sent off for his part in an altercation with Alan Shearer. Keane was waiting for Alan in the tunnel after the game and had to be dragged away by his teammates.

I didn't play in that game. In fact, I missed the first few months of that season. At the end of the previous campaign, I'd had surgery on a stress fracture in my shin. They took a piece of bone from my hip, put it in my shin and pinned it all together. I began to train with the team again in the build-up to the new season but I broke down when the muscle ripped away from the shin bone.

I was still recuperating when the club decided they were going to take the squad away to Marbella for a winter break. I knew all about the temptations of Marbella by then and so I didn't particularly want to go. I said I'd rather stay in Newcastle and continue with my rehab there. The club said I had to go.

So we beat Aston Villa at home on the first Saturday in November and the next day we flew out to Malaga. We were staying at a resort called La

Quinta in San Pedro de Alcantara, a few miles from Marbella. There was a friendly fixed up against Recreativo Huelva for the Wednesday, which I wouldn't be involved in because of my injury.

The day after we arrived, I had a training session with one of the physios in the morning and then Craig, Carl Cort, Andy Griffin and I went out for lunch in Puerto Banus. We were in a restaurant down in the port, not far from the Sinatra Bar where people stand outside in the evenings, watching the flash cars parading and the beautiful people wandering by. We had some lobster and we started cracking on with the drinks. There was no game the next day so we were in the clear.

We had been in there for three hours, sucking back vodka and oranges and a few beers, when I got a call from Tony Toward, the team administrator. He said we had to be back at the hotel by 7pm for a meal. He didn't say why. He just said 'be back for the meal'.

We were pissed by then. We didn't want to go to the meal. We'd just had a meal. So we carried on drinking and drinking. We were gone. We got back to the hotel about 7.30pm and there was no one around. So we went to the bar and ordered four vodka and oranges and four cigars and stuck them on Freddy Shepherd's room.

After a bit, we went upstairs, got changed and waited for the other lads to come out of their meal. When they showed up, Speedo said we were in trouble. It turned out it had been a meal in honour of Newcastle's former chairman and owner, Sir John Hall. I didn't think too much of it. We all went bar-hopping around Marbella, got in about 3am and went to sleep.

It felt like I had barely put my head on the pillow when I was woken by this heavy, urgent banging on my door. I peered at the clock. It was 6am. I was sharing with Carl Cort and I looked over at him and said: 'Who the f***'s that?' The knocking went on. So I got up and opened the door and it was Tony Toward. He handed me a sheet of paper. It was the itinerary for a flight home.

The phone started ringing. It was Craig. He and Andy were being kicked out as well. We even had to arrange the trip to the airport ourselves. Now, for a footballer used to having everything done for him, that was serious.

We were all brutally hung-over and it wasn't a pleasant journey home. The other lads managed a bit of gallows humour about it but I was just sitting there, thinking 'this is not good'.

I'd been through the fallout from Ayia Napa. I knew what was coming. I knew the news would get out fast and that there would be a backlash. In many ways, what happened in Marbella, which was relatively innocuous, marked the beginning of the idea that there was a group of players in Newcastle who were out of control.

The fact that we had missed a meal in honour of Sir John Hall fed this idea that we had no respect for the club and its traditions, and that we were a group of blinged-up brats beyond the reach of a decent old football man like Sir Bobby Robson.

His decency and wisdom was used as a counterpoint to our foolishness and fecklessness, and it was the beginning of the notion that we viewed him with scorn and amusement. That was wrong, but it stuck and we did enough stupid things to make sure that impression never quite faded from the public mind.

When we got to London, we got the Tube over to King's Cross and then caught a train up to Newcastle. We were all still feeling rough. When we got to Newcastle, we got in a taxi and the 'Three Legends' show was on Century Radio, a phone-in that was hosted by Bernie Slaven, Malcolm Macdonald and Eric Gates, great players representing each of the North East clubs.

They were slagging us all off and saying that we were a disgrace. The usual stuff. It was interesting hearing that from Malcolm Macdonald, who wasn't exactly renowned for his abstinence himself. You know you're in trouble if he's calling you a disgrace.

When we got to my house in Durham, it was surrounded by reporters and television crews. So I went to stay at Andy Griffin's place. We were in limbo for a couple of days because everyone else was still in Spain, and so the media feeding-frenzy around us grew and grew.

The day after we got back, Jonathan Barnett called and said that a story was about to be printed in one of the papers that the four of us who had been sent home had been in a brothel with prostitutes. I started crying. I thought about what my mum was going to say. I thought 'this isn't happening'.

'OK,' Jonathan said, trying to calm me down. 'Where did you go?'

I told him the name of one of the bars we'd been to.

'That bar's a brothel,' he said.

'Yeah, all right,' I said, 'it might have been a brothel, but we didn't know that and there were no girls involved. We just went for a drink.'

I could see that it didn't look great. It was carnage. Griff was married. Carl Cort was married. And there's a story about us being in a brothel. In the end, I think Graham Shear, our legal representative, managed to make sure the story said there was no suggestion that we had gone to the bar for sex and that we were just having a drink, but the lines had already been blurred.

When the rest of the players came back from Marbella, the four of us who had been sent home were summoned to the chairman's office at St James' Park. Freddy Shepherd wasn't happy. It wasn't just that he was annoyed by the fact that we'd missed the dinner. He was also livid about the stories that had surfaced in the paper.

It turned out that the bar we'd been to in Marbella, the one that the papers were calling a brothel, was the same place where he and Douglas Hall, Sir John's son, had been stitched up by the *News of the World* some time earlier. It was the place where he'd called Shearer 'Mary Poppins' and made some unflattering remarks about Geordie women.

The stories in the papers now were about us, but they kept referring to Freddy's own misadventure there. He was livid about that. Freddy went into one about it all and Craig gave him some back. 'I know you bastards ordered vodkas and cigars on my room,' Freddy said at one point. That lightened the mood a little. Even he started laughing then.

Despite the run-ins I had with him and the trouble I caused him, I always liked Freddy. The fans gave him stick from time to time, but he genuinely loved the club and he put his money where his mouth was. Newcastle is a big club and he made sure there were times during his tenure when it punched its weight. It's been hard to say that under Mike Ashley.

At the end of 2001, as I was regaining my fitness and getting back into the team and we were challenging at the top of the table, Freddy called Jonathan Barnett and said he would like to start discussions early about negotiating a new contract.

I still had two years left on my existing deal, but Sol Campbell had made his Bosman free transfer from Spurs to Arsenal in the summer of 2001 and that had concentrated the minds of a lot of chairmen on the need to tie their best players to their clubs and not allow their contracts to run down.

I picked Jonathan up from the station in Newcastle and it was a quick drive to the ground. I hadn't spoken to him about the new deal.

'How much do you want?' he asked.

I knew that there was talk that Shearer was on £42k a week. I was on £20k.

'I want £35k a week,' I said.

'I'm going to ask for £55k a week,' Jonathan said.

'Cool,' I said. 'You're the boss.'

I dropped him off at the stadium for his meeting with Freddy. He said he would probably be an hour and then he would ring me. I drove off. I'd gone about half a mile when my phone started ringing. It was Jonathan. 'Come and pick me up,' he said.

I went back, collected him and asked what had happened.

'I sat down,' Jonathan said, 'and Freddy asked what I wanted. I told him £55k and he said that was impossible. So I thanked him for his time and walked out.'

I panicked. Jonathan told me not to worry. He said he was going to catch a train back to London so we headed for the station. His phone rang before we got there. He put it on speaker. It was Freddy. 'I'm sorry I lost my rag,' he said. 'Look, come back, and I'm sure we can sort something out.' Jonathan looked over and winked at me.

They had another discussion and Freddy said he would have to speak to his board and the rest of the directors. A few months later, towards the end of the season, we had an away game and Freddy had flown down with the team so he could meet Jonathan at the hotel and finalise the deal.

I was in my room with one of the lads when I got a text from Jonathan. He said he had agreed a new four-year deal for me that worked out at about £60k a week. It was £12 million over four years. I read it and started doing somersaults on my bed. 'What the f*** are you doing?' the other player said.

I handed him my phone. 'Read that,' I said.

They are good at what they do, my agents. It just goes to show how much power players have got. Bear in mind that I had missed half of the season with injury and they were still able to negotiate a deal of that size for me.

Everything was changing so fast in our league. A series of events had come together to boost players' earning power beyond our wildest dreams and now I was cashing in. I didn't question it. I didn't question whether I was worth it. You're worth whatever somebody's willing to pay you.

I understand why people think that footballers being paid that kind of money is obscene. I know that it's ridiculous that we are paid more than nurses or teachers or firemen and people who give so much to society. And when I got older, I tried to use my money more responsibly.

But back then I just knew that the money sloshing around in English football meant that clubs were willing to pay me the kind of money that I'd only seen on Monopoly boards before. I didn't question it. If somebody is willing to pay you that kind of cash, you're not going to turn it down, are you? I just revelled in it.

It helped me that we had a fantastic season in 2001–02. Craig's arrival had made a huge difference and he and Alan were working brilliantly together up front. Laurent Robert was providing a lot of assists and we were playing terrific, attacking football.

I came back into the first team in December in the midst of a run of six wins in seven league games that took us to the top of the table at Christmas. We beat Leeds 4–3 at Elland Road on 22 December and I know Sir Bobby attached a lot of significance to that result because it suggested we had overtaken Leeds as one of the main challengers to the dominance of Manchester United and Arsenal.

Top at Christmas. We started to dream of the title. We were back in the situation of being everyone's second-favourite team again for a while, partly on the back of the romance of it being Sir Bobby who was leading us and partly because of the type of positive football we were playing.

We lost to Manchester United and Chelsea over the holiday period, but then we came back with another strong run of results and were still right in the mix at the beginning of March.

Then Craig got injured in a game against Sunderland and we lost successive matches to Arsenal and Liverpool without scoring a goal. I missed those games, too, with a stress fracture of the foot, and when we drew at home to Ipswich in our next game, it meant we were suddenly eight points behind the leaders, Manchester United.

I got into another scrape around that time. In the week leading up to the Arsenal game, I had been training with the physios as I worked my way back from the injury. On the day before the game, which was a Saturday evening kick-off, I trained with the first team. After training, Sir Bobby called me into his office and said I'd looked so sharp that he'd been tempted to put me on the bench but had decided against it.

So I made plans to go to Manchester on the Saturday with Carl Cort and Wayne Quinn. We thought we'd do a bit of shopping in the afternoon and then go out to a couple of bars and clubs in the evening. There was a rule that when you had a home game, you were supposed to go to the stadium to watch, but if you weren't in the squad it was a bit of a grey area. I went to Manchester.

Around lunchtime, I was in a clothes shop somewhere when I saw I had a voicemail. I listened to it and it was Sir Bobby. 'Hiya, son,' he said. 'I've been thinking about it and I'd like you to be on the bench.'

I thought 'oh God'. We were supposed to be at the ground three hours before kick-off. I looked at my watch. It was 1.30pm, which meant that in theory, I had an hour to get to St James' Park.

There was no way I was going to make that, so I decided I'd rush back and pretend I hadn't heard my voice mail and get there about 4pm. I jumped in my car and drove back along the M62 and the A1 like a maniac.

**Left:** With my cousin Emma: I look rather pleased with myself. She's not impressed. The story of my life.

**Below, left:** An early picture of me and my sister, Kirsha.

**Below, centre:** The grave of my brother, Mario, who died at birth.

**Below, right:** My mum was allowed to hold Mario just for a few minutes after he died.

Me, Mum and Kirsha. Note the gold chain. I was already the King of Bling. Note the fake Christmas backdrop, too.

**Left:** With my mum and dad and Ipswich Town boss George Burley, signing YTS forms in his office at Portman Road.

**Right:** An early game for Ipswich against Sheffield United in the Division One play-offs.

**Left:** Celebrating one of my first goals for my home-town club.

**Right:** With David Johnson on the pitch at Portman Road. I'd just discovered that we had missed out on automatic promotion to the Premier League.

**Above:** Scoring a goal for Newcastle in the Tyne-Tees derby despite the best efforts of Paul Ince to stop me. Incey was one of my favourite players when I was growing up.

**Right:** Sir Bobby Robson giving me instructions on the touchline at St James' Park.

**Below, left:** The tackle by Southampton's Tahar El Khalej that ruined my chances of doing myself justice at the 2002 World Cup.

**Below, right:** If I look haunted, it's because this was the first game after I'd refused to play right wing for Sir Bobby. The crowd was baying for my blood.

**Left:** Celebrating scoring against Bolton after Sir Bobby's dismissal and trying to win the fans back ov

**Top:** Me and Lee Bowy going at it in the game against Aston Villa at S James' Park.

**Above:** We were haule in front of the press after the game. Graem Souness made us face the music.

**Left:** I had a hunch I was going to score at St James' Park agains Spurs on 23 Decembe 2006. I was right.

**Left:** Stricken on the pitch at the Memorial Ground in August 2007 after the tackle that effectively ended my career.

**Below:** Carried off on a stretcher a few minutes into my debut at QPR.

**Right:** Playing for Middlesbrough, my last club.

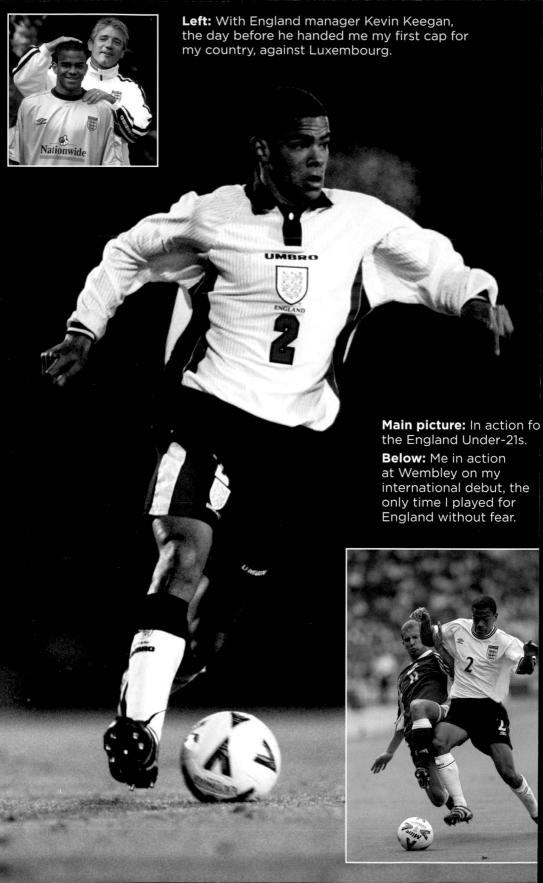

**Left:** With England manager Kevin Keegan, the day before he handed me my first cap for my country, against Luxembourg.

**Main picture:** In action for the England Under-21s.

**Below:** Me in action at Wembley on my international debut, the only time I played for England without fear.

**Left:** With England manager Sven-Göran Eriksson at our 2002 World Cup training base near Kobe, in Japan.

**Below:** Making my World Cup debut in England's opening game against Sweden. It took me about five minutes to realise I was nowhere near match fit.

**Left:** Playing against Thomas Gravesen in our second round demolition of Denmark.

**Below:** With Hollie at our wedding ceremony at Helmingham Hall.

**Below:** Leaving the *I'm a Celebrity* jungle camp in December 2015.

**Above:** Me with my four kids, from left to right, Kie, Kaden, Kody and Lexi.

**Above:** Father Christmas' bushy eyebrows giving the game away. Me, Hollie and our gang.

Somewhere along the way, my phone rang and Sir Bobby's name came up. I didn't answer it.

I had to go home to Ponteland, which is north of Newcastle, so I could get my club suit, then drive back. I walked into the stadium looking as casual as I possibly could, still pretending I knew nothing about Sir Bobby's plan to put me on the bench. It was about 90 minutes before kick-off by now.

I saw Sir Bobby as soon as I walked in. 'Did you get my message, son?' he said. I played dumb and shook my head and tried to look surprised. He was apologetic. He said he was going to put me on the bench but he'd had second thoughts. I went up to take my seat in the stands, feeling like a nervous wreck. I just about got away with it.

Dennis Bergkamp scored one of the greatest goals in recent English football history in that game so it wasn't a wasted journey, but the 2–0 defeat was a blow.

Successive draws against Aston Villa and Fulham meant that all dreams of the title were definitely dead, and we started to worry about whether we would even clinch a place in the top four, which would be our passport to Champions League football the following season and the realisation of a dream for me.

Chelsea were breathing down our necks in fifth place but when we scrambled a draw against Blackburn Rovers on 23 April, it put us out of reach of our pursuer. It was a big thing for us to break into the top four and smash that cabal of Manchester United, Arsenal, Liverpool, Chelsea and Leeds.

It was a great achievement for Sir Bobby, too, particularly when you considered that our back four was weaker than a lot of the defences in the league. We had made the top four and we had done it playing good football. There was still a game at Southampton to play on the last day of the season, but my mind started to turn towards the 2002 World Cup.

## THE WORLD CUP

## 12

I couldn't wait to get out to South Korea and Japan for the 2002 World Cup. I had made the final England squad, as everyone expected me to, I was in good form and I was playing for a Newcastle team that was on a roll. I was full of confidence and I was looking forward to travelling out to Dubai with the rest of the lads for the holding camp before we flew out to the Far East.

It was the last great football dream I had to fulfil, I suppose. I had played for Ipswich, I had played in the Premier League, I had played for England, I was going to be playing in the Champions League and now I was about to be part of the greatest show on earth when it came to sport. For me, the World Cup was the pinnacle of the game.

I felt lucky to be fit and well. Gary Neville and Steven Gerrard had already been ruled out with injuries and there were still doubts about other members of the squad, particularly David Beckham. The entire nation had been plunged into panic when a tackle from an Argentine midfield player, Aldo Duscher, had broken Beckham's metatarsal in Manchester

United's Champions League quarter-final second-leg tie against Deportivo La Coruna in April.

Becks wasn't our best player but there was no doubting that he was our talisman, and he was the captain, too. The nation held its breath when he was injured. Uri Geller was recruited to stroke pictures of David's foot and help heal it and the England manager, Sven-Göran Eriksson, had to go into battle with the Manchester United boss, Sir Alex Ferguson, just to name Becks in the squad.

I had no worries like that. I'd missed the last qualifying game of the campaign, when Becks scored that impossibly dramatic late equaliser against Greece that meant we qualified automatically for the 2002 finals, but I was fighting fit now and hoping that I might be rested for Newcastle's last game of the 2001–02 season away at Southampton in the second week of May.

We had already qualified for the Champions League so I thought I might be allowed to stay back in Newcastle, but Sir Bobby Robson soon put paid to that. We had recorded nine away wins that year and Sir Bobby said we owed it to the thousands of fans who would travel down from the North East to the South Coast to put out a full-strength team and go for the tenth win.

So I started the game. In the first half, we played exactly like a team that has nothing left to play for and we were 2–0 down at the interval. Sir Bobby gave us a huge rollicking in the changing room and when we came back out, we were flying.

Alan Shearer got one back for us ten minutes into the second half and a couple of minutes after that, we were attacking again. I was flying down the wing when Tahar El Khalej cut me down with a brutal double-footed tackle that sent me flying and got Sir Bobby off the bench, ranting and raving at the referee, Andy D'Urso.

There was a big melee around El Khalej as I lay on the ground, and I was told later that Alan had been particularly angry. I knew straightaway there was something wrong with my knee. I was in a lot of pain. El Khalej was sent off and I was stretchered off. I just couldn't believe it. I thought my dream of playing at the World Cup was over.

I left The Dell on crutches and the medics said that they thought I had damaged my medial ligament but they weren't sure quite how seriously yet. I went to meet up with England at The Grove the next day. My agent, David Manasseh, drove me because I couldn't get behind the wheel with my injury.

The England physios assessed me and they said I had a strained medial ligament and it was going to be a month or six weeks before I had a chance of being fit again. There were less than three weeks left before Sven had to hand in the squad list to Fifa, so it seemed as if I had no chance. I was devastated.

Sven came into the medical room. 'I'm so sorry, Kieron,' he said. It couldn't have been easy for him and it wasn't great news for his team, either. I was seen as the best solution to the troublesome question of who to play on the left side of midfield and now it looked like I was out of his plans.

He was just about to walk out of the room when Dave piped up. 'Sven,' he said. 'Look, I'm sorry to be a pest but you don't have to name your final squad until 31 May, so couldn't you postpone your decision on Kieron until then? He could come along and train and who knows, he might make a miracle recovery. Some people are quick healers.'

Sven thought it was a great idea. I was reprieved. I didn't know for how long, and it was still a long shot that I would be fit in time, but at least I could give it a go. I wanted to give it absolutely everything. I thought it might be my only chance to play at a World Cup and I worked as hard as the injury would let me.

The rest of the squad flew to Dubai, but I returned to Newcastle to work with the physios there. Then I flew to Dubai on the FA plane that was picking the other lads up and travelled with them to the island of Jeju, off the southern coast of South Korea, where we were to be based for a few days.

That was where things started to get complicated in terms of selection. My situation had improved dramatically and it was starting to look as if I had a decent chance of making the final squad. We played a game against South Korea in the Jeju World Cup stadium in Seogwipo on 21 May and even though I didn't play any part in the game, the physios had me running up and down the steps in the empty stands at the training session the day before.

Trevor Sinclair, who had come to Jeju as standby for me and obviously thought I only had an outside chance of making it, was now told that he wasn't going to be in the final 23-man squad. They wanted him to stay on until 31 May but, understandably, Trevor didn't want to hang about, effectively waiting for someone else to get injured, so he flew home.

Then, while we were still in Jeju, Danny Murphy broke a bone in his foot in training and was ruled out of the tournament. Trevor had just touched down back in England when he was told he was flying straight back to the Far East to join up with the rest of us in Japan.

We had another warm-up game five days later. This time, it was in Kobe, which was to be our base for the tournament. We drew 2–2 with Cameroon, courtesy of an injury-time equaliser by Robbie Fowler, and then, after a few days' training, we headed for the outskirts of Tokyo, where we were to play our opening game of the tournament against Sweden in Saitama.

I was so happy to be involved. I started on the bench and came on for Darius Vassell 16 minutes from the end with the score at 1–1. Even though I was only on for a quarter of an hour, it soon became evident to me that I was nowhere near fit. I had missed the acclimatisation in Dubai and hadn't played a game for a month when the tournament started.

I thought I was fit, but when I got out there in the heat and the humidity of Japan at that time of the year, I realised I had made a big mistake. Would I have done it again? It's really selfish, but I think I would. If you are being asked if you think you are fit enough to play in a World Cup and you know your place depends on your answer, you are always going to say yes.

As far as the team went though, it was probably the wrong choice. I didn't realise that until I got out on the pitch in Saitama. But then it hit me: I was miles away. I was blowing hard. Even Becks, who'd had longer to get back than me, was struggling. It was a big ask for us, but at least he was given matches in the tournament to get fit.

I played bits and pieces. I didn't get on in the other group games against Argentina and Nigeria but we got through to the knockout stages and we were doing OK. We had Rio and Sol anchoring the defence, Scholes and Nicky Butt in the heart of midfield and Michael Owen and Emile Heskey up front. We thought we had a chance.

I came on for Scholes in the round of 16 tie against Denmark and played most of the second half. It was a good time to come on. We were already 3–0 up and there was a party atmosphere among the England fans in the stadium in Niigata. Our minds were already starting to drift towards the quarter-final against Brazil and we didn't add to our lead.

The night before the Brazil game, I sat in the physios' room with Becks and Rio and we all felt that if we could get past this game then we would win the tournament. The problem was that that was rather a big 'if'. Brazil started that game in Shizuoka with Ronaldo, Rivaldo and

Ronaldinho up front and Cafu and Roberto Carlos as full-backs. Those players alone are going to be enough to beat most sides.

The rest of them weren't mugs, either. Lucio and Roque Junior were decent centre-halves. Edmilson and Gilberto Silva were solid in the heart of midfield. And if you've got Ronaldo, Rivaldo and Ronaldinho up front, solid in midfield is all you need.

I was on the bench again but when Michael put us ahead midway through the first half, I really thought we might have a chance. We held the lead almost until half-time, but then Rivaldo equalised and Ronaldinho put them ahead with a free-kick from 40 yards that sailed over David Seaman's head when it should really have been a routine catch.

I came on for Trevor Sinclair with just over half an hour to go and a minute later, Ronaldinho was sent off for stamping on Danny Mills. That gave us more hope of an equaliser, but we suffered in the heat again and it was difficult to put them under real pressure.

We might have had a numerical advantage, but I still struggled to contain Cafu on the left. I was nominally playing left-midfield but I was tracking back so much to cover his runs that I felt like I was playing at left-back for most of my time on the pitch. If I'd been fully fit, I might have been able to cause him some problems, too, but it was the limit of what I could do to nullify his threat.

It was a desperate disappointment when the final whistle blew, but we were beaten by the better team. Even with ten men, they had been able to keep us at arm's length and none of our big players had great games. Once again, we had come close but had been found wanting when it really mattered.

I was pleased to have played in a World Cup, of course, but I found it hard to get over the disappointment that haunted me of being unable to do myself justice in the Far East. I was nowhere near fit and I felt bitter about the tackle at Southampton that had ruined my chances of being effective on the biggest stage in the game.

I knew as we embarked on the qualifying campaign for Euro 2004 that my chances to lay claim to a starting place were probably going to be limited as well. I liked Sven, but you knew before you joined up with England what the starting line-up was going to be and in my case, that meant I knew I wasn't going to be in it.

Sven's first-choice midfield was always going to be Beckham on the right, Frank Lampard and Gerrard in the centre and Paul Scholes on the left. I always thought it was disrespectful to Scholes that he had to go on the left. That was one of the biggest crimes ever.

When you talk about Gerrard, Lampard and Scholes, Scholes was the best of the three of them and yet he was the player who was asked to give way and was shunted out wide. I'm not saying it was an easy decision over which one of the three to drop, but whatever the correct decision was, sacrificing Scholes was wrong.

Scholes was the best player I played with. On one occasion when we were training with England, we played a game of one-touch. Now one-touch is about as hard as it gets, because you have to have pictures in your mind of where everybody is so that you can play the ball to them instantly. It is almost like you have to have eyes in the back of your head.

Scholes was the absolute master of that. In that particular exercise on that day, he scored three or four goals – and I'm not talking tap-ins. I'm talking 25-yarders-lodging-in-the-stanchion-type goals.

When the session was over, the rest of the England players formed a guard of honour for him and clapped him off the pitch. I'd never seen the players do that before and I never saw it again. Scholes was so quick upstairs. He was so sharp in the mind.

Other nations would have used him as their fulcrum. People like Xavi and Zinedine Zidane counted Scholes as their favourite player. But we didn't have a football culture that appreciated him properly.

So we wasted him by putting him on the left. We banished him to the margins and in that way, as in so many other ways, we were the authors of our own downfall.

## 13

# THE GAMBLER

Not too long after we got back from the 2002 World Cup, a story broke in one of the English newspapers that Michael Owen had run up debts of £30k during the tournament in card schools at the England team hotel and that I was the man to whom he had to pay the money.

I felt sorry for Michael. As is often the case with news stories, there was a grain of truth in what was printed but they had got some of the facts wrong. The truth was that Michael had offered to be the bookmaker while the England squad was in Japan and so he had taken all the bets from the players.

I'd done pretty well and had a couple of spectacular wins. I put a £500 bet on South Korea to be drawing with Italy at half-time and to win the game. Michael gave me odds of 16–1 and the bet came in. So that was £8,500 he owed me straightaway.

But Michael made money from other people in that tournament. That's what happens when you're the bookie. You win some, you lose some.

I think he probably came out around even in the end. In fact, he was probably a few quid up, so the notion that he ran up debts was wrong.

The story did hint at a wider issue within the England squad. The amounts of money that we gambled in my time in the England set-up grew more and more extreme as the years went by, until it got to the point where I thought there was a huge danger it was destabilising individual players and potentially affecting our results.

The amount of gambling that went on within the England set-up is one of those issues that has often been hinted at but never fully explained or laid out in detail. Maybe that's because the sums we started to wager when we were in Portugal at Euro 2004 and around some of the qualifying games for Euro 2008 were eye-wateringly huge.

People seem to think it began in the Kevin Keegan era, and I have heard stories about race nights and that kind of thing. I was never involved in that. I don't know if it was just that I went to bed before it began in earnest or whether it was exaggerated, but in my experience the levels of gambling under Keegan were fairly tame.

There were card schools going on, sure, but the players used to play in the communal areas at Burnham Beeches in full view of everyone else. To me, that was a sign it was all under control. By the time we got to Euro 2004, we were gambling such large sums that we knew we couldn't possibly do it in public. So we gambled secretly in each other's rooms, behind locked doors.

When Keegan was the manager, everything seemed relatively sedate to me. Alan Shearer and Gareth Southgate were part of a card school, but I don't think they played for money at all. They played a game called 'Hearts'. Some of the other players were in other games and I think the sums were relatively small, a couple of hundred quid here and there.

I fancied myself as a bit of a card player but I was new to the squad then and I didn't have the confidence to get involved in any of the games, certainly not the ones that the manager was involved with. When Keegan quit and was replaced by Sven-Göran Eriksson in January 2001, things stepped up a notch.

It was still manageable. It never got over the top. Generally, it was me, Michael, Teddy Sheringham, David James and Wayne Bridge and sometimes Robbie Fowler. The stakes were higher than they had been under Keegan but we're talking about a maximum of a couple of grand in a hand.

I know that sounds pretty excessive, but, given the wages we were on, that was not out of control. Maybe a couple of people were a few grand down at the end of a tournament, but it was nothing that was going to be in their head and making them panic.

At the 2002 World Cup, we were staying in Japan at a hotel on an island an hour away from Kobe and there was nowhere else to go and nothing to do. Players get bored in situations like that. To make things more exciting when the tournament started, Michael set himself up as the bookie and he'd print out pages from the *Racing Post* with odds on the matches. The players and staff had a bet on the games.

That was good fun and I don't think anyone was massively up or down. I guess I was up relatively handsomely, but the fact that I had a cheque for £30k on the plane home didn't mean I was £30k up. That didn't take into account what I had wagered in the first place. Everything that happened out there in the Far East was good fun.

But the levels that we reached at Euro 2004 were just ridiculous. There were four or five of us who played, but the sums were so large that I'm not going to name names. There were no limits on what we'd gamble or what we'd chase to win our money back if we'd lost.

The only restriction that we imposed upon ourselves was that we stopped playing cards 72 hours before a game. That was telling, I think.

It was an unconscious admission that playing cards for obscene amounts of money could be just as damaging – probably more damaging – to you mentally and physically than going out for a few drinks.

It was an acceptance that it was very hard to get your mind back on an important game if you had lost hundreds of thousands of pounds to a teammate a couple of nights before. And that is the kind of money I'm talking about. Gambling that kind of money, usually on games of three-card brag, was routine at Euro 2004.

As I said, we didn't gamble in the public areas at the team hotel, which was on the outskirts of Lisbon. We went to a room and shut ourselves away. We were like clandestine drinkers, hiding ourselves to get wasted. Except at that tournament, the drug was gambling and there was a sizeable band of us that was addicted.

We didn't gamble with cash by then, either. That simply wasn't practical. The table would have been groaning with notes if we'd done that. We gambled with IOUs and kept a record of how much each individual player owed the pot. That was another reason why the sums became so absurd, I think. Sometimes, it didn't seem real.

It was usually three-card brag but if there were four of us, we would deal out 13 cards each and then every player makes four good hands and passes a card on. If you have got the best first hand, you win a point, and then the best second hand and so on.

It started off tamely for the first few days and then the numbers, especially in three-card brag, got mind-blowing. The way that brag works is that each player gets three cards, and each player has the option of betting or folding. If there was a previous bet, the player must contribute at least that much more to the pot to stay in.

It continues until there are only two players left, at which point either player may double the previous bet to 'see' his opponent. At this point, the two hands are revealed, and the player with the better hand takes the entire pot. If there is a tie, the player who is seeing loses.

The best hand is three of a kind, or a prial, followed by a straight (or running flush), a run, a flush, a pair and a high card. The best running flush is Ace–2–3. The best prial is a prial of threes. The thing with brag is that you might all think you've got a good hand. So people tend to keep going. No one is going to stack their hand if they think they have got a good hand.

When we got into the swing of things at Euro 2004, the opening stake was usually a couple of hundred quid. We'd stake that without even looking at our cards. It's called betting blind, and it's an early test of nerve. Once we'd looked at our cards, we would start betting at two grand a pop.

I'll give you an idea of the kind of money that was changing hands. After a week or so in Portugal, I was £46k down. Then one night, we were having a game of three-card brag and it was clear that a few of the lads thought they had good hands.

I peeked at my cards. I lifted up a corner of the first card and saw a two in a black suit, then a three and then a four, all in black suits. So I knew I had a straight. We went round and round and round and round. No one was folding. People were going £2k open, £2k open, so it was like £10k per round.

One person folded. At that point, I had a proper look at my hand and it was all spades. So I had a running flush. Only a prial could beat it. Player A finally saw me. He had a run, but not in the same suit, so I won. And in that hand, I went from £46k down to more than £50k up. So there was £100k in that one hand.

I was earning £60k or £70k a week at Newcastle by that stage, but when I was £46k down, it was a horrible feeling. I hated it. It was in my head. It affected me. Yes, we shut down 72 hours before a game but still, it's on your mind. It was out of control.

By the end of Euro 2004, it had got to the stage where one player was so massively down that he was begging other players to do deals. 'Would you take 30 grand for the 50 grand that I owe you?' he was saying. That kind of stuff. Most of the time, people helped him out. I don't know how much he was down but it would have been a few hundred grand.

The amounts of money we were playing for were such that, if someone had a string of bad days, they could have been half a million pounds down easily. That's just at one tournament. Some people chase their losses and that's when things can get dangerous.

I can't talk about how it affected the other players, because I don't know. I don't think it affected relationships within the squad. I didn't notice any breakdowns between individuals because of it. But we were at a major tournament. How can you go into an important game and not have that playing on your mind?

I don't care if you're worth £10 million or if you're worth £20 million. To be owing half a million pounds in gambling debts off the back of one tournament is an awful lot of cash for anybody. You're supposed to be in the shape of your life at a tournament, but if you're in that kind of debt, your head is going to be a mess.

I only played seven minutes in the entire Euro 2004 tournament, against Switzerland, in the group phase, so it wasn't an issue for me. But if you're a lot of money down, I don't see how you can go out against France, say, in one of the biggest games of your life and play your best football.

I think I was a couple of grand up or down by the time we got knocked out by Portugal on penalties in the quarter-finals. The player who lost the most was down by more than £100k. I think he clawed some money back in the last couple of weeks of the tournament.

It is clear to me that gambling is an issue in football. Players get bored. Players spend too long in hotel rooms. Players have too much disposable income. It's obvious: we are problem gamblers waiting to happen. Only last year, I read a piece in the paper by John Hartson, who once had a big gambling problem. He said he'd had calls from six Premier League managers asking him to help players who were struggling with betting issues.

There was a card school at Newcastle, too. We flew to most away games so we gambled on the plane. The amounts weren't as big as they were with England, but there was one game of brag that finished as a stand-off between Craig Bellamy and Laurent Robert that ended up with about £40k on the table.

Michael Chopra, who went on to develop a serious gambling problem, blamed that Newcastle card school for his issues, which began when he was a teenager at the club. He mentioned me and Craig and Titus Bramble as the main players in the school. He said his gambling debts had led to him being threatened by underworld figures.

There's another reason why footballers gamble a lot, too: because we're the kind of competitive people who think we can always be good at something. People say cards is luck, but I think it's skill. I think I'm good. I think all the players who were in our card school at Euro 2004 thought they were good, too. And that's the problem.

You go into it and you think you're going to win. I like playing cards. I don't like to gamble on horses. If I do gamble, I gamble on things I'm in control of. Even the bookie thing with Michael Owen at the 2002 World Cup – that's me thinking I know my stuff.

If anything, things got even more extreme with England under Steve McClaren. The card school wasn't as big but the stakes were. We were playing in each other's rooms, behind closed doors again.

We didn't qualify for any tournaments with McClaren, which was probably a blessing in disguise for one of the lads in particular. If he'd been away for a few weeks, if he'd had more than just a few days at one qualifying match to rack up his debts, he would have been bankrupt by the end of it.

This player hadn't been involved with England so much under Sven and it was a real bonus when McClaren started picking him. I loved it when this lad was in the squad. He was either the unluckiest card player I'd ever seen or the worst. I think he was the worst. I was just happy to take his money.

Every time we met up with England, I smashed him all week. It got to the point where he owed me so much money that he asked me if he could pay me back in instalments. I said that would be fine, so he set up a standing order to deal with the payments.

I think maybe he had a joint account with his missus and he didn't want her to know. Poor bloke, he must have kept thinking his luck would change, but it never did. For a while, I got standing orders or bank transfers from him every month.

I played my final match for England against Germany at Wembley on 22 August 2007. I came on for Alan Smith in the second half. We lost 2–1. It was the last of my 33 caps. A week later, I broke my leg playing for West Ham in a Carling Cup tie at Bristol Rovers.

Still, the standing orders from my international teammate kept rolling in. At least I won at something when I was with England.

# THE FERRARI

## 14

When I was a kid, I had two big dreams. One was playing for England. The other was owning a Ferrari. I'd achieved the first one and so when I got back from the 2002 World Cup, still fresh from signing that big new Newcastle contract, I thought I'd treat myself to a new car.

I went to a fancy dealership in Newcastle city centre called Formula One. I ordered a bright red Ferrari F360 Modena and paid £120k. When I got it, it was an incredible thrill. It was a symbol, I suppose: a symbol of youth and wealth, of power and arrival. It was a car driven by a guy who had it made.

I didn't just use it for special occasions. I drove it everywhere. I drove to training in it. I drove it down to the Quayside when going out clubbing. I went to the shops in it. Looking back now, I laugh about how conspicuous I must have been wherever I went, but I didn't think about that then.

I didn't buy it so I could say: 'Look at me, Larry Large.' It was just that it had always been my dream. It had been something I thought impossible when I was growing up in that backstreet in Ipswich. Something that was beyond my reach. Now I could afford to own one. It meant a lot to me.

I must have stuck out like a sore thumb driving that thing around in Newcastle. If I had been playing for a London club, then fair enough: there are Ferraris everywhere you go in London. But in a goldfish bowl like Newcastle, they saw that car coming and thought: 'Here's Kieron Dyer.'

I drove it back and forth to Ipswich a few times, showed it off to my mates and let them all have a go in it. I knew they'd always wanted a Ferrari, too, so it was like we could all live out a bit of our dreams through my good fortune.

It gave me a lot of pleasure seeing them behind the wheel of that car. That was always a big part of the thrill of earning a lot of money for me. It was giving my friends access to things that would otherwise have been out of their reach. It was sharing things with them that I know they would have shared with me if it were them who had got lucky.

The truth is that, if any of us won millions on the lottery when we were in our early twenties, for many, especially men, one of the first things we would spend it on would be our favourite fast car. Well, by that stage, my wages were at a level where it felt like I was winning the lottery every week.

There were some things about the Ferrari that I didn't enjoy. There was no comfort to it. You were so low down that you felt every bump in the road and I nearly lost the back end a couple of times when I was going round corners in the days after I had got it.

It almost felt like you should have had a separate driving test to teach you how to drive it. There was so much power in it and so much acceleration that it was particularly ill-suited to city driving. It was absolutely pointless having it in Newcastle really, certainly from a practical point of view. But I didn't really do practical back then.

I always felt like I was on the edge when I was driving it. It wasn't really a city car. It would have been nice to take it down to a track somewhere and give it a proper thrash. But who thinks with common sense when you're a 23-year-old behind the wheel of your first Ferrari? It had raw power, so who cares if it was a bumpy ride. It was rapid: that was the main thing.

I got it in October 2002, and as Christmas approached, I was starting to get used to driving it. We beat Fulham at home on the Saturday before Christmas to go fourth in the table and I made the first goal for Bellers and won a penalty, which Shearer missed. There was plenty to celebrate, and on the Sunday night I drove the Ferrari down to a nightclub called Julie's, near the Quayside, which was a popular haunt with the players.

I'd already had a couple of scrapes in fast cars by then. The year before, my Mercedes S500 hit a Vauxhall on the A1 near Newcastle's training ground in Chester-le-Street and a man in the Vauxhall was taken to hospital with a minor head injury.

In July 2001, I was fined £1,000 and banned for two months by magistrates at Chester-le-Street after the police clocked me doing 104mph on the A1 on 8 April while I was listening to the US Masters golf on the radio on my way back to the North East from Ipswich. I'd been to visit my son and I was driving back home to the apartment I had in the Stamp Exchange in Newcastle city centre.

I was a big Tiger Woods fan and I was listening pretty intently to the BBC commentary. Tiger won it to claim his fourth Major in succession and complete the Tiger Slam. My lawyer tried to turn that into an extenuating circumstance, which didn't seem to go down particularly well with the magistrates.

My brief, Barry Warburton, told the court my Mercedes was designed for cruising on Germany's autobahn. 'It is double-glazed and it is totally silent even at the speed Mr Dyer was travelling at,' he said. 'He is keenly interested in golf and was apprehended just at the time Mr Woods managed to win the American Masters.'

It was around that time that the chairman of the bench told me to take my hands out of my pockets. It seemed he hadn't been impressed by the description of how luxurious my car was. I didn't think that was a particularly good omen, either. I didn't cut a particularly remorseful figure afterwards. 'What can I say?' I told reporters, 'I'm a Tiger Woods fan.'

It is strange to think of that now. Even the defence offered on my behalf somehow sought to stress how much money I was earning, how luxurious my lifestyle was and how smooth and sleek my car was. It was as if everyone was blinded by a footballer's celebrity. Maybe we were so used to people saying 'yes' that it came as a shock when a magistrate wasn't swayed by the presence of a footballer and the tales of his wonderful life.

I got off lightly with a big fine. It didn't hurt me particularly because I was earning so much. I didn't really notice it. Maybe that's why I came out with that crack about being a Tiger fan. If they'd really wanted to punish me, they should have done what they did to Wayne Rooney last year and sentenced me to 100 hours of community service. That might have made me think about it a bit more.

I got another fine and six points on my licence two weeks before the weekend when my mate Curtis came to visit. This time I was caught doing 80mph in a 50mph zone near Grantham, in Lincolnshire, in my BMW M3. It reads a bit like I was trying to set a record for how many different cars I could get caught speeding in.

The night after the game against Fulham, I had been in Julie's for a few hours when Curtis asked if I'd take him out for a couple of circuits of the city centre in the Ferrari. It was around 1am by that stage, but like a moron, I said I would. It was parked round the corner in a car park so we wandered over and climbed in.

I thought we'd take it around the city centre and then over the Swing Bridge across the River Tyne, past the Baja Beach Club. That was a Geordie institution and one of my favourite places, too: the beach cafe upstairs, the dancers dressed as everything from the *Sister Act* nuns to the Village People, the shark head above the entrance. It was kitsch but it was fun.

We'd head there on Mondays sometimes, if we didn't have a mid-week game. I wasn't as in to the music there because it was all Chesney Hawkes, Madonna and Bryan Adams but it was a laugh. We even had the club Christmas party there one year. Jermaine Jenas went as Superman, Carl Cort was Batman and I was dressed up in a wig and black-rimmed glasses with a red velvet suit as Austin Powers. That was a decent night.

Curtis was buzzing about being in the car, so I wanted to try to give him a decent spin. It was tricky to get a good speed up in the city centre because the streets are tight and narrow and there are lots of bends, but the acceleration still pinned Curtis back in his seat now and again and that V8 engine was roaring away. What a goon I must have looked like.

Soon enough, I came flying around a corner and whizzing on to the little Swing Bridge on the Quayside, going over the River Tyne from Newcastle to Gateshead. As we got on to the bridge, the back end just got away from me and started spinning.

I know now that you're supposed to turn into it to correct a spin but I didn't know that then, and I'm not sure I would have had the presence of mind to do it even if I had known. I just let it go and waited for the inevitable. It seemed to be spinning for an eternity. I braced myself and then it smashed into the barriers of the bridge.

It kept spinning and smashing everything in its path. All the airbags popped out and ballooned into my chest and face. There was white powder spraying around. I wondered what the hell that was. Eventually, the Ferrari came to a halt. Instinctively, I started patting myself all over my body to see if anything was broken. I felt OK. I wasn't in any pain. I didn't think I had done myself any damage.

Everything was still for a second. The CD changer was changing songs when we crashed and it was going on to this Usher album called *8701*. I'd just smashed my Ferrari up, the front of it was all buckled and there was smoke coming from it, and all I could hear was this smooth, smooth voice whispering into the night.

'Eighty-seven oh one,' Usher was saying softly. *'Man, it's been a long time coming . . . we had a good time, we've grown together, who would've thought we'd stay down this long, heh? This is my chance to share my world with you, and I know you're gonna like it. Are you ready?'*

It kept repeating. All I could hear was that soft voice saying *'eighty-seven oh one'* over and over again. It wasn't long before Usher's sweet nothings were replaced by the urgent shouts of Geordies. The bridge we'd crashed on was right in the centre of Newcastle's nightlife area.

There was the Newcastle Quayside on one side and the Baja Beach Club on the other side and loads of people were on the scene quickly. It felt weird seeing everyone coming out of the clubs. It was like they had been taken out of their natural habitat.

Some of the onlookers recognised me straightaway and urged me to flee the scene. 'Run, run,' they were saying. I think they must have assumed that I was drunk, because they started saying they would take the rap for me. That's how loyal Geordies are. I might not exactly have been their favourite but that didn't matter: they would do anything for their team.

I told them I was OK and that I didn't need to get out of there because I hadn't had a drink. By that time, I had also become aware that Curtis was in trouble. He was in shock. He opened the passenger door and tried to climb out but his legs crumpled beneath him and he fell on to the tarmac.

'I'm paralysed,' he was screaming. 'I'm paralysed.'

I was beside myself now. I went over to try to help him. I touched his legs but he started screaming again.

'My legs, my legs,' he was saying. 'I can't feel my legs.'

The police and the ambulance turned up. Curtis was on the floor, moaning and wailing. By this time, the whole of Julie's and most of the Quayside seemed to be on the bridge. The police asked me if I had been driving the car. I said I had. I hadn't had a single drink, so I took the breathalyser test without any anxiety and passed it. It was a small relief, I suppose, but it was still a chaotic scene.

When I got out of the police car, Curtis was on the stretcher and they were giving him oxygen. This was getting way out of hand. By that stage, Jermaine Jenas and Nobby Solano had turned up. Titus said he was going to go to the hospital with Curtis.

I started to feel a bit shaky myself. It was partly worry about what had happened to Curtis and a bit of delayed shock. I watched the ambulance drive off towards the hospital and then one of the other lads offered to take me back to my place. We all went there and sat waiting for news of Curtis. Those were an anxious couple of hours.

Eventually, Titus called. My heart was in my mouth when I picked the phone up. He said Curtis had a bit of whiplash and a bruised hip. That was it. They were going to discharge him. He wasn't paralysed. I hadn't ruined his life. I felt a huge surge of relief.

The police analysed the scene and took measurements of the skid marks on the bridge to gauge whether I should be charged with dangerous driving, but they decided that I had been within the speed limit and that they were not going to take the case any further.

The bad news was that my beautiful red Ferrari was badly damaged. It wasn't worth me claiming it on insurance. Because I was so young, making a claim would have ramped my insurance premium up to about £16k a year. So I took the hit on it. The repairs cost about £45k and I had to suck it up.

It had turned out to be one hell of an expensive test drive. I couldn't even tell myself Curtis had enjoyed it. He'd had the fright of his life and so had I. I got rid of that car as soon it was fixed.

## THE GIRL

By the autumn of 2002, I had moved out of Newcastle and was living near the training ground in Chester-le-Street. I had finally started to see a little bit of sense and accepted that I might be asking for trouble living in or around the centre of Newcastle. One Saturday night, after a game, Carl Serrant came round for a couple of drinks.

Carl had been a Newcastle player but he had moved to Bradford Park Avenue and he said he wanted to watch *Popstars: The Rivals* because one of his teammates, Martin Pemberton, was going out with a girl called Kimberley Walsh, who was part of the TV show.

So we watched the show and Kimberley sang a song called 'Emotions', and then towards the end they announced that a girl called Cheryl Tweedy, from Newcastle, was going to sing 'Nothing Compares 2 U'. I thought she was great so I asked Carl to get Pembo to speak to Kimberley and get me Cheryl's number.

By the next morning, I had her number and I rang her that afternoon.

We hit it off straightaway and we spoke on the phone for a couple of hours. She was quite nervous and shy and I did most of the talking. I knew how busy she was going to be, so I wished her luck with making it into the band that was going to be formed and said I'd keep in touch.

By the end of November, they had finalised the line-up for the girls' band, which was to be called Girls Aloud. Cheryl was the first one to be chosen. The rest of the girls were Kimberley, Sarah Harding, Nadine Coyle and Nicola Roberts and they set off on a promotional tour to try to get their debut single, 'Sound of the Underground', to number one at Christmas.

I kept in touch with Cheryl and we worked out that we might be able to meet up in mid-December when the girls were appearing in Newcastle. They were staying at a hotel next to Newcastle Airport that night and I was flying home from a Champions League match against Barcelona at the Nou Camp.

Things were going well for me that season. I was finally playing in central midfield, where I had always wanted to play, and the team was performing well. I had formed a good partnership with Jermaine Jenas at the heart of the side and we complemented each other nicely.

For once, we got off to a flier in the league. We crushed West Ham 4–0 on the opening day and even though we lost a couple of matches, we went on a run of five wins in six matches which put us near the top of the table, and we thought from quite early on that we might actually have a shot at the title.

It was a big thrill for me to be playing in the Champions League, too. Just lining up on the pitch at Dynamo Kiev's ground in mid-September and hearing the Champions League anthem before the game made me feel that I had taken another huge step forward in my career. I had played for my country and now I was a Champions League player.

We thought we were going to blow everyone away. We were playing in a 4–4–2 and we had so much pace. It was the same as the Kevin Keegan era: we thought we could outscore everyone. But Kiev soaked up all our pressure, hit us on the break and won the game.

Then we lost at home to Feyenoord and away to Juventus. It was a thrill to play at the Stadio delle Alpi. I was inspired by it. I played in the hole behind Shearer and I was on fire. Edgar Davids couldn't get near me that night.

It was one of those evenings when the ball just wouldn't run for us. I ran the whole length of the pitch and pulled the ball back for Laurent Robert for a tap-in but he hit a defender on the line. Shearer had a goal disallowed for offside against me, even though I wasn't interfering with play. Alessandro Del Piero scored twice and we lost 2–0.

No one had ever lost their first three games in the Champions League and still qualified and everyone said there was no way back for us. Newcastle under Sir Bobby Robson didn't play by those rules, though, and we beat Juventus and Kiev in the next two games to leave our qualification for the next phase hinging on winning away against Feyenoord at the De Kuip in Rotterdam.

We went 2–0 up through Craig Bellamy and Hugo Viana and seemed to be cruising into the next round. Then Feyenoord hit back with two quick goals and we were heading out of the competition. We had entered the last minute of the match when we got a free-kick deep in our own half.

It was pumped forward and when Alan Shearer won a superb header on the edge of their box, I ran on to it and took it past a defender and suddenly I was in on goal. I side-footed my shot to the goalkeeper's left and I thought all was lost when he dived to push it away. But Craig was on it in a flash and rammed it over the line.

That year, the format of the Champions League was such that we went into another group phase rather than a straight knockout and we were drawn with Inter Milan, Barcelona and Bayer Leverkusen. The top two teams in the group would go through to the quarter-finals.

We got off to the worst possible start as Craig was sent off after six minutes of the opening game against Inter at St James' Park when Marco Materazzi trapped him with a classic piece of gamesmanship. Materazzi pinched him, Craig reacted by swinging his arm and Materazzi went down like he had been shot. Craig was sent off and we lost the game 4–1.

The next game, we had Barcelona at the Nou Camp but it rained and rained and the game was called off because the pitch was waterlogged. The idea was to play it the next day, but Sir Bobby called us in and said we could do that or we could go home and rearrange it for a later date.

It was funny because all the players who knew they were in the side wanted to play the game the next day. All the players who had hoped to be in but hadn't been selected wanted to play it at a later date. We played it the next day in the end and we were taught a bit of a footballing lesson.

Craig and Alan were both missing because of suspensions and we had Shola Ameobi and Lomana LuaLua up front in a 4–4–2. Barcelona played their 4–3–3 with Juan Román Riquelme in the hole. So that meant Gary Speed and I were up against Thiago Motta, Xavi and Riquelme, which was pretty funny.

We were chasing shadows most of the game. It was one of the most exhausting matches I've ever played in from that point of view. I thought it was bad chasing Paul Scholes around a football pitch, but Xavi was just 'wow'. If you press someone like him, he will pop it around you and get it back. If you stand off him, he'll split your defence with a 30-yard through ball.

So you become so hesitant that you don't know what to do. You end up in no man's land and it becomes mentally exhausting. There weren't many players that confused me like that and left me unsure how to deal with them, but Scholes was one and Xavi was certainly another.

They went 1–0 up early and then I drifted a pass over to the back post for Shola to equalise. Patrick Kluivert put them back into the lead before half-time and then they scored again just before an hour had elapsed – a goal that I was blamed for.

A corner came over from the right and Motta rose highest and glanced it towards goal as Shay Given came out to try to punch it away. I was guarding the back post, but I was so tired by that point that I hadn't noticed I was standing just behind the goal-line.

I got to Motta's flick and hooked it back into the box but only after it had crossed the line. I thought I'd done OK at the time, but when I watched it back, it didn't look great. I was so mentally tired, I couldn't even move my feet. It was embarrassing.

The boss had 25 emails the next day to say I should be suspended from the club. It was the old accusation that I didn't care enough about the club and I wasn't trying hard enough. The boring truth was that I was exhausted after chasing Xavi around the Nou Camp for an hour.

We got back to Newcastle Airport about 1am and Cheryl had stayed up to see me. It was all a bit furtive. I hadn't told any of the other lads I was going to meet her, obviously, so when we all jumped in our cars, the rest of them drove off and I just drove across the car park and parked outside the hotel. I wandered through the foyer with my hood up.

I knocked on her hotel room door and when she opened it, I was taken aback by how pretty she was. We talked most of the night. We just watched a bit of TV and chatted. The time flew by and I didn't leave until about 6.30am.

She was based in London by then and they were working every day on the promotion of their single. Just before Christmas, it was announced that 'Sound of the Underground' had made it to number one

We had our first date around Christmas. She got a bit of time off to come back up to Newcastle to see her family and we went to the cinema complex at the Gate in the centre of Newcastle to see a movie. She was so nervous because it was our first proper date that she turned up and admitted she'd had a few drinks to calm her nerves.

Cheryl was a great girl. I liked her a lot, but we never made anything public. If I went down to London to see her, we would never walk into a club together or be seen together. I think people got an inkling that we were seeing each other. There were rumours for sure, but it was never confirmed and we never talked about it.

Whenever I met up with England, the boys asked me questions about her. Ashley Cole asked a million and one questions. He was fascinated by her. When they got together and married, it all started to make sense. He was always keen on her and desperate to get to know her.

Only a few of my friends knew about me and Cheryl. I didn't want it to be broadcast in the papers and nor did she. I think the Girls Aloud manager wanted them all to distance themselves from footballers because footballers have a certain reputation and it wasn't the kind of association they wanted for a new and vibrant girl band.

I suppose that time was pretty much what they now might call Peak Newcastle for me. I was going out on dates with a beautiful pop star, I was earning money beyond my wildest dreams and I was playing the best football of my career in a successful side. It was a brilliant time.

When the Champions League resumed in February, we rallied and beat Leverkusen home and away. I missed the game in the San Siro against Inter with a tight hamstring but JJ, Jermaine Jenas, played in my place and played superbly and we got a 2–2 draw.

If we'd won, qualification would have been back in our hands again, but when we went into the last game against Barcelona, we knew the odds were against us. We had to beat Barcelona and hope that Leverkusen got a result against Inter.

I had to do the press before the tie with Barcelona at St James' Park and they all made a big thing of how I owed the club because of my botched clearance at the Nou Camp in the first meeting. I gave them all the soundbites they wanted.

When the game came, I ran my heart out. Even Xavi looked at me at one point and said: 'This is impossible, how are you still running?' I was a man on a mission. Craig came back from suspension and he must have had six one-on-ones and missed them all. It was one of those nights. We lost 2–0 and the Champions League adventure was over.

We still had a chance in the Premier League, though. Between the end of December and the beginning of March, we went nine games unbeaten and won seven of them. When we played Manchester United at St James' Park in the second week in April, Arsenal were top, but I still believed we had a chance of pipping both them and United to the title.

When JJ put us ahead in that game with a screamer, I really started to believe but then Ole Gunnar Solskjaer equalised, everything fell apart and United scored four goals in the space of 13 minutes. Scholes got a hat-trick that day, but I also felt that the coaches had got the game-plan wrong for us.

They had said they wanted Jonathan Woodgate to man-mark Ruud van Nistelrooy, but as the first half wore on, Van Nistelrooy twigged what was going on and basically played as a winger.

Woody didn't know whether to stay with him or revert to his normal position. It was a mess and it was one of the reasons why Scholes had so much space to work with. United were superb, obviously, and they went on to win the title, but I didn't feel we helped ourselves.

We watched the video back afterwards and Sir Bobby and the other coaches tore into us and said how poor we had been and how bad all United's goals were from a defensive point of view. When their analysis finished, I was expecting Speedo or Al to say something in our defence, but no one did. So I chipped in.

I said I thought we all accepted that we had played poorly, but that maybe the coaching staff ought to admit they got it wrong as well. They got confrontational straightaway. I pointed out that it had felt as if we were playing with one centre-half a lot of the time and that Ryan Giggs had a field day coming in from the left.

Sir Bobby went ballistic. He said I was questioning whether he knew the game. I said of course I wasn't. I had just been pointing out that our best centre-back was playing right-back. But Sir Bobby went into meltdown and one of the coaches, Dave Geddes, said I was out of order.

I had to go and see Sir Bobby afterwards to explain what I was trying to say. I wasn't criticising him. I just didn't understand why we couldn't accept that we were all at fault. I suppose I was searching for that old Terry Venables favourite, a bit of collective responsibility.

Sir Bobby was in a gentle mood. He talked to me as if he was humouring an idiot.

'Look, son,' he said, 'it's just that I don't think you were right to criticise our tactics after the game.'

'What do you mean?' I said.

'Well, Woodgate was man-marking Van Nistelrooy,' he said.

'Yes,' I said.

'Well,' Sir Bobby said, 'Van Nistelrooy scored a penalty but he didn't score from open play, did he?'

'No,' I said.

'In fact,' he said, 'did he have any chances at all?'

'No,' I said.

'Exactly,' he said. 'So my tactics were spot on.'

He winked at me and then he thought of something else.

'Who were you playing against in the game, son?' he said.

'Scholes,' I said.

'How many did Scholes score, son?' he said.

'Scholes got a hat-trick,' I said.

Sir Bobby winked at me again. I was speechless for a second and then the two of us just started laughing and laughing.

Our part in the title race was over after that. United beat Arsenal by five points in the end and we were nine points further back in third place. Still, third place was quite an achievement. It was the best we ever did in my time at the club, and if you consider what the expectations are there now, it shows you what a special time it was.

The kind of season we had was recognised at the Professional Footballers' Association Awards that year. I was voted on to the PFA Premier League Team of the Year, Jermaine Jenas was named Young Player of the Year, Alan picked up the Premier League Player of the Decade Award and Sir Bobby was given a Lifetime Achievement Award. It was Newcastle's night.

My dates with Cheryl had carried on all through that spring and into the summer. Like I said, she was a great girl, an absolutely great girl, but my personal life was complicated at that time and I wouldn't say we were ever really boyfriend and girlfriend.

There was a time a bit later in 2003 when she wanted me to get more serious, but I couldn't do it, because by then I was harbouring another secret. I had got another girl pregnant and I could never have got serious with Cheryl knowing that I was about to have a child with someone else.

To be honest, I would have liked to get more serious, too, but I knew I had to deal with the fact I was going to become a father again. I knew that Cheryl deserved better than me. I also knew that if I tried to ignore the other things that were going on and throw myself into a proper relationship with her, she would only get hurt. And I didn't want that.

So the thing with Cheryl kind of fizzled out. I'm pleased that she seems so happy in her personal life now, because any of the bad things you see written about her simply aren't true. I just wasn't a good fit for her, because I couldn't commit to her. There were trust issues as well. She wanted more and I couldn't give her any more.

Nothing will ever change my mind that she's a great person, though. When the Grosvenor House Hotel scandal broke in 2004 and I was going mad with the worry of being implicated in something I hadn't done, she sent a card to my house saying that she was thinking of me. And five years after we stopped seeing each other, when my sister was sent to prison, she sent a big bunch of flowers and a card to my mum. How she got hold of mum's address, I have no idea. That just emphasised to me what a great heart she has.

When she was touring with the Black Eyed Peas, I went to watch her show at the O2 Arena in London and got a message to her PA to ask if there was any chance my kids could get a picture with her. After the show was over, she came straight up, which made my kids' day.

Six months or so after we stopped seeing each other, I started to read stories about how she was going out with Ashley Cole. Ashley and I had been really close until then, and we'd go out in London all the time. After he started going out with Cheryl, we would text and talk but we were never close friends again.

## THE DAUGHTER

# 16

I had known Zoe for ages. She had grown up in Ipswich, like me, and when she moved to Fulham, in west London, we remained great friends. If I was in London for a game, she'd text, I'd go round, we'd have a meal and a drink and then have some fun.

Neither of us was looking for any commitment. Besides, I was going on dates with Cheryl at the time and enjoying her company more and more and beginning to think that maybe that might get serious.

One night in the summer of 2003, I went round to see Zoe and she told me she was pregnant. To say it was a shock is an understatement because we were never serious. Because I was an England footballer and because I'm a jerk, I was worried the story would come out and make big news.

She said she definitely wanted to keep it because she'd had trouble getting pregnant in the past. I didn't try to change her mind, but I stormed out of the house because I was in shock and she had to chase me down the road, pleading with me to talk about it.

I wanted to find out if I was definitely the father, so I persuaded her to have a test at a clinic in London. I didn't want to wait for the results of a DNA test. I was a footballer. I wanted everything and I wanted it now. I wanted her to have the test even though there was a risk to her and the baby, and in the end, reluctantly, she agreed. I feel ashamed of the way I acted.

Zoe was so co-operative. She must have been feeling insecure and uncertain herself, but when I arrived at the clinic, she tried to talk to me and, like an idiot, I blanked her.

I was so stubborn and stupid, I didn't even look at her. The more I think about it, she was the one doing me a favour. She did the test and, sure enough, the results showed that I was the father. I still felt as if I was in shock.

I was worried about how my friends and family would react. She didn't want to rock the boat. She was planning to move back to Ipswich anyway, and she knew that if it got out that I was the father of her child, she might get harassed by the press. She was the one who came up with the idea of keeping the whole thing a secret. Coward that I am, I thought that was a good idea.

I wasn't there when she went into labour on Valentine's Day, 2004. I was in New York. We had been knocked out of the FA Cup by Liverpool in the fourth round and so we were given some time off over the weekend of the fifth round and I flew to the States with Titus Bramble and our pal, Lennie.

I was in my room at the Peninsula Hotel when Zoe called and said she'd had a baby girl. She said she was going to call her Lexi-Belle. I didn't tell Titus or Lennie what had happened, but I did go out to celebrate. I was happy and relieved that Zoe and Lexi were OK but I was worried, too, about the way I was leading my life.

My dad had already told me that I had brothers and sisters all over the place around Ipswich, from his various liaisons with different women. A lot of my best friends' dads have kids with six or seven different women. I'm not stereotyping black men but it was just the way it was in the circles I moved round in Ipswich.

I started looking at myself. Kie was born at a time when his mum and I weren't even together. Now I had Lexi with someone I thought I was just having fun with. I was going down the same route as my dad and I wanted to stop.

My brother turned up on my doorstep when I was 12. I had never met him and he turns up and says, 'hi, I'm your brother.' I didn't want that for my kids. I didn't want to be someone who has kids with five or six women. But here I was, aged 23 and I had two children with two baby-mothers already. I thought to myself: 'Just keep it in your f***ing pants.'

So my daughter, my only daughter, was a secret for four years. Zoe moved back to Ipswich when Lexi was born and when I came back from Newcastle to see Kie or my friends, I would go around to Zoe's when it was dark and sneak around the back so no one would see me, like some sort of cat burglar. I was being totally and utterly absurd.

There were times when we had to indulge in farcical role-play. I'd bump into Zoe and Lexi at a wedding, say, and express surprise that she'd had a child. 'Oh, I didn't know you'd had a baby,' I'd say for the benefit of others. 'Congratulations. How you doing now? Oh, you've moved back to Ipswich. I didn't know.'

When Lexi was three or four, I had a row with Zoe over something petty and refused to see her, and Lexi got caught in the middle of that. I was stubborn and stupid and I wouldn't knock on Zoe's door. I sacrificed seeing my daughter for a year. I will never get that year back.

That was me all over. In the first two or three years of Kie's life, I'd go down to Ipswich when I had a weekend off. But the truth is, I didn't have weekends off very often. I should have been going every weekend.

But, oh, the lads wanted a night out, or, oh, it's a great night at Julie's on Sunday. Oh, I want to show off in the Ferrari with some of the lads on Saturday night and, oh, I've just crashed it on a bridge. There was always a reason not to go to see him and I always found it.

I wish now, of course, that I'd gone back to Ipswich on every single day off I had, but I wasn't emotionally smart enough to do that. I should have driven down or got my mum to bring him up. I still regret that bitterly. I look back and think 'what were you doing, you stupid twat.'

I played at being a dad, really. I didn't take it seriously. I made gestures, but that was all they were. I threw a bit of money at it and thought that was enough. I wouldn't see Lexi for a while, but I'd send Christmas presents down for her. One year, Zoe phoned my mum. She was exasperated. 'Who the f*** does he think he is?' she said.

She was right, of course. She was absolutely right. The pity is that I didn't realise it earlier. I had my second son, Kaden, in May 2006 during a period when I was back with Kie's mum. By 2008, I was living back in Ipswich with Kai, Kaden and their mum, and one night I was going out to a party thrown by a jeweller called David Bell. I was still a bling boy back then. I hadn't spoken to Zoe or Lexi for about a year.

Before I got to the party, I got a phone call from my mum. She said she had some bad news. Zoe and Lexi had been at a kids' party and Zoe had developed a migraine. She used to get migraines all the time. She took Lexi back home, but then Zoe had a convulsion of some sort and collapsed on the floor.

Lexi was three or four at that time and she was there alone with her mum, basically watching her mum dying in front of her. She got her mum's phone, worked out the security code and rang one of Zoe's friends, Marsha. She told Marsha that her mummy wasn't waking up and so Marsha rushed round to the house, found Zoe and called an ambulance.

My mum said that Zoe was on her way to Addenbrooke's Hospital in Cambridge and that the prognosis was not good. They thought she was going to die. I couldn't believe it. I was consumed by a mix of shock and fear. And, of course, guilt. Lots and lots of guilt about how I had behaved, and lots of fear about whether it was now going to be too late to put any of it right.

I thought about my daughter, having to go through all that on her own. I thought about how brave she had been and how clever and how quick-thinking. And then I felt more guilt that I had played such a small part in her life and if this was a brave, resourceful little girl, it was everything to do with her mum and nothing to do with me. I rang Neville and sobbed uncontrollably for what seemed like an eternity.

I didn't know what to do next. I hadn't spoken to Zoe for a year and I was aware that if I phoned her mum or her sister – who must have already had me down as a waster – and started weeping about what was happening, I was going to look like even more of a loser to them.

If I started showing an interest now, I thought they would think: 'What the f*** does he care?' But I wanted to do it. This was serious and if it made them think even worse of me than they already thought, it didn't really matter. I didn't have a lot to lose. I wanted to be able to support them if they needed it.

I rang Zoe's sister, Donna, and she picked up. They were on their way to Addenbrooke's and it was still not clear whether Zoe would make it. But she survived the journey to the hospital and had to be rushed into emergency surgery. It was touch and go but thankfully her condition began to stabilise. An aneurism in her brain had burst and she was in a coma. The doctors said she was lucky to have survived. I think it was her wanting to see Lexi again that kept her alive.

After a few weeks, I asked Zoe's mum and dad if I could see Lexi. I knew it was difficult for them, particularly because Zoe wasn't able to make the decision for herself. They said they would think about it. I spoke to her dad and he just asked me to promise him I would always be in Lexi's life, whatever happened with Zoe.

I promised him that straightaway. I started taking Lexi to see her mum while she was lying in hospital in a coma. If Zoe had died, I would have wanted Lexi to come and live with me. But Zoe didn't die. Her mum stayed with her in the hospital and one day, after about three months in a coma, Zoe woke up.

She had suffered partial paralysis and she is now still confined to a wheelchair. She was hoping that she might be able to walk again, but the doctors have told her that is not going to happen. So she is in a wheelchair but she is alive and she is a wonderful mum to Lexi.

When Zoe came out of hospital, they told us that she would need full-time care. Her mum and dad had a small place and they had to sell it. Zoe needed a place that was wheelchair friendly. She needed a bungalow, essentially. Her mum and dad couldn't afford one and they became really distressed about the idea of having to put her in a care home of some sort.

I spoke to Donna and said I would like to buy a bungalow for them. I didn't think they would take it, because I knew they were proud people. I told them it wasn't for them. It was for my daughter. If I had been honest with them, maybe it was for me, too.

Maybe it was to try to make up for lost time. Maybe it was to try, in some small way, to make things right again and to wash away some of that guilt I felt. So don't think it was an unselfish act on my part. It was selfish, in its own way. Is there any such thing as an altruistic gesture? Or is altruism, in whatever form it takes, always wrapped up in making a person feel better about him or herself? I don't know.

When I told Zoe's parents I would buy the bungalow, her mum burst into tears. I think it was just a huge relief. The weight had been lifted off her and we have formed a great bond ever since. Zoe even came to my wedding and I see Lexi, who is 14 years old now, whenever I want, which is more than I deserve.

I still feel great guilt about the way I behaved towards her and her mum, but I'm trying to make up for it. I'm lucky I got a second chance.

# 17

## THE GROSVENOR HOUSE HOTEL

At the end of September 2003, we played a match against Arsenal at Highbury on a Friday night. It was shown live on Sky and was a decent game. It was the only time in my career that I got the better of Ashley Cole and I had a hand in both our goals but we still lost 3–2. Thierry Henry scored a late winner from the penalty spot.

It meant that we had gone the first six games at the start of the season without a win. We had been knocked out of the Champions League by Partizan Belgrade in the third qualifying round and Sir Bobby Robson was coming under a bit of pressure.

I still wanted to go out in London that night, though. It was a Friday night, it would have been rude not to. I wasn't planning a big one. Just a few drinks. Some of the lads headed straight back to Newcastle but we didn't have another match for eight days, so a few of the boys stayed down and made their own plans to go out.

I'd arranged to meet a friend of mine, Lucy, after the game. I got her and her brother tickets for the match. She lived in Essex but she had a place in London as well, and the plan was for us to go out for something to eat and then go back and chill at hers.

After the game, I met her and her brother in the players' lounge. She said she'd forgotten the key to her house, so I figured we'd just book a hotel room instead.

Titus Bramble was there with his mum and brother, but I didn't know what his plans were, and Lucy and I headed off into town. We went to the Grosvenor House Hotel in Park Lane because it was somewhere I had stayed before. I went to reception and asked if I could book a room.

I was talking to the guy behind the desk and sorting the room out when my mobile phone rang. It was Titus. He asked me where I was staying. I told him and he asked me if I'd book a couple of rooms for him, too. I explained the situation to the guy at reception and he said it was fine.

He said I just had to leave a credit card to guarantee all the rooms and then when Titus arrived, he could take over the booking. I rang Titus back and said there were two rooms reserved in his name. I didn't think anything more of it. Not thinking anything more of it was always part of my problem.

I went up to the room and got changed and Lucy and I went out for something to eat. We met up with my agent, David Manasseh, and went to a bar called Sketch, just off Regent Street. I was wearing combat jeans and a t-shirt that had 'Hip Hop' printed across it. A paparazzo took my picture. Lucy and I got a cab. We went back to the hotel and straight to our room.

When I got up on Saturday morning, I rang Titus and asked where he was. He said there were a few of them in his room, including a guy we all knew called Nick Meikle, and he'd see me in the lobby. I took Lucy downstairs and arranged a taxi for her and she went home. I waited around until Titus and Carlton Cole, who was on loan with Charlton Athletic at the time, appeared and we all went shopping in town.

Titus said they'd had a good night. He said a girl had come back to one of the rooms with Nick and Carlton. He said the girl was up for it and that he and Carlton and Nick had all slept with her.

I wasn't shocked. I was a veteran of Ayia Napa, after all. Anyway, that kind of behaviour was fairly common among the footballers of my generation and the girls we sometimes attracted. The way Titus was talking about it, everybody had had fun. They were all consenting adults.

That evening, we went out to a couple of bars and clubs and Rio Ferdinand and David Beckham's sister Joanne and some of her friends came out with us. The first time I set foot inside Titus's room was on the Sunday morning, when I stopped in before heading off to King's Cross to catch the train back to Newcastle ready for training on the Monday. I'd had a great weekend.

On Monday morning, I got up and looked at my phone. I had three or four missed calls from my agent. I called him. 'Have you seen the *Sun?*' he asked me.

The story was splashed all over the front page. It alleged that a group of footballers had been involved in a gang-rape at a London hotel. A 17-year-old had told police that she had gone back to the hotel for consensual sex with one man and then been attacked by up to six others.

The article didn't name any footballers. I told David it was nothing to do with me. I told him the truth about going straight back to the hotel with Lucy on the Friday night and what I'd been up to on the Saturday. He was relieved. 'Good, good,' he said.

I put the phone down and opened my curtains. There was an army of photographers outside the gates of my house. I phoned Titus and asked him what the hell was going on. He said he hadn't seen the *Sun.*

I drove to training and the photographers were snapping away as I left. There were even more reporters and cameras outside the training ground. Inside, everyone was asking what on earth was going on. John Carver came in and said Sir Bobby wanted to speak to us all.

Sir Bobby stood up in the meeting room and said the police had called Freddy Shepherd. Freddy wanted to know if any of us were involved. Titus put his hand up and said the story was made up but that he might be one of the people that it was referring to.

The gaffer went mad and started saying how irresponsible it was and how appalled he was, but Craig asked him to hear Titus's side of the story first. Titus was embarrassed but he explained what had happened and said there was no rape.

We had another meeting after training and Sir Bobby said he wanted to give us a chance to come clean. He asked Gary Speed if he was there. Speedo said he wasn't. He asked me if I was there. I said 'no'. He asked Shola and Shola said 'no'. Sir Bobby said the police had told him I was involved and that Shola was involved, too. Shola laughed. 'I wasn't even in London,' he said.

The gaffer said the police wanted to interview me. The next day, things started to move fast. The *Sun* did a massive follow-up and printed a picture of me walking out of a club on its front page. It pixellated my face so they could say that they had protected my identity, but a load of people recognised me in the photo. The headline said: 'England Star in Rape Claim', or something like that.

I was nearly in tears by now. I was getting text messages from family members saying I was a disgrace. People were openly talking about the fact that I was involved. That night, we were summoned to Hull for a police interview but it was cancelled.

The Attorney General, Lord Goldsmith, ordered the newspapers not to identify either Carlton or Titus in case it prejudiced any future trial. It was a fair decision, but it also meant that the speculation over who was involved spiralled out of control and my name was dragged into it more and more.

The story got bigger and bigger. There was a media feeding frenzy. I was named in the starting line-up for the home game against Southampton the following Saturday. We won 1–0 but I felt everyone was watching me and assumed I was guilty.

I felt under huge pressure to give my version of events. I was desperate to clear my name, but I also knew that to do so would heap even more pressure on Titus and Carlton Cole. I was also told that, legally, it was advisable for me not to comment.

It was like I was trapped in a nightmare. There were even suggestions at one point that Sir Bobby was going to resign over the incident. Critics were rounding on him and saying that the young players at the club were out of control and Newcastle was a symbol of all that was wrong in football.

The day after the Southampton game, the *News of the World* ran an interview with Nick Meikle. He told the paper that I was not there when the sex with the girl took place, but he did go into lurid details about the world of sexual excess he said we inhabited and the way that girls would be shared around by footballers on nights out.

He said that the practice of sharing a girl was called roasting. I hadn't heard that term before, but I recognised what he was talking about. Some said roasting referred to the fact that the woman in question was treated like a piece of meat.

There was another, more graphic, interpretation which held that the term originated because one man would have sex with the girl from behind while she was performing oral sex on another man. So it was like she was being spit-roasted. You can pick which explanation you prefer.

Either way, it shone a rather unpleasant light on footballers' lives and 'roasting' entered the English language as shorthand for the depraved antics of players who had so much money that they felt they could treat any woman like a piece of dirt.

In this new world where celebrity was everything, the Grosvenor House Hotel incident was portrayed as celebrity's most disgusting moment. It was held up as a mirror to a society that had become obsessed with fame and being associated with it. It was even used by some as an excuse to accuse women of degrading themselves with footballers and their friends.

It was called 'football's worst scandal of the decade' and, inevitably, those who said footballers should be role models for our young people outdid themselves in their angst. I've never agreed with that role model stuff. Don't look up to me. Look up to your parents. Look to them for guidance, not to a young footballer. If you're a mum or a dad, don't expect me to bring your kid up for you. Do it yourself.

My son Kie is going on his first lads' holiday in the summer and the way he behaves is my responsibility. I want him to have fun, and even though there is precious little room for me to be holier than thou about anything with him, it would be stupid if I didn't at least tell him about what some of my experiences have taught me.

We haven't chatted about it yet, but before he goes I will tell him that there is a line that you cannot cross when it comes to respect for women. I wasn't involved in the incident at the Grosvenor House Hotel but some of the same lessons can be applied to it as what happened in Ayia Napa. Just because something is consensual doesn't necessarily mean it's right.

In Newcastle's next league game, on 18 October, we played our local rivals Middlesbrough at the Riverside. The Middlesbrough fans didn't hold back with me. They were brutal. Every time I touched the ball, the same chorus rang around the stadium. *'Who's the rapist on the wing,'* they chanted, *'who's the rapist on the wing?'*

I like to think I'm quite mentally strong, but when you're innocent and you can't come out and tell your side of the story because there's an investigation going on, it is really hard. I felt like I couldn't handle it any more and I rang the club and said I wasn't coming into training.

Sir Bobby stuck by me, though. He promised that the club would support me and he told me that training and playing was the best thing for trying to keep my mind off what was happening. He persuaded me to come in and, gradually, the truth began to emerge.

Titus and Carlton had been arrested on 10 October and I was interviewed by police. I was told I was a witness, not a suspect. I was questioned by a male detective and a female detective and they asked me in great detail about what had happened that Friday night and the exact timings of my movements.

When the female detective started interrogating me, she got right to it with her first question. 'Have you ever had anal sex?' she said. I nearly choked on my glass of water. The questioning went on for about three hours. It was a proper grilling.

I had to go into everything that happened in the 48 hours after the game. They asked me if I ever went into the rooms of Nick, Titus or Carlton. I had to draw a diagram of which areas of which rooms I had been in because they had fingerprinted them.

It felt to me as if they thought I was lying. They contacted Lucy and interviewed her. Rio and Joanne Beckham got interviewed as well to see if any of the lads had been talking about it when we met up on the Saturday night. When I got out of there, I felt like I'd been on the wrong end of an interrogation by Jack Bauer.

Around that time, the ban on naming Titus and Carlton was lifted and so I was able to give my side of the story at last. I released a long statement. It was long because I had a lot to get off my chest. None of the papers printed it in full but some did include extracts.

'Recently,' I said in the statement, 'there has been much press coverage as to my supposed involvement in an alleged incident at the Grosvenor House Hotel on the weekend of 26 and 27 September.

'Despite intense pressure, I have respectfully maintained a dignified silence whilst the police have been undertaking their initial investigations. I now feel it is appropriate for me to set the record straight and put an end to the massive speculation ...

'Unfortunately, the fact that my name was mistakenly attached to someone else's room has provoked wild speculation. Furthermore, I was appalled by a supposedly "blurred" photograph of me that appeared during a storm of publicity which had suggested that I was at the centre of the criminal investigation.

'I was obviously identifiable generally and also from the photograph, as has been proved by the vast amount of e-mail, chat room/website and references elsewhere to my alleged involvement, as well as comments made to me by many people.

'This whole matter has been very distressing for me. To make matters worse, my family and friends have been hounded, and my reputation has been damaged in the most public way possible.

'Until now, I have felt trapped and it has been very frustrating that I have been unable to clarify publicly the facts, which clearly exonerate me, whilst the police conduct their enquiries. Additionally, amidst the volume of press coverage there have been many inaccurate and defamatory reports published, which has been massively hurtful.

'I will now make clear a number of points: I have not been fined by Newcastle United Football Club nor reprimanded by its management, directors or chairman. My teammates are fully aware that I had nothing to do with this and reports of them launching personal attacks on me are categorically untrue. I had no involvement in this matter, let alone being "at the centre of it" as suggested ...

'I have, from the very beginning, had a number of witnesses who can and have corroborated my whereabouts which prove I had no involvement in the alleged events. I recognise that the claims being made by the woman involved are of the most serious nature, and warrant a thorough investigation, that is without doubt.

'I do not wish to trivialise these serious allegations. It is for this reason that I have not stated my position until now. I am grateful to be given this opportunity to set the record straight.'

In January 2004, it emerged that neither Titus, nor Carlton Cole, nor Nick Meikle would face charges after the Crown Prosecution Service concluded there was insufficient evidence to proceed, but the inquest into the way footballers behave around women still rages today.

I don't think the culture has changed that much. The Ched Evans case showed that. Evans, who was a Sheffield United player, and his friend Clayton McDonald, who played for Port Vale, were accused of raping a woman in a hotel in Rhyl in May 2011.

McDonald was acquitted but Evans was initially found guilty and served a prison sentence. Even though he was acquitted after a retrial, the case touched off many of the same emotions that came to the fore during the furore over the events at the Grosvenor House Hotel that night in September 2003.

Yes, it was a relief to get my statement out there to the public and make my innocence clear but to this day, when people talk about the Grosvenor House Hotel incident, they always think I was involved.

My lawyers commissioned research about the way the case was

reported and it showed that even though my face had been pixellated in the front-page image that was printed of me in the aftermath of the incident, 98 per cent of people they questioned said it was me.

It was also repeatedly said that I paid for the rooms. That was wrong. I reserved the rooms and paid for my own room. Titus paid for the rooms he took. My lawyers sued some newspapers and I was awarded a significant amount of money, but the damage was already done.

## THE GUILT

# 18

There was more than one man to blame for the demise of Sir Bobby Robson at Newcastle United, but in the public mind it was always me. In the public mind, I was the spoiled, blinged-up little brat who spat my dummy when Sir Bobby was at his most vulnerable because he asked me to play right-midfield. In the public mind, I precipitated his fall.

I wasn't blameless. I admit that. I have spoken several times already about the guilt I feel over mistakes that I have made in my life. My role in the sacking of a man I admired and revered more than any other man in football is something that I will always regret, too. I had my reasons for behaving the way I did, but I wish now that I had acted differently.

Sir Bobby was fired by Newcastle United on 30 August 2004, but the causes of his departure had their roots in far more disparate issues than my argument with him about his desire to pick me on the right side of midfield for the opening game of the 2004–05 season. The truth is that the knives had been out for him for a while.

In a way, Sir Bobby paid for his fantastic achievement in leading the club to its third-place finish in 2002–03. That season was testimony to his talent as a manager and as the supreme man-manager of his era. We had a good side but it had serious flaws, and for us to finish that high was a result of Sir Bobby building a team that was far more than the sum of its parts.

That achievement, however, created exaggerated expectations. Sir Bobby had given Newcastle's fans and its board a taste for the high-octane thrill of the Champions League and those nights against the giants of Europe like Barcelona and Inter Milan. Sir Bobby had made Newcastle feel part of football's elite again and everyone wanted it to stay that way.

So it was a massive blow when we lost to Partizan Belgrade in the third qualifying round of the Champions League at the start of the 2003–04 season. We beat them 1–0 in Belgrade in the first leg, but they beat us by the same score back at St James' Park and the tie went to penalties.

We missed our first three spot-kicks. Alan Shearer blasted his penalty wide. I took the second kick but the keeper guessed correctly and dived to his right to push my effort away. Jonathan Woodgate took the third and the keeper saved it easily. The shootout still went to sudden death, but when Aaron Hughes lifted his kick over the bar, Milivoje Ćirković sent Shay Given the wrong way and we were out of the competition before the group stages had even begun.

Sure, we went into the Uefa Cup and had a decent run to the semi-finals, where we lost to Marseille, but the glamour wasn't the same. And in the league, even though we had another decent campaign and were always in and around the top four, we struggled to match the consistency and the results of the previous season.

Other things got in the way, too. The Grosvenor House Hotel stuff didn't help. It was a distraction for me and for Titus, and for the hierarchy at the club. It didn't lead to any charges for anybody, but it fuelled the fire of people saying that Sir Bobby couldn't control his players and that he was too lenient when it came to our behaviour.

I was also struggling a bit with my fitness. Before the start of the 2003–04 season I was diagnosed with a condition called auto-immune hepatitis. The immune system around my liver needs help to boost it up because once something attacks my liver, my immune system doesn't fight it off. They'd missed it when I passed my medical for Newcastle.

That diagnosis led to all sorts of rumours circulating that I had caught a sexually transmitted disease, which I hadn't. It's not something you catch. They put me on the highest dosage of Prednisolone steroids and another fairly heavy-duty medicine called Azathioprine. It brought me out in spots.

I got my bloods taken every two weeks but I was still allowed to play and, gradually, my dose of steroids went down and down as my bloods went back to normal.

I came off the medication altogether for a while, but the problem is that if you then get a virus and something attacks your liver, it's going to flare up. So I will probably be on medication for the rest of my life. When I got more injuries later in my career, the medication I was on for the auto-immune hepatitis slowed down my recovery.

We were still in with a chance of making the top four until very late in the 2003–04 season. We thought we had put ourselves in the box-seat with a home win over Chelsea at the end of April but then we lost to Manchester City and drew with Wolves.

When we drew with Southampton in the penultimate game of the season, it meant we could no longer catch Liverpool, who were in fourth place. We played them on the last day of the season and drew, which meant we qualified for the Uefa Cup, but there was a dreadful air of anti-climax around the place. I knew we would be under pressure right from the start of the following season.

We signed a few players over the summer to try to push on. Patrick Kluivert, Nicky Butt, James Milner and Steven Carr all arrived. Kluivert was the marquee signing, but there was a feeling around the club that he wasn't really Sir Bobby's choice. That caused some unease, and when Gary Speed left for Bolton, we lost someone that everyone in the dressing room looked up to.

I liked Speedo. He was a proper bloke. He would always come and check on the younger players and make sure they were OK. He was like the club captain for me. He led by example in training and he looked after me on the pitch. 'You get on the ball,' he said. 'I'll do your dirty work for you.'

Craig Bellamy said he felt it was the beginning of the end of everything that team had achieved when Speedo left, but he wanted to play first-team football and central midfield was suddenly looking like a very crowded area of our team. Butt's arrival meant that he, Jermaine Jenas and Lee Bowyer and I would all be competing for two starting spots at the heart of the team.

Craig was fretful, too. All the talk in pre-season was that Kluivert had been bought to form a dream-team attack with Shearer. Craig had been our best player for the last two seasons, so you can imagine how that made him feel.

Things started to go awry when we hosted a pre-season tournament at St James' Park at the end of July. Our first game was against Rangers and I started in the centre of midfield, with Lee Bowyer, and Craig was up front with Alan. At half-time, Sir Bobby said he was going to take Laurent Robert off and he told Craig he was moving him to the left.

Craig was nearly in tears. It wasn't that he refused to do what Sir

Bobby said. It was more like he was pleading. 'No, no,' he was saying, 'the fans are begging for Shearer and Kluivert but I've been unbelievable, I want to play up front. I know what's going to happen, don't do this to me, I'm not a left winger.'

Kluivert wasn't even involved that day, but Craig was convinced they were going to try to engineer it that he would move to the left when the season began so that Shearer and Kluivert could play together. He kept pleading with Sir Bobby not to move him.

It was going on and on and the interval was nearly over. It was getting ridiculous and there was no resolution in sight. 'Gaffer,' I said, 'why don't I go on the left and you put Nicky Butt in the centre and then sort out this stuff with Bellers afterwards.'

So I was on the left. I played well, we beat them 4–2 and I scored a goal in the last minute. After the game, I thought the shit would hit the fan but nothing was said. It was just 'see you Monday'. Craig was my best friend, so it wasn't like I wanted him to get into trouble, but I was surprised that there was no inquisition about what had happened.

That was a fortnight before our opening game of the season against Middlesbrough at the Riverside. On the Thursday before the match, Sir Bobby started giving out the bibs for the first team and Jonathan Wood-gate turned to me and said: 'It looks like you're playing right-mid.'

He was right. We started going through our shape and it became obvious that Nicky Butt and JJ were going to be playing in central mid-field. I was sulking badly. I'd played well in central midfield the previous season. In fact, I'd made the PFA team of the season once more on the back of my performances in central midfield, and now the same old crap was happening again and I was being shifted out to the flanks.

It had become a big mental block with me. I preferred centre-midfield because when you play out wide, you rely on other people to give you the ball. In centre-midfield, you get on the ball automatically. You have more influence. I always felt I was more trusted when I played in the centre. I felt I was more valued, and I thought it was where I was best.

I also felt as if I was being punished for being so accommodating during the match against Rangers. I'd done the right thing there and helped out when there was a problem. I'd solved an issue. So everyone else got to choose their position if they stamped their feet, but I was the one who was sacrificed. That's how it felt to me.

I didn't say anything to Sir Bobby during training. I sulked through the session and left the training ground without having a shower. I rang the gaffer that Thursday night and he didn't pick up so I left him a voicemail.

'Gaffer,' I said, 'you know I don't like playing on the right. Other players tell you they are not playing certain positions and it's no problem. But look, you have just signed James Milner as a right-midfielder, so if you don't think I'm good enough to be in the team in centre-midfield, then fair enough, but why don't you just play James Milner right-midfield, because he wants to play there and I don't.'

I left it at that and I didn't hear anything back from him that evening. He pulled me over on Friday morning and said he had got my message. I said I was sick and tired of being messed around.

'But, son,' he said, 'James Milner's a young lad.'

'Listen,' I said, 'I'll play there, but my head's not right. I'm pissed off.'

'Well, you need to get your head right if you're going to play,' he said.

'My head's not right,' I said, 'and I'm sick and tired of being the fall guy.'

On Saturday, he named the team and I wasn't in it. I was on the bench. I was kind of relieved I wasn't playing right-midfield. He had picked Milner there. We played really well that day, especially JJ in centre-midfield. I was thinking 'bloody hell, I'm not getting my place back any time soon.'

We were 1–0 up and Sir Bobby told me to warm up. I came on in the 68th minute for Milner, and Sir Bobby told me to play right-midfield. That's where I played. So in the end, I didn't really refuse to play there at all, although I accept that's a bit of a grey area.

I was standing on the touchline, waiting to come on, and my mind was whirring.

'I know you'll do a job,' Sir Bobby said.

Five minutes after I came on, Middlesbrough equalised. Then, seven minutes from the end, Alan put us ahead with a penalty and it seemed that we had won the game. I thought everything might be all right. Winning matches has a happy habit of smoothing over problems in teams.

Three minutes from the end, I looked over at the touchline and the board was up, signalling that Kluivert was coming on for Alan. My mind started whirring. I should only have been thinking about the game, but I knew I was about to face a decision.

Al was captain and now that Speedo had gone, I was the vice-captain. So I realised Al was going to give me the armband. Either way it wouldn't look good: if I put the armband on and the story came out about the fuss I'd made about not wanting to play on the right, the fans would lynch me. But if I didn't put it on, it would be obvious there was a problem.

Al gave me the armband. I was looking around for senior players, but there weren't a lot there. Shay Given was in goal and the only outfield option for being captain was Aaron Hughes. So I ran over to him and flung the armband at him. 'I'm not putting that on,' I said. 'You have it.'

In the last minute, I got isolated one-on-one with Boudewijn Zenden on the right touchline. He took me on and as I tried to go with him, I slipped. It wasn't just a stumble. I fell flat on my face. It was like a comedy moment where somebody steps on a banana. Zenden was away. He had a lot of time and a lot of space and his cross bounced to the back post where Jimmy Floyd Hasselbaink headed it in for the equaliser.

I'd had quite an afternoon. I'd told Sir Bobby I didn't want to play right-midfield, I was left out, I refused the captain's armband and I messed up for Middlesbrough's last-minute equaliser in the Tyne–Tees derby. That was pretty good going, even for a trouble magnet like me. I was devastated. I knew I'd let everybody down.

Sir Bobby disappeared to do his post-match press conference and when he came back, he took me aside. 'They know, son,' he said. He said there were pictures of us arguing on Friday and they had put it to him that I had refused to play right-wing. He said he had told them that was lies.

That was Sir Bobby all over. Even though I'd let him down by messing up for the second goal and by not playing, he was still protecting me.

Sure enough, the next day, there was a big article in the *News of the World* about how I refused to play. I think Henry Winter did a massive piece slaughtering me in the *Daily Telegraph*, too. He wasn't alone. I felt distraught about it all. I couldn't come out and tell my side of the story, because if I did, I would be throwing Craig under the bus. So I had to take it.

There was an international break after the Middlesbrough game and I joined up with England for a friendly against Ukraine. My luck wasn't improving: the game was at St James' Park, where it appeared I had quickly become public enemy number one after what had happened on the opening day.

I came on at half-time for Steven Gerrard and when my name was read out over the loudspeaker system, the whole stadium booed. It was brutal. I played all right and we won 3–0 but, if I hadn't known already, I realised that I was in for a rough ride.

Freddy Shepherd came to see me at the training ground a couple of days later. He warned me this was serious and that I was going to get booed every time I touched the ball. There were reports that I was going to be transfer-listed and that Newcastle wanted to offload me.

Newspapers had a laugh reporting some stunt where I had been put up for sale on eBay. The largest offer, apparently, was £10k.

Our next league game was Tottenham at home. I came off the bench and got absolutely pelted by the fans. When the crowd are on you like that, it's hard to play. I think I'm strong, but it gets to the stage where you don't even want to touch the ball. We lost 1–0.

Jermaine Jenas picked up a strain in the Spurs game and so I started in the centre of midfield in the next game, at home to Norwich, on the Wednesday night. We threw a two-goal lead away and drew 2–2. I was so bad that day, it was actually hard to believe. I could barely kick the ball, let alone pass it accurately or run with it.

After about an hour, Steven Carr played the ball in to my feet and I tried to nick one round the corner and it kind of bobbled off my shin and went up into the stand. The crowd booed like hell. I looked over to the dugout and I saw a board come out and I was praying it was number eight. 'Please be number eight,' I was saying to myself. 'Please be number eight.'

It was number eight. A massive roar of approval came from the Newcastle fans when they realised I was being substituted. The Norwich fans were absolutely loving it, too, seeing an Ipswich boy going through this hell. It was awful. The whole thing was desperate.

I went straight down the tunnel when I came off. I was already in the bath by the time the lads came into the changing room. I sat in the bath until about midnight. I wondered what the hell I was going to do. The physios, Derek and Paul, were the only ones still there. They took pity on me and offered me a beer. I didn't want a beer.

'Stay strong and get through it,' one of them said, but I thought there was no way to get over this. The way I was playing, that eBay bid was £10k too high.

The next game was Aston Villa away and we travelled down on the

Friday. We all knew that if we lost this game, Sir Bobby would probably be fired. You could tell. People were starting to talk about the names of the candidates to take over from him.

Sir Bobby came to my room that evening and said he was going to leave me out to take the pressure off me. I tried to point out it was an away game and that the away fans tend to be more supportive and get behind the whole team.

'I want to do a job for you,' I told him. 'I owe this to you.'

'No,' he said. 'I have made my decision.'

Sir Bobby dropped Shearer that day as well and played Kluivert and Bellamy up front with Butt and Bowyer in the centre of midfield and JJ on the right. We played so well that day. We were leading 2–1 at half-time but we missed a couple of chances and every mistake we made was punished. We lost the game 4–2.

Sir Bobby was fired on the Monday after the Villa game. We were all in training and he came in to say his goodbyes. He had been so good to me and I just felt overwhelming guilt about the way it had all ended. When he said goodbye to me, I couldn't even look him in the eye.

I could see how hurt he was. He thought he could have turned it around, but now he had lost the job at the club he loved more than any other. It wasn't like he was my manager. It was like we were family. It was a bit like we were father and son. I let him down, but he still protected me. I suppose that's what a father would do for his boy.

I had let Sir Bobby down so many times: the Ayia Napa stuff, getting dragged into the Grosvenor House Hotel thing, not playing on the right. And yet he always stood up for me. He wouldn't let the press say a bad word against me. He was always loyal to me.

As a player, Sir Bobby made me feel loved. There were better coaches but there was nobody who was a better man-manager. He got the best out of everyone. There were other managers I was scared of and other managers I respected, but Sir Bobby was the best I ever played for.

When Sir Bobby died at the end of July 2009 after a long battle with cancer, I was on a pre-season tour of Asia with West Ham. There was a minute's silence in his honour before the game we were playing in and I stood there on the pitch, crying.

## 19

## THE ENFORCER

A lot of names were thrown around amid the speculation over who would be Sir Bobby's successor at Newcastle. Steve Bruce and Terry Venables were the favourites and David O'Leary and Gordon Strachan were mentioned, too. But Freddy Shepherd had another candidate in mind.

I think he wanted someone to keep the Brat Pack in check and make sure we didn't throw any more tantrums. He wanted an authoritarian. He wanted someone who would bring an end to all the scandals and the bad behaviour. He wanted someone who would put the fear of God into us. He went for Graeme Souness.

On 5 September 2004, in the middle of an international break, it was announced that Souness would be leaving his post as boss of Blackburn Rovers and that, after he had taken a week off so as to let the scheduled league game between Blackburn and Newcastle pass without him, he would start as manager of Newcastle on 13 September.

There was a certain amount of trepidation about his appointment among the players. He had a reputation for being old school. He didn't take any prisoners. He had been one of the best players of his generation when he was captain of the great Liverpool teams of the 1970s and 80s. He is probably among the top five Liverpool players ever and that's quite an accolade.

Let's not underestimate what a player he was. He won everything in the club game. He had everything as a midfielder and as a leader. Even a player as great as Kenny Dalglish has talked about the aura that Souness carried with him, and he still carried that as a manager.

When Dalglish scored that sublime winner in the 1978 European Cup Final at Wembley against FC Brugge, it was Souness who supplied the equally sublime pass, chesting the ball down on the edge of the box, buying himself a few seconds with a feint and then sliding the ball through for Dalglish to apply his genius.

Souness was also a hard man. Some of his tackling was so brutal, it was eye-watering. He generally wore the air of a man with whom a young player ought not to mess. He insisted on total commitment at training. Sometimes, he took that to extremes. We had all heard the stories about how he had tried to breathe a bit of fire into his star striker at Blackburn, Dwight Yorke.

Souness had grown impatient with Yorke during a five-a-side and he hurt him with a tackle. 'Even if he had not intended it, the effects of his actions could easily have matched his threat to break my leg,' Yorke wrote later. Andy Cole, who was also at Blackburn then, said the gash in Yorke's shin was so deep you could see the bone. And this was one of Souness's own players.

The bookies quickly drew up a list of odds for which player would be first out of the door at Newcastle. I was the favourite. Craig and Laurent Robert were not far behind. Everyone thought that Souness would probably set his sights on the King of Bling and make an example of me.

In that context, my first real dealings with Souness were hardly ideal. There had been pictures in a newspaper that appeared to show me doing up my flies in the street in Newcastle after a night out. I was accused of urinating in public and I was told I had to report to a local police station. Souness said he was coming with me. My heart sank.

So Newcastle's player liaison officer, George Taylor, drove me and the new manager to the police station, and Souness and I were ushered into an interview room where two officers were waiting to talk to me. It wasn't the best way to make a good impression with the boss.

The senior policeman of the two acted like he was Dirty Harry. He said I'd be leaving the room in handcuffs and that they were going to throw me in jail for what I'd done. This was for peeing in the street. The claims were absurd, by the way. It was just an opportunistic photograph that gave the wrong impression.

I told him it was complete nonsense. They said they had CCTV footage of me doing it. I said: 'No you haven't.' I knew they didn't have any footage because I hadn't done it, so it was impossible. The senior officer started shouting at me like I was a little kid.

Maybe he believed the paper. Maybe it was a set-up. He just tried to bully me into admitting to doing something I didn't do. In the end, I told him to charge me or stop wasting everybody's time. They wanted me to accept a police caution to make the whole thing go away, but I refused.

The whole time, Souness just sat there and listened. When we left the police station, we walked back to the car in silence. Souness got in the front seat and I got in the back. He turned around to look at me.

'If I ever have to come to a police station again because you have stepped out of line,' he said, 'I will beat you up.'

I kept my mouth shut. He wasn't messing around. He was serious. I thought: 'I'm not saying a word here.' By the time we got back to the training ground, he was in a filthy mood. He got out of the car and looked back at George. 'Tell the players I'm calling a meeting now,' he said. 'I'm sick and tired of this shit.'

He was about a month into the job and there were a few other items on his agenda by then, too. Around that time, we had played Charlton in the league at The Valley and Souness had substituted Craig during the game. The television cameras had caught Craig muttering 'f***ing prick' in his direction as he walked off.

Souness didn't see it or hear it, but he was alerted to it by the press. He expressed his surprise to them and was clearly irritated that they had caught him off guard a little. When he was shown footage of what had happened, he was livid. There had also been stories about an altercation between Craig and Nicky Butt before the England–Wales game at Old Trafford a week or so earlier. Souness wasn't happy about that, either.

We all convened in the meeting room and Souness stood up to talk. I hadn't had time to tell the other players what had happened at the police station, or what Souness had said to me afterwards, but I was hoping everyone was going to take the hammering we were going to get and keep quiet.

'When I was on the outside, looking at this football club,' Souness said, 'what I saw was a very talented team, exceptional football players, but people who are out of control and think they are above the law. Let's take a typical week of my life since I have been Newcastle manager.'

He looked over at me. 'I have just been to the police station with this little prick,' he said. 'It's probably normal for him to be back and forth to the police station all the time, but it's not normal for me. It's not my preferred way of spending a spare hour or two.'

Then he moved on to Craig and Butty. He said he had heard about their altercation and that Butty had threatened to beat the shit out of Craig. 'I wish he had beaten the shit out of you,' Souness said.

Craig had been warned by Dean Saunders, Souey's assistant, not to answer back, but it wasn't in Craig's make-up to keep quiet. He started protesting that there hadn't been any argument. I tried to get his attention. I was drawing my hand across my throat, telling him to shut up. He ignored me.

'See, this is the problem,' Souness said. I could see he was about to go. He mentioned a few of the trophies he had won and some of the clubs he had played for. 'And then someone like you calls me a f***ing prick,' he said to Craig. 'I'll f***ing knock you out.'

He went towards Craig and tried to grab him by the throat. 'In the gym now,' he said. 'Let's sort this out like men.' Alan had to pull Souness off him. That was the first time in my life I've seen Bellers completely speechless. They never made it to the gym, but it knocked the stuffing out of Craig. It made me sit up, too.

Souness was actually really good for me. I got on with him and Saunders straightaway. I was physically afraid of him, for a start, and I think that helped. I didn't want to cross him, partly because I believed there would be physical consequences if I did. I'd seen the proof.

Even though I had my best times with Sir Bobby, I think the full season I had with Souness was the best football I played. I do think it was because I feared the man. You couldn't cut any corners or slack off in any game. In that meeting, he put down a marker. He wanted a confrontation to put people in their place. That's why I didn't say a peep. I had never come across anyone like that.

Souness helped me to rehabilitate myself at Newcastle, too, which was no mean feat. Even I had thought that was a lost cause after I had become the object of so much scorn because of the perception that I had played a pivotal role in the departure of Sir Bobby.

I was at a low point when Souness was appointed manager. I started the Uefa Cup first-round tie against the Israeli side, Bnei Sakhnin, his first official match in charge, and missed an easy chance in the first ten minutes when I half-volleyed the ball over the bar from a Laurent Robert cross. There were more boos and groans.

Then, midway through the second half, I pulled my hamstring and limped off. The joy I felt when I realised it had gone was a bit scary. It was the first time in my life I was happy to get an injury. As I was walking off, I just thought: 'Phew, I'm out of the firing line for a few weeks.' My confidence was totally shot.

Souness was expected to run me out of town, but he did the opposite. I came back into the team after my hamstring injury healed and played in the home game against Manchester United in mid-November. I played on the right and got booed again pretty much every time I touched the ball. We had a warm-down the next day and Souness called me into his office.

He asked me why I always drifted inside and didn't like playing in that position. He said he thought it was a mental thing with me. He said he could tell I was playing with fear, and I told him it wasn't easy playing in front of 50,000 people who are jeering you.

Souness said he knew what it was like. When he and Alan Hansen played for Scotland, he said, they used to get booed, too. It hurt Hansen but Souness said he made sure he got on the ball as much as he could.

'If you're a midfielder,' he said, 'and the centre-half gets the ball, run and get it off them. Get it off everyone. Because the more times you get on the ball, the quicker they'll get tired of booing you. You have to be brave, drown out the boos and think "if you're going to boo me, I'm going to love it, I am going to get on the ball so much that you are going to spend the whole game booing."'

That always stuck with me and I felt like I reached a turning point when we played Portsmouth at St James' Park a couple of weeks before Christmas. I started right-wing, and early in the second half, Laurent Robert came on for James Milner and I moved into the centre.

Every time Titus Bramble or Aaron Hughes had the ball in our central defence, I ran to get it off them, and even though the fans weren't happy with the fact that we were drawing the game, the boos for me started getting quieter and quieter. Souness came in afterwards and said he had decided I was better in the middle than on the right and things got better and better for me after that.

Unfortunately, it wasn't quite the same for Craig. I could see early on the way that the relationship between Craig and Souey was going and I was devastated about it. Craig was my best friend in the team and I also thought that he was an even more important player than Shearer for the side.

I know that sounds ludicrous when Alan was scoring 25 to 30 goals a season, but I don't think Alan was the same without Craig in the team. Craig did so much work and made so many unselfish runs and pulled so many defenders out of shape with his pace, that he made Alan's job a lot easier than it would have been without him.

But Bellers found it hard to come to terms with the departure of Sir Bobby and, by his own admission, he never really gave Souness a chance. The two of them just rubbed each other up the wrong way, and their clashes formed a dramatic backdrop to an ordinary league season.

It all came to a head in late January, when we played Arsenal at Highbury. Craig and Souness were bumping heads a lot and Craig had walked off the training pitch the week before. There was an argument and they ironed it out, and Craig was put back in the squad for the Arsenal game.

Craig knew he wasn't in the starting eleven before we got to the stadium, but then Souness told him he wasn't even going to be among the substitutes. A Sky reporter asked Craig if he was injured and Craig said he wasn't. Craig then got it into his head that Souness was hinting to the media that he had refused to play that night.

The next day, Craig invited Sky Sports to his house for a proper interview. I rang him up and begged him not to do it. The fans loved Craig and weren't that keen on Souness, but he was overplaying his hand with this. Even Craig admitted later it was one of the most ridiculous things he had ever done.

He accused Souness of telling 'a downright lie' about him and that was the end of his time at Newcastle. He moved to Celtic on loan on the last day of that transfer window.

We didn't have a particularly good season in the league, but we moved out of trouble at least and climbed towards mid-table. And we went on decent runs in the FA Cup and the Uefa Cup that obscured some of the other problems we had.

I was happy with my form, too. I was playing on the right, but I felt as though I was always involved and that I was finally fulfilling my potential. I was relatively clear of injuries and that felt blissful. It was a glimpse of the way my career might have gone had that period free of problems lasted longer.

My confidence had come back and I was a better wide player than I had ever been before. The crowd got off my back and began to applaud me when I did good things again. That made a big difference. I came to realise that I could have a big influence on games even if I wasn't playing in the centre.

Stephen Carr was a massive help to me, too, because he was a proper right-back and I knew I could rely on him for help with the defensive side of things. That, coupled with the fact that the manager had given me the freedom to express myself, made me feel everything was on the up again. My friends had started to ask me why I never took people on any more, but now they stopped.

Souness told me and Laurent Robert that we were the new creative sparks in the team and that we were the ones who had to make things happen. When the ball was in the final third, I had free rein to try what I wanted. The fans responded. I was the kind of player they had seen when I first arrived at Newcastle.

Everything was pointing in the right direction again. We had Sporting Lisbon in the quarter-finals of the Uefa Cup and Manchester United in the semis of the FA Cup. Alan announced that he was postponing his retirement for a year, and even though we were struggling in the Premier League, there was some optimism about the future.

I was 26 and I felt like I was learning to take more responsibility for my career. On 1 April, an interview with me was published in the *Independent*. The shoutline was: 'From petulant playboy to being at the heart of Newcastle's revival under Graeme Souness, Kieron Dyer tells Simon Williams how he has worked to restore the glitter to a career that was on the verge of collapse'.

I feel a little for Simon Williams now. With the benefit of hindsight, it wasn't the best-timed story. The next day, we played Aston Villa at home. By the end of it, all the glitter was gone.

## THE FIGHT

## 20

I always got on well with Lee Bowyer. I still do. I didn't really know what to expect when he arrived at St James' Park in the summer of 2003 on a free transfer from West Ham United. He had a chequered reputation as a bit of a bad boy, but I knew it wasn't worth taking rumours like that particularly seriously. I thought I'd judge for myself.

Bow was signed by Sir Bobby Robson to strengthen our midfield, but his move wasn't universally popular with the Newcastle fans. I think most people recognised he was a good player, but he had been involved in a high-profile court case a couple of years earlier that had made some supporters squeamish about him wearing the shirt.

Bow and Jonathan Woodgate, who both played for Leeds United at the time, were accused of grievous bodily harm with intent after an Asian student Sarfraz Najeib was badly beaten up following a chase through Leeds city centre in January 2000. Bow was also accused of affray.

The family of the victim claimed it was a racist attack and a friend of

Woodie's was jailed for six years for GBH. Woodie himself did 100 hours of community service after he was found guilty of affray. Bow, who had continued to play for the club during the trial at Hull Crown Court – and played extremely well – was cleared of all charges.

That inconvenient detail didn't stop people levelling all kinds of accusations at Bow and assassinating his character. He was called a racist, but he wasn't a racist. I could tell that straightaway. I know this sounds like a cliché but his best mate was black and Rio Ferdinand, who had played with him at Leeds, could not speak highly enough of him. I liked him immediately.

The media have portrayed him in a certain way, and sure, he had his moments. But Frank Lampard had his moments, too, and now people say he was the perfect football role model. I suppose it helps that Frank fulfilled his potential and that he was an unbelievable player. That encourages people to forget his past misdemeanours.

Bow wasn't racist but he did have a nasty temper. He was quite laid back in many ways, but once he went, he really went. He is the kind of lad who wears his heart on his sleeve. He cares about his football and about the result and he is passionate about winning. Sometimes, that passion boiled over, and when it did, you just had to stand back and watch the show.

We both started the home game against Aston Villa on 2 April in central midfield. The mood around the club was improving. We had won six home games on the bounce in all competitions, we were in the semi-finals of the FA Cup and the quarter-finals of the Uefa Cup and we hadn't lost a game since the end of January.

We were still firmly in the bottom half of the table but we had started to climb away from trouble, and there was a celebratory mood at St James' Park that day for other reasons, too. The week before, Shearer had announced that he was postponing his retirement and the Geordie nation rejoiced.

All in all, there were expectations that it would be a fun afternoon. Villa were above us in the table but not by much, and it felt as if, with our resurgence, they would be there for the taking. It didn't really work out like that.

Juan Pablo Angel scored for Villa in the fifth minute and it went downhill from there. We didn't play well enough to get back into the game and about 20 minutes from the end, Gareth Barry put Villa further ahead from the spot after a comical bit of defending from Steven Taylor led to a penalty.

On another day, Taylor's play-acting would have made plenty of headlines. It was one of the best examples of its type. When Darius Vassell nicked the ball off Nicky Butt on the halfway line, broke away and went round Shay Given, Tayls had rushed back to provide the last line of defence.

Vassell hit his right foot shot well from about six yards out and Taylor, who had only been on the pitch for about 20 minutes after replacing Andy O'Brien, threw himself to his left and batted the ball away with his left arm. It would have been a decent save had he been the goalkeeper. But he wasn't.

Tayls still wasn't giving up though. As Vassell appealed for handball, Tayls fell backwards dramatically, his legs tucked underneath him as if he had been shot. He seemed to fall in slow motion and as he fell, he clutched his stomach as if that was where the ball had wounded him.

If it hadn't been such a bad situation, it would have been brutally funny. He lay there writhing around for a couple of seconds, holding his stomach as if his guts would spill out if he didn't. The referee, Barry Knight, wasn't fooled for a second. He marched straight up to him and showed him the red card.

Barry tucked away the penalty, and a few minutes later, he scored again from the spot to put the game well and truly out of reach. We had the first leg of our Uefa Cup quarter-final against Sporting Lisbon coming up and this was hardly ideal preparation. It was about to get a lot worse.

Even though the game was gone, we kept pressing to get a goal back. The crowd was on our case, which they had every right to be, given the farce that was unfolding in front of them, and we were all wound up by the fact we were getting so badly beaten. Out on the pitch, tempers were fraying.

Not long after Villa's third goal, Bowyer came to show for the ball when I had it on the right. He was available, sure, but I thought there were better options. I dribbled inside and passed the ball across the pitch to another teammate.

It wasn't as if I did something reckless. It wasn't as if I had tried something ridiculously ambitious instead of passing to him. It wasn't as if I had given away possession. But when I didn't pass to him, Bowyer went crazy.

'Pin, f***ing pass me the ball,' he screamed at me.

'What are you talking about?' I said. 'I didn't give the ball away.'

'You never pass me the ball,' he said.

I don't know where that came from. It was just frustration probably. Bow was as fierce a competitor as anyone. He hated losing and this was a humiliation. I told him to do one. He chuntered at me a bit more. I let it go.

If I had ignored him and played the ball to an opponent or hoofed it out of play, I would have held my hands up and said sorry. I would have understood his anger if that had happened, but it hadn't.

A few minutes later, I got the ball again, in a similar position. He came short to show for it. He wanted me to lay it square to him, so he could whip it round the corner for a striker to run on to.

I thought there were better options. It wasn't anything personal. You make a decision in a split second in a football match, and I didn't think we were most likely to threaten their goal by me playing the ball square to him in that situation.

So I played the ball up to one of the centre-forwards. Again, it wasn't a silly pass or a hit-and-hope ball lumped upfield. We kept possession. It wasn't anything special, but in the context of the game, it was progress. Bow didn't think so. He went absolutely nuts.

'F***ing hell,' he yelled, 'you never pass me the ball.'

I was starting to get wound up now because I hadn't done anything wrong. We were losing 3–0 at home, I was keeping possession and I had Bow raging on and on about me not passing him the ball. So I lost it.

'The reason I don't pass you the ball,' I said, 'is because you are f***ing shit.'

It was below the belt but he was doing my head in. As soon as I said that, his whole demeanour changed. He had gone and I knew he had gone. I was half-watching the play, because we still had the ball and we were attacking, but out of the corner of my eye, I could see him marching towards me. His eyes were bulging.

We were only about 10 yards from the bench and I could see Souness on the touchline and hear him shouting 'don't do it' at Bow. But Bow couldn't hear anything by then. He kept on coming.

I grabbed him by the shoulders and the neck to keep him off me and then he started raining in punches. It was like slow motion. When the punches were hitting me in the head, all I was thinking was: 'I cannot believe he is hitting me in front of 52,000 people. What the f*** is he thinking?'

I was holding him and trying to let him punch himself out. I thought it was just going to be handbags. It's the kind of thing that might happen in training but not in a match. No one in their right mind would do that, but Bow had lost his mind in those few seconds.

I think he hit me about four times. The punches didn't hurt. I was just thinking: 'I can't believe this nutter is doing this.' But by the time the fourth punch came in, I thought: 'f*** this', and launched one back at him.

The other players gradually realised something bizarre was happening and Gareth Barry rushed in to restrain Bow and drag him away. Bow's shirt was ripped down to his chest and he was still snarling and snapping and trying to get himself free.

Stephen Carr got hold of me and led me away. I was relatively calm, but I looked over at Bow again and he was frothing and raging. I didn't even realise at the time that you could get sent off for fighting your own teammate on the football field.

It wasn't as if there was much precedent. Derek Hales and Mike Flanagan had a famous fight during a match at The Valley when they were Charlton teammates, and Graeme Le Saux smacked David Batty when they were playing for Blackburn Rovers against Spartak Moscow, but even those incidents sent out an inconsistent message.

Hales and Flanagan were sent off but neither Le Saux nor Batty saw red. Still, I know now that it doesn't matter who you fight with on the pitch, one of the opposition or one of your own, because violent conduct is violent conduct, whoever you aim it at.

Barry Knight was having a busy afternoon. He came over and showed me the red card. I turned away and walked towards the tunnel. There was a short delay and then he sent Bow off, too. Shearer walked alongside him for a few paces, muttering in Bow's ear. I don't think it was particularly complimentary.

I started to feel angry. Bowyer had attacked me. All I had done was defend myself. I was wrong for saying he was rubbish, but that happens all the time in the heat of the moment. Your own teammate trying to beat the living daylights out of you in front of a capacity crowd isn't quite so common.

So I waited at the entrance to the tunnel, ready to fight him. As I stood there, I saw that our two masseurs, Lenny and John, two big, big men who worked in prisons and could look after themselves, had appeared to chaperone us back to the dressing room.

Bow came down the tunnel and I went towards him.

'You think you're so hard . . . come on then,' I said.

'F*** off, Pin,' he said.

He was starting to look a bit miserable about the whole thing.

'No,' I said, 'if you want to give it out there, let's have it now.'

I ran towards him but John grabbed me and picked me up and slung me over his shoulder like a little kid being given a fireman's lift by his dad. My feet were dangling in the air. John took me all the way to the dressing room like that before he put me down.

When we got there, Steven Taylor was sitting there by himself. He looked confused at first. He thought the game must be over, but John told him we had been sent off. He asked what for and John told him for fighting each other. Tayls was buzzing about that. He probably realised it took the heat right off him for his B-movie antics.

John and Lenny put a couple of benches across the middle of the changing room to keep Bow and me apart. We just sat there calling each other a string of horrible names. It seems childish now, I know. It was childish. But at the time, all I could feel was fury.

Eventually, we heard the final whistle. We heard the crowd booing and then there was the clatter of studs and the sound of someone running up the corridor. It was Jean-Alain Boumsong, our French defender. He was livid. He had obviously run straight off to confront both of us.

'You want to fight?' he said. 'Then fight now. Fight now.'

I didn't say anything, but inside I was thinking: 'Yes, yes, let's fight now.' I was still consumed by rage about what had happened.

Shearer was the next one in. He was fuming, too. I had never seen Al so angry. He was calling us both 'selfish pricks' and going mad. He had realised straightaway that because we had both been sent off for violent conduct, we would miss three domestic games, one of which would be the FA Cup semi-final against Manchester United, which was a fortnight away.

Al was desperate to win some silverware for his home-town club. It was one of the great dreams of his career and he knew that we had probably sabotaged it. Without both me and Bow, our chances of beating United had taken a big hit.

I started to calm down. My lust for revenge over Bowyer began to disappear. It was replaced by the gathering horror that I was going to miss an FA Cup semi-final. The sheer stupidity of the whole episode crashed down on me. What a mess.

Souness came in soon after that and he said he was going to go upstairs to watch the footage of the incident. He said if he saw what he expected to see, we were going to have another fight on our hands because he would come back down and batter both of us. The way Souness was, I kind of believed him.

It was also starting to dawn on me that having won the fans back, I would be a villain in their eyes again now, and all that hatred they felt towards me would come flooding back. I still felt I had done nothing wrong, but it was clear it was one of those situations where that wasn't going to count for much.

Eventually, Souness came back down and said I was exempt from blame. He turned on Bowyer and laid into him. I was relieved but I actually started to feel sorry for Bowyer. He was being hung out to dry.

Freddy Shepherd was the next one in. He was furious with Bowyer, too. He told me I should have head-butted him. You wouldn't get a lot of Premier League chairmen offering that advice. Freddy and Souness both said the club would appeal my red card.

Souness said both of us had to accompany him to his post-match press conference, so we shuffled up on to the dais with him like a couple of naughty schoolboys with their headmaster. We were both in club suit and tie. We mumbled apologies to the fans, our teammates and the club and then walked off the stage together while Souness continued talking to the press.

I had one other person to deal with. My mum had come up to Newcastle to watch the match. How's your luck. I can only imagine what she was thinking while she watched me and Bow fighting each other, and it was a bit awkward when we met up for the journey home. I couldn't exactly ask whether she'd enjoyed the game.

We got in the car to drive back to Ipswich, and like a moth drawn to a flame, I turned Radio 5 live on to listen to the post-match phone-in. What an idiot. A lot of the callers were saying Bow and I should never play for the club again. I had gone right back to square one with the supporters.

Then my mobile phone rang and it was Bow. He was brilliant. 'Pin, I'm so sorry,' he said. 'I lost my head, I should never have done it. It was my fault. Now I'm f***ed and it looks like you are, too.'

At training on Monday, the press came to the training ground and Souness made us to do this stupid, corny handshake. I thought that made it worse. People laughed at us for doing it. Not long afterwards, I lost my appeal against the sending off.

Then a fan made a complaint to the police, so they wanted to do Bow for assault. I had to go to the police station and the police were begging me to press charges. I was never going to do that. He was in enough trouble as it was. Freddy told him that they were going to fine him six weeks' wages and if he didn't accept that, they would sack him.

Bow stayed at the club until the end of the following season and then moved to West Ham. I joined him there not long afterwards and we remained friends. We're still friends. I see him now and then, usually at a Sir Bobby Robson golf day in Portugal, and we get on brilliantly. We just had one mad moment.

THE TEARS

# 21

Five days after the fight with Lee Bowyer, I started the first leg of the Uefa Cup quarter-final against Sporting Lisbon at St James' Park. The match was heavy with the symbolism of reconciliation and the fans seemed to be amused by it more than anything else.

Midway through the second half, when we were leading thanks to an Alan Shearer goal, Souness substituted me. Inevitably, he decided that Bow should be the one to replace me. All the anger had long gone from both of us by then and we shook hands as I ran over to the touchline. The crowd roared its approval.

That's one of the things about our game: principles don't last for long in football. The previous weekend, Bow, in particular was being vilified by the Geordie faithful and by the club for his part in our scrap on the pitch. Freddy Shepherd was talking about fining him tens of thousands of pounds.

Now, less than a week later, he and I were being entrusted with important roles in the biggest match of the club's season so far. As with most businesses, principles only go so far in football: if a club thinks a player can help it win a game and earn more money, their sins are swiftly forgotten.

There were no more goals in the first leg and we won the match 1–0. We knew the tie was finely poised. We weren't in great form by then. The Villa defeat had hit us hard and we lost again at Spurs the following Sunday. Our season would be on the line in the space of five days with the matches away at Sporting and then the FA Cup semi-final at the Millennium Stadium.

We believed we could do it in Lisbon, but on the eve of the match Laurent Robert, who had been substituted in each of the last three games and had been playing particularly poorly, decided the time was right to do an interview criticising the team and saying that we were a lesser side than the one which had lost to Marseille in the semi-finals of the competition the previous season.

'Are we better this year than last year?' Robert said. 'No, I don't think so. Are we the same? No, probably worse. I don't think we are playing as well this season as last. We have not played well in the last three games.

'We have been very, very bad. We were awful against Aston Villa and we lost at Tottenham and we were not playing good football. It is difficult to explain why we are playing so badly, but we have to get out of it quickly.'

We were in Lisbon when the story broke. Souness got all the papers faxed over from England, and when he saw what Laurent had said, he got on the bus which was taking us for a light session and strode up to the back to confront him. He screwed up the papers and threw them at Laurent. 'You're a disgrace,' he shouted at him. 'Get the f*** off this bus.'

I understood where Souness was coming from. He had every right to be angry. He was asked about the comments that day and he left no one in any doubt that he was disgusted with Laurent.

'Once again,' he said, 'we have had to take our eyes off the ball because of the selfish attitude of one of our own players. We have been sidetracked by a selfish player at a time when this club is playing its two most important games for 35 years, and that is totally unacceptable, not only for the management team of Newcastle United and its players but also the supporters.

'When Laurent Robert plays badly, he always seems to blame someone else. I mean, was it my fault he played so poorly at Spurs? What Laurent Robert has to do is to look at himself first, and if he is not playing well, he should try harder.'

When the team was announced that day, Laurent wasn't in it. He wasn't on the bench, either. This was Souness being old school. I understand why he did what he did. He had to discipline Laurent in some way, but I also felt that leaving him out altogether was self defeating.

We still had plenty of firepower. Patrick Kluivert only played one season in Newcastle, but I know Souness rated him. Technically, he was one of the best players I have ever seen. In training, his finishing was unbelievable. But as you see now with Wayne Rooney, when you get to a certain age, you can't do the things you used to be able to do.

Look at Alan Shearer. I don't put him in the best eleven I have ever played with. That's not an insult. I have an unbelievable amount of respect for Al and there is no doubt that he was an icon and a brilliant striker. But I never played with Alan when he was at the peak of his powers.

He was still a fantastic player at Newcastle, but I missed the very best of him. I played with Michael Owen for England Under-20s and a young Owen was the best striker I played with. Kluivert? He was on the way down when he arrived in the North East. He came for ridiculous money and a swansong and, Newcastle being Newcastle, he had a good time.

Kluivert was on the bench that night, but leaving Laurent out meant Souness had to play Jermaine Jenas on one flank with Charles N'Zogbia on the other. JJ could play the position, but he was not Laurent Robert. JJ was better in the centre. As it turned out, Sporting decided to play a high line that evening. It was a night made for Laurent to be curling passes and crosses into my path.

I put us ahead after 20 minutes when I ran on to a ball over the top of the Sporting defence and tucked it between the goalkeeper's legs. We were making plenty of chances and I put another effort just wide soon afterwards. We were 2–0 up on aggregate and things were looking good.

But then Niculae gave the Sporting fans some hope by equalising on the night with a decent header five minutes before half-time. We were still confident of hanging on to get through, but then with about half an hour still to go, I was sprinting down the line and I felt a stabbing pain in my hamstring. I came off a few minutes later and Kluivert replaced me.

Titus Bramble had had to come off a few minutes before me with an injury, but the two of us sat on the bench and agreed that we should still go through. With our away goal, the odds were still stacked in our favour and the scores were still level after 70 minutes.

Then everything went wrong. Kluivert missed a decent chance to put the tie out of reach and then Sporting scored three goals in the last 19 minutes to knock us out. It felt like a vicious sucker punch. Souness said later that if we had kept our starting eleven on the pitch, we would have won. He was probably right, but it didn't have much relevance by then.

I still loved Souness. I owed him a lot. I liked his style. Sometimes, he'd have his top off in the gym and he'd be doing the chest press and it was like 'boom'. I was thinking 'my God, this guy'. Then he'd join in a five-a-side and if some of the lads were taking it easy a couple of days before a game, he'd be snapping at them in tackles, trying to get them fired up.

He was great for me but he could rub people up the wrong way. A more pragmatic manager would have found a way to discipline Laurent

Robert and play him against Sporting Lisbon and we probably would have won the game, but that wasn't the way Souey thought. If someone crossed the line with him, they were finished.

The Sunday after the defeat to Sporting, we lost to Manchester United in the FA Cup semi-final in Cardiff. It our second 4–1 defeat in the space of four days. It was also the end of our season. The United of Keane, Scholes, Van Nistelrooy and Ronaldo were just too good for us and, with half our first-choice team missing, we had no chance.

I came back after my hamstring injury for a league game against Middlesbrough at the end of April, but ten minutes before half-time, I felt it go again and I had to come off. That was the end of my campaign, too. I didn't play again that season.

At the end of the season, Souness told me he wanted to build the team around me for 2005–06. He told Freddy Shepherd the same thing. I only had two years left on my contract, so I signed a new four-year deal with no wrangling and no fuss. I was excited about the season ahead.

I didn't know then that the minor hamstring injury, which I first felt in the second leg of the Uefa Cup clash with Sporting, was going to cost me a year of my career.

We reported back for pre-season and I did the whole programme with no problems. We were in the Intertoto Cup and the day before the first game against FK Dubnica in Slovakia, I felt my hamstring again and Souness sat me out of the game. They told me not to risk aggravating the injury.

I felt worried about the injury, but not as worried as I should have been. It seemed like it was just a niggle that would soon clear up. Other things were going well at the club. Towards the end of the summer transfer window, we signed Michael Owen from Real Madrid and Albert Luque from Deportivo La Coruna to add to the recruitment of Emre from Inter Milan and Scott Parker from Chelsea. On paper, we had a brilliant team.

But then everything started going wrong. I came back into the team for the home game against Manchester United at the end of August and lasted 38 minutes before I did my hamstring again. Emre had torn his hamstring 15 minutes earlier. A couple of weeks later, Luque ruptured a hamstring and was ruled out for more than two months. The season was falling apart almost before it had begun.

The physios were puzzled that my injury was lingering on. They sent me to Hans-Wilhelm Müller-Wohlfahrt, the guy who had been the Bayern Munich club doctor for the past 38 years and who had treated sports stars like Paula Radcliffe, José María Olazábal, Usain Bolt and Kelly Holmes.

Müller-Wohlfahrt was famous for his controversial treatments, including apparently injecting his subjects with cell parts from the foetuses of calves and juices from a turkey's head. I'd also been told he wasn't afraid of using a needle fairly liberally.

He sent me for an X-ray on my back and MRIs on my back and hamstrings. He thought he had found the problem. He said one of the joints needed manipulating and that was causing the problem. He gave me about 20 injections in my back.

I had gone to Germany with Derek Wright, Newcastle's head physio. Derek is a portly guy and when he saw me after the second day of injections, I could hardly walk. I was hobbling around like a 100-year-old. Derek laughed. 'You move like me now,' he said.

When we left, I was confident that the problem was over. Müller-Wohlfahrt has a good reputation and he said I should be fine. He told me to do normal rehab to build strength and then proceed as normal.

But the first game back, I felt my hamstring again. I was close to tears. I was doing everything I was told to do and none of it was working. Souness sent me to a guy in Nottingham next, and when that didn't work, there was another guy waiting in the queue.

I made the odd appearance here and there. I came on as a substitute for a game at The Hawthorns at the end of October. The front six who finished that game were Solano, Parker, Emre, me, Shearer and Owen. That was the line-up Souness had dreamed about, but nobody was fit long enough for it to have the impact he desired.

We did win that game 3–0, and a few minutes after I came on, I was one-on-one with Darren Moore. I did a stepover and glided past him, got to the byline, cut the ball back and Michael Owen smashed it in. But as I saw the ball hit the net, I felt my hamstring again.

I had got to the stage where I was embarrassed to say I had got an injury. It was the first time that I played on just to get to the end of the match so I didn't have to walk off the pitch. There were 12 minutes left and I thought I'd rather play with a hamstring tear than face the walk of shame.

At the end, everyone was buzzing because of the result and I asked our masseur, Lenny, to give me a massage on the hamstring. I was trying to convince myself that it was just a bit tight. I didn't say anything to anybody else. I tried to pretend it hadn't happened.

The players who played in the West Brom game had a warm-down on the Monday. The substitutes, and those who hadn't been involved, trained normally. So I was out training with a grade-one hamstring tear and Souness was going mad at me, because he could see I wasn't putting everything in.

'Kieron,' he was yelling, 'you have to train how you play because we need you to get fit and get match toughness.' I knew I couldn't do that. So I just walked in and I was crying all the way to the physio's room. I was inconsolable and I was embarrassed.

There were all sorts of specialists. I went to see lots of guys. None of them worked. It got to the point where it felt we were halfway through the season and I hadn't played.

The prognosis seemed to be getting worse and worse. The club began to think it might be a hip problem. If it was, they were worried it could be career-threatening. I was getting distraught about it. The best advice seemed to be to rest it for longer and then have another go at coming back.

The club wanted to take pressure off me. They said they were going to put a statement out saying I was out for the foreseeable future because I was dealing with a medical problem. They did it with the best intentions, but in a rumour-factory like Newcastle, it was probably the worst thing they could have done.

All sorts of theories started to circulate about the reasons for my absence. The rumours spread fast, to the point where people began to believe they were fact. It was being said that I was suffering from cancer. Other people were reporting I had AIDS. It went on and on and got more and more fantastical.

So I had ex-girlfriends and ex-partners on the phone saying: 'Oh my God, do I need to get a check-up, do I need to get an AIDS test?' I tried to reassure them that I just had a hamstring problem, but I'm not sure they all believed me.

My best mate Neville rang me. He was practically in tears. He asked me if I was dying. I reminded him of all the false stories that had been printed about me when I was out in Ipswich and he was out with me. He knew they weren't true and so I told him not to believe this either.

'Please tell me you haven't got cancer,' he said at one point. The whole thing got totally out of control. I think some people still believe there was some truth to it all, but there wasn't. Newcastle did it for the right reasons, but it allowed the media to fill a vacuum.

The hamstring problem got so bad that I thought about retiring. Apart from my own selfish reasons for wanting to restart my career, it was killing me that I couldn't help Souness, because I knew how much he believed in me and what a central part he had been intending me to play in Newcastle's season. As 2005 rolled into 2006, we took one point from a run of five games and Souness's job started to come under real pressure.

We played Manchester City away at the beginning of February 2006. I took a fitness test the day before the game, and even though I could feel my hamstring was still not right, I told Souness I wanted to play. I told him I knew he needed to win the game and that I'd play through pain. He appreciated the gesture, I think, but he said no.

City absolutely battered us that day. They were two-up by half-time but it could easily have been four or five. There was a big 'Souness Out' banner among the away support and the fans were singing for him to be sacked as the players went in at half-time.

I thought Souness might give the players a massive bollocking at half-time but he didn't. He seemed resigned to the fact that it was coming to the end. I think he knew what was coming. So he was fatalistic in the dressing room at the interval. We were a bit better in the second half, but not good enough to turn the game around. City won 3–0.

That result left us 15th, six points above the relegation zone, and the next day Souness was sacked. I was gutted about it. He had put a lot of faith in me and I couldn't get on the pitch for him. I had let him down.

Souness called a brief meeting after he had been fired. There was no shouting this time. No offers to fight anybody. It was a very different mood. Dean Saunders, his assistant, was in tears. Football doesn't wait for you. That's the game.

## 22

## THE LONG GOODBYE

In the aftermath of the sacking of Graeme Souness, Freddy Shepherd appointed the head of Newcastle's youth academy, Glenn Roeder, as caretaker manager. Alan Shearer, who was in his final year as a player, was appointed as his assistant. They started to turn around the club's fortunes straightaway and in the next five league games, we won four and drew one. The worries about relegation were gone.

In the middle of that winning run, I made my first start since August in an FA Cup fifth-round tie against Southampton. Alan was injured so Roeder drafted me into the team for a match that was loaded in significance for me, not just because it was another chance to try to prove the hamstring problem was behind me, but also because George Burley, my former boss at Ipswich, was the Southampton manager.

Ten minutes into the game, I felt my hamstring go again. I was distraught but I didn't tell anyone. I couldn't tell anyone. Once again, it was too embarrassing. I played on as best I could despite the stabbing pain in the back of my leg whenever I tried to accelerate. It was an ordeal, but it wasn't as bad as having to walk off the pitch before half-time again.

My head was all over the place, but I didn't play too badly. I faded a bit in the second half but with 20 minutes to go, Charles N'Zogbia made a great run from deep and slipped me in behind the Southampton defence. I slotted the ball past Bartosz Białkowski in the Southampton goal and jumped into the crowd to celebrate.

Even though I knew I was injured, there was a lot going through my mind when I was celebrating with the fans. It felt like a release after playing through so much pain during the game and, I suppose, a sense of triumph that I'd managed to score despite being injured. It had been a long time since I had had anything to celebrate on the pitch.

I also thought I was coming to the end of my career. I didn't play in the next game against Charlton but after the match I told Roeder I wanted to call it a day. I told him I couldn't do it any more. I couldn't cope with a career that had become a continuous cycle of hope and despair. If there were an end in sight to it, it would be different, but no one could seem to cure the problem.

I liked Roeder. He was the opposite of Souness in many ways. He was not as authoritative and not as sure of himself, but he had interesting ideas about the game and he was a good coach. He had a decent managerial career, but he was probably too nice a bloke to be an outstanding success.

Roeder pleaded with me to go and see a physio called John Green, who he had worked with when he was the manager of West Ham. I told him I was done with specialists but he begged me to do it and he was insistent that this guy would be able to help me. It was clear he had a lot of faith in him, and so, because I liked Roeder, I decided I'd give it one last go.

So off I went down to London with a sheaf of scans, my collection from all the times I had been to various clinics during that season. John Green's clinic was in Chadwell Heath at the time, and when I walked in, it looked like an absolute hovel.

The machinery looked old and it was all crammed into a little box room. It wasn't like all the state-of-the-art places that had made the previous diagnoses about my injury. I thought I might as well get the train straight back home.

John asked about my history and my medication, and when I said I had been told the medication might be affecting my recovery, he said poor physios and doctors use the medication as an excuse because, if they can't do their job properly, that's their get out of jail card – it must be the medication. He said medication might slow down the healing but it wouldn't stop a grade-one strain healing.

I stripped to my boxer shorts and he assessed me. He said my left glute, the muscle in my buttocks, wasn't working. He asked me to tense it. I couldn't. So the result was my hamstrings were very strong because they were doing all the work and taking all the load that the glutes should have been taking.

But if your hamstring is doing everything, if it's taking a much heavier load than it's supposed to, eventually it's going to pop. John thought that was a good sign. His initial prognosis was that all we would have to do to get rid of the problem was activate the glute.

Next, we went into central London on the Tube to see a radiologist, Dr Jerry Healy, who analysed the scans. I told him about my history: I get a grade-one strain, do four or five weeks rehab, come back and then first game back, I do it again.

He put the scans on the screen and turned on the light. He said it wasn't a grade-one strain. He said I had paratenonitis. He said my tendon was so inflamed where my hamstring was taking all the strain that when

I started sprinting in a match situation and loading it again I was getting the sensation of being stabbed in the leg.

Paratenonitis, apparently, refers to inflammation of the paratenon, which is a thin membrane around the tendon. The paratenon helps the tendon glide up and down smoothly. It is most commonly associated with the Achilles tendon and often afflicts runners, but mine was an issue higher up the leg.

The stabbing feeling I was getting in my hamstring was where the tendon in my hamstring was inflamed. So every time I ran, I was getting that pulling, burning sensation. I couldn't sprint the way I wanted to without pain, but I could just about carry on.

So I hadn't been pulling my hamstring at all. It just felt like it. You can't really keep playing with a proper hamstring strain, so the paratenonitis made perfect sense as a diagnosis. At last, the mystery was solved.

When I had heard what Dr Healy had said, I asked what was next. I thought they might say an operation and another long period out. He said I'd have a steroid injection, rest the leg for a few days and then I would be good to start training again and begin the process of trying to regain fitness.

I don't know why the glute wasn't working in the first place. It might have been something to do with injuries I'd had in the past. They said they would get it working again through simple exercises. I had to squeeze my buttocks together, tilt my pelvis a certain way, be more aware of my posture, use a cushion to help me sit upright. It would be as simple as that.

I was relieved and slightly disbelieving, but I was also angry. My season had been a waste of time. I'd played 13 times for the club but most of those had been ruined by the injury, one way or another. A good manager and a good man had lost his job and I had been accused of being too fond of the treatment table.

As a player, you have to put your trust in medical professionals. Sometimes, they get it wrong, but the fans don't see that. They just see what they think is an injury-prone player and so that's how they label you. They don't see the fact that maybe the player is paying for someone else's mistake. They just see a well-paid lad who they think is shirking.

In those situations, the player takes the brunt of all the moans about injuries and no one says anything about the doctor. Anyway, by the time what was wrong with me had been properly diagnosed, the season was all but over. It was a write-off.

Roeder had taken us from 15th to seventh in the Premier League table and he was offered the job full time at the end of it. There was a wrangle about whether he could take the job because he didn't have a Uefa Pro Licence, but when it was pointed out that he had been studying for it when he was struck down with a brain tumour in 2003, the other clubs relented and gave permission for him to be appointed.

I spent the whole of the run-up to the 2006–07 season with John Green in London, working on getting fit again and building up the glute so it was fully functioning. I was ready to come back into the team in late September, but then I contracted another bizarre injury in training. Not for the first time, I felt I was cursed.

We were training the day before what was to have been my comeback game and we were slaloming in and out of poles that had been planted in the turf, working on our sprints. Nicky Butt was running in front of me and he stood on one of the poles and it snapped back in my face and hit me in the eye.

I lost vision in that eye for 48 hours, which was long enough to start worrying that it wasn't ever coming back and that I was going to be blind in that eye. I missed that game, and then I wasn't allowed contact for another game, and then I had to build my fitness up yet again.

I finally made my latest comeback at the end of October 2006 in a Carling Cup tie against Portsmouth. I played my first league game for seven months a couple of weeks later against Manchester City and it felt so good to be playing without pain again.

We had become a rather ordinary side by then. Alan had retired by now, Michael Owen was missing for most of the season with the knee injury he sustained playing for England at the World Cup the previous summer in Germany and our front two for that City game were Antoine Sibierski and Shola Ameobi. We were lacking quality all over the pitch.

We were in the bottom three by the time I got back into the side. We had lost at home to Fulham, Bolton and Sheffield United by then and it was a struggle to drag ourselves up the table. At least I was fit and able to contribute, but it was not a season that the Toon Army will remember with much fondness.

For once, I could look at myself and say I played well. I'd had my share of feeling I'd let managers down, but that season I put a proper shift in. I even got back in the England squad. Obafemi Martins and Scott Parker were immense that campaign, too. Between us, we kept Newcastle out of trouble.

I scored at The Emirates in my second league game back in the side in a 1–1 draw against Arsenal that gave us a bit more optimism about the season after the dreadful run we'd been on. We won three games on the spin after that and moved clear of the relegation zone again.

Maybe I deserved it after everything that had happened, but despite the way I was playing, I was still made a scapegoat when things went wrong in games. I was the one who got picked on and moaned at if the team wasn't playing well. I did everything I could to win the fans back over, but it felt as if their minds were made up.

Three games from the end of the season, Roeder gave me the captaincy for the game against Reading at the Madejski Stadium. I'd had my problems with the armband before so I was a bit apprehensive about it, but I took it as a great honour and ran my socks off, as usual.

We lost 1–0. I didn't have a great game, but I tried my best. Afterwards, the phone-in callers all seemed scandalised that I had been handed the armband. 'Dyer doesn't care,' I remember one of them saying. 'How can he be captain when he doesn't try a leg?'

That was what was always thrown at me when I was at Newcastle. I didn't care and I didn't run. I don't know why people thought either of those things. Maybe it was my body language. Maybe it was the fact that people had decided I was a waster and were blind to the work I did.

But in my whole career at Newcastle, I was in the top three in running stats in distance travelled and high intensity – every season. I was running more than James Milner, for a start, who was always held up as the epitome of grit and effort.

Roeder was sacked after our last home game of the season – a 2–0 defeat to Blackburn Rovers – and Nigel Pearson was given the job of caretaker manager for the final match against Watford, who had already been relegated to the Championship.

We were warming up in front of our fans in the away end before the game and the fans sang everyone's name except for mine and Stephen Carr's. They hated Stephen Carr for some reason. They even sang Antoine Sibierski's name. He'd only be there for nine months and he hadn't been tearing up trees. He'd done OK but he wasn't exactly Alan Shearer.

I'm not blaming them for that. It's up to them who they like and who they don't like. I think the Newcastle fans just had enough of me.

I'd been there a long time. I'd had plenty of ups and downs, plenty of scandals, plenty of injuries, plenty of bad publicity, and they were bored of me. Sometimes, people just outgrow each other.

When I'd come back into the team that season, we were struggling like hell. I didn't score that many goals, but my performances were good and I helped keep the team up. But I knew by the end of the season that I had outstayed my welcome.

I scored the only Newcastle goal of the game that day in what was a meaningless draw for both teams. I didn't even bother celebrating. It was the end of the affair. I knew I was going to leave. I'd made my mind up and I think the fans had, too.

A couple of days later, I went off to meet up with England. I came on as a sub in the first game at the new Wembley, the friendly against Brazil. Mike Ashley had bought the club from Sir John Hall and it had been announced that Sam Allardyce was going to be the new Newcastle manager. Before the game, he came to see Michael Owen and me at The Grove.

He told us both how important we were to his plans. Sam loves his data and he could see from the statistics, as well as his own experience, that I was a high-intensity player. I know part of the reason he had been sacked by West Ham was that they didn't like his style of play, but I was impressed with how advanced he was with his use of stats.

It doesn't surprise me that he has success wherever he goes. Look at what he did with Sunderland and what happened when he left. Look at how he kept Crystal Palace up. I became a fan of his very quickly and I suddenly felt a bit torn. I wanted to leave, but I wanted to give Sam a chance, too.

Scott Parker left to sign for West Ham at the beginning of June. Scottie was an inspirational leader, but the fans had bought into the idea that he was too negative when he had the ball and they used to jump on his back when things weren't going well. When West Ham came in for him, he decided to leave.

I was still there when the pre-season programme began and I played in the second game against Carlisle United in late July. I was getting off the coach outside Brunton Park and there were loads of Geordies around, giving me stick. One of them shouted out to me as I came down the steps. 'You prick, Dyer,' he yelled.

We drew the game 1–1 and Sam Allardyce shot off straight after the match. I was in the dressing room with Nigel Pearson and I told him I wanted to leave.

Nigel said he'd pass on the message to Sam, and when Sam spoke to me, he was reasonable about it but he said he needed to find a replacement before they sold me.

I already knew that West Ham wanted me by then. They had been bought by an Icelandic consortium headed by Björgólfur Guðmundsson, a billionaire businessman, who had been the chairman and owner of the Icelandic bank, Landsbanki.

The Icelandic owners were throwing money at the club and giving the manager, Alan Curbishley, what sometimes seemed like an unlimited budget. As well as signing Scottie, they had also bought Lucas Neill, Freddie Ljungberg, Craig Bellamy, Matt Upson and Julien Faubert. They were also paying big wages.

When Faubert, who was a right-sided player, ruptured his Achilles tendon in a pre-season friendly, Bellers phoned me and asked if I'd consider going to West Ham. I thought it might be a bit of a backwards step from Newcastle, but it was hard to deny that they were a side who seemed to be brimming with new ambition.

I'd be close to home, too. I could live back in the Ipswich area. I had just bought a house that was half an hour away from the West Ham training ground. I was 28, so I knew this would probably be my last big contract, and they were willing to pay me more than £80k a week. So I asked Bellers to tell Curbishley to ring me and soon afterwards, I got a call.

I asked him where he saw me playing, because I didn't want to play on the right-wing. He said they had just lost Faubert so I might be needed on the right for a bit, but in the long term, he saw me playing in the centre of midfield. We talked about my wages and Curbs wanted to be sure I actually wanted to come to the club.

A few days later, my agent called to say a fee – I think it was about £6 million – had been agreed between the two clubs and I travelled down to London for a medical. Because of my hamstrings and my injury history, they made sure it was comprehensive. It lasted for two days, but I got through it without any problems.

After the second part of the medical, I went down to the West Ham training ground to take part in a training session with my new teammates. When I got there, Curbs came out looking worried. 'I'm sorry, Kieron,' he said, 'but you need to leave. Mike Ashley has pulled the plug on the deal. It's all off. You need to get out of here.'

I phoned my agent and he said that someone from West Ham had been out at a casino in London the night before and had been bragging about how they had taken Mike Ashley for a ride by getting him to sell them a current England international for £6 million. It turned out one of Ashley's best pals was playing the same table.

The comments got back to Ashley and he called the whole thing off. A businessman like him isn't going to take too kindly to being mocked for a decision, and when I got back to Newcastle, Sam said there was nothing he could do and that I might have to stay.

That wasn't an option for me. By then, everyone knew I wanted to get away. It was public knowledge that I had been down to West Ham and had been close to signing for them. That increased the negativity towards me in Newcastle. I didn't have a problem with that. I understood it. But it made life a bit uncomfortable.

That pre-season was the first time I came across Joey Barton. I kind of like Joey but we had an argument almost straightaway. I hated losing in five-a-sides and during one match in training, I was on the same team as Joey and Charles N'Zogbia.

Charles was struggling a bit and I was moaning away at him.

Joey said. 'Leave him alone. He's only young.'

'Who the f*** do you think you are?' I said to him. 'I seem to remember you stubbing a cigar out in some kid's eye.'

Joey brushed that aside. 'You think you're f***ing Pelé,' he said dismissively.

'I am f***ing Pelé, compared to you,' I said.

A couple of days before the end of July, we played a friendly against Juventus at St James' Park. I did OK and we won 2–0. After the game, our cars were driven on to the side of the pitch so that we could get to them without having to interact with the fans.

Yes, I realise how that sounds now.

Anyway, as I was driving out of the ground, my car got pelted with eggs. That was nice. My home was vandalised – eggs again –and I generally took a lot of flak. Surprisingly enough, I didn't really fancy living there much longer, so I told Sam I wouldn't live in Newcastle any more. I'd commute from Ipswich.

I know it sounds ridiculous. In fact, I know it was ridiculous. But I wanted to make it plain that I wasn't going to give up on the move and let some crap surrounding chairmen's egos get in the way. I didn't want to go on strike. I would never have done that. But I did want to do everything I could to force the move through.

So I hit on a plan that demonstrates the excesses of the times. When Souness was manager, he had told a few players about a scheme where you pay for the use of a private jet by the hour. I think a lot of golfers use the same scheme. I bought 50 hours' worth. My agent had got married in Marbella that summer and I used up three hours going out there and back. I had 47 hours left.

So I got into a new routine. When I finished training in Newcastle at 1pm, I got a cab to the airport and hopped straight on to the private jet and flew back either to Stansted or to an airfield even nearer Ipswich. A mate would come and pick me up and drive me home.

For the return journey, I had a driver from the North East called Lawrence who had a van and he would leave Newcastle at 3am and come and pick me up at home. I got in the back of the van, lay down, pulled my duvet over me and went to sleep for a few hours. We would pull up at the Newcastle training ground at 9.30am and I'd hop out with my pillow and my duvet and go and get changed. We repeated that routine while the situation played out.

The season began and I was still flying to and from Newcastle training by private jet. I'd have done it all season if I had to. But then West Ham lost their first game of the season at home to Man City. They were well beaten, too, and Curbs described the performance as 'unbelievably flat'. He increased the pressure on the West Ham hierarchy to resurrect my deal, and the next week, the transfer finally went through.

Perhaps it was a fitting way for my time at Newcastle to come to an end. Travelling to and from training by private jet was a neat symbol of the massive wealth that had flooded the game. Football was going mad and we were going mad with it.

I didn't feel any nostalgia about leaving Newcastle. Not at all. I had been there eight years. It had run its course. I had seen all my friends go. I had seen the treatment meted out to people like Jermaine Jenas. They killed the kid. They are great fans in many ways, but they'd had enough of me and I'd had enough of them.

# THE TACKLE

23

By the time I got to West Ham in the summer of 2007, I had begun to wise up. I had looked at players like Craig Bellamy and Gary Speed and how they took care of themselves and nurtured their careers and thought that I needed to do the same. They were people I admired, and the dedication and the commitment they were showing had an effect on me.

I was 28, so I was no longer a kid. I started to get a sense that this wasn't going to last forever and I wanted to make the most of it. Like anybody who starts to grow up, I developed an awareness of my own mortality. I didn't think I was invincible any more.

I had realised I couldn't just do what I wanted and then go out on the pitch and play. I knew that would have repercussions on my fitness. I wanted to give everything I could to my career. I wasn't interested in all the stuff around the game any more. I wasn't interested in glitz or bling. I wanted to dedicate everything to football.

I was still in the England squad and I thought there was a lot more for me to achieve. I knew I had lost a lot of time to injury in my career already, but I thought now that I was starting to look after myself, there was no reason why I shouldn't be able to avoid more lay-offs and be healthy for a good five or six years.

It seemed to me that West Ham were going places and I wanted to be part of their rise. There was a lot of optimism around Upton Park at that time, I had a lot of friends at the club and I thought there was no reason why this should not be a golden period in my career. I was coming into my prime. I felt excited about the future.

This process of change had begun in my last couple of years at New-castle. I very rarely went out. I still had a couple of drinks now and again, but crucially I stopped getting drunk. I was the first into the training ground every day and the last to leave. I started doing a lot of strength work. I ate healthily and was much more careful about nutrition. I became a model professional.

In fact, I went from being one of the least professional players to one of the most diligent and conscientious. I did everything I could to give myself every chance of being the best I could be on a Saturday afternoon or a Wednesday evening. Going out wasn't fun any more. I just changed. Finally, I got smart.

I wasn't interested in Ayia Napa or which club was open on which night, or doing shots or chucking beer over my friends. I understood at last that football was at the heart of everything and that football was the thing that I loved more than the nights out and the parties.

My stats proved I cared. No one who didn't care could produce the running numbers and the high-intensity numbers I was delivering. I was back around my kids all the time now and I was with my friends in Ipswich, who had always been a good influence on me.

When I signed for West Ham, I didn't think it was professional for me to be driving for 45 minutes to the training ground from my house and

45 minutes back, so I employed two of my best friends, Milo and James, as my drivers. I gave them a weekly wage, which helped them along. I was becoming a proper man. I was putting things in place. I was doing the right thing.

That was the greatest irony of my career: when my mindset was like that, I could never stay fit. Some people might say that I'd stored up problems with the way I'd lived my life earlier in my career and it was simply that I reformed too late. There may be some truth to that. Maybe I deserved what I got.

Benjamin Franklin, one of America's Founding Fathers, said that 'life's tragedy is that we get old too soon and wise too late'. I like that, but I prefer the Mike Tyson version. I love boxing. I love the big fights and I love the wisdom of fighters. 'I didn't understand me 15 years ago,' Tyson said a few years back. 'I got old too soon and smart too late.'

Tyson also said this: 'Everyone has a plan until they get punched in the mouth.' And I was about to get punched in the mouth. I had only been at West Ham a few weeks when the blow came.

I loved it when I arrived at the club. Craig and Scottie and Lee Bowyer were all there, so it was easy to settle in to the dressing room. Lucas Neill was a great skipper who was big on organising events to bring the squad closer together – go-karting, meals with the players and their families – and there was a good camaraderie there straightaway.

I had a couple of days of training before West Ham's second game of the season, which was away at Birmingham City. I liked what I saw on the training pitch. I was very impressed with Mark Noble. I hadn't seen much of him before but he was a clever, neat, stylish midfielder with a great attitude.

Bobby Zamora was a terrific lad, too. I didn't realise he could be as funny as he was. He was the life and soul of the dressing room and I couldn't wait to sprint out at St Andrews and get my season up and running.

The atmosphere at the club was a long way from the idea that we were just a collection of mercenaries who had gone there because the Icelandic owners were throwing money at the situation. Yes, I was on better wages at West Ham than I had been on at Newcastle, but only just, because I had been on terrific wages at Newcastle as well.

A lot of us were on pretty big wages at our previous clubs. I still had two and a half years left on my contract at Newcastle, but I had needed a new challenge, and with West Ham making the investments they were making and signing quality players, I thought they were going places.

Inevitably, I started on the right of midfield at Birmingham. That was fine. Alan Curbishley had been straight with me about needing cover for Julien Faubert while he was injured, so I was expecting it.

I got on fine with Curbs. I respected him as a manager for all the work he had done up to that point. He had kept Charlton Athletic in the Premier League for six years, and as soon as he left, they had been relegated. The season before I arrived at West Ham, he had masterminded a great escape from relegation, helped by Carlos Tevez, who then left for Manchester United.

I played OK on my debut at St Andrews. I started on the right of a four-man midfield that also included Noble, Hayden Mullins and Matty Etherington. Bellers and Zamora were up front and the team had a decent look to it. I should have had a penalty in the first ten minutes when I was impeded by Stephen Kelly as I tried to run on to a ball from Bellers, but the referee waved my appeals away.

Noble scored the winner in the 70th minute with a penalty. I should have made it 2–0 near the end when Craig slipped me in after a counter-attack, but I miscontrolled the ball and the keeper smothered it. Never mind, we had points on the board and it was a good away win.

I felt encouraged. I had played 90 minutes for a start and I was feeling good physically. I was a bit undercooked because of the farce of commuting from Newcastle to Ipswich by private jet and sleeping in the van on the way to training, but I was getting closer to being as sharp as I knew I could be.

The following Wednesday, I played for England against Germany at Wembley. I came on for the last half-hour of a 2–1 defeat. I didn't know it then, but it was my last cap. The next Saturday, I made my first West Ham appearance at Upton Park in a 1–1 draw against Wigan Athletic. It wasn't a great performance, but I was feeling good. I played another 90 minutes. I was getting sharper and sharper.

I looked back at a report of the game recently and it mentioned I had been 'enjoying the freedom of Upton Park' during the first half. It felt like that, too. I felt energised by the move and I loved the West Ham fans. It was early days, but it felt like everything was going to work out.

After the game, Curbs called me into his office. He said he was pleased with the way things were going with me. We had a Carling Cup tie against Bristol Rovers at the Memorial Ground coming up on the Tuesday night and he said he wasn't going to play me. He knew my recent injury history and he wanted to keep easing me back. He wanted to protect me. He was going to give me the night off.

I pleaded with him to be allowed to play and he said he would think about it. On the day of the game, he invited me up to his hotel room and asked me if I still wanted to play. He said it was up to me. He said he'd still prefer to rest me, but if I was desperate to play, he was willing to put me in the side.

My rationale was that I wanted to get to a point where I was 100 per cent match fit and I thought playing at Bristol Rovers was probably the final step. I'd be ready after that. I thought I'd be playing centre-midfield, too, and that was a big thing for me. I was still fixated on making sure I did everything I could to nail down that position as soon as I could.

So I said again that I wanted to play. It was probably the biggest mistake I ever made. Curbs said OK and we put out a strong team. The midfield was Bowyer on the right, me and Mullins in the centre and Luís Boa Morte on the left. Up front we had Craig and Bobby. We hadn't quite been firing properly in the league and it was a selection aimed at fine-tuning a few things.

Bristol Rovers were a League One side. They had been promoted from League Two at the end of the previous season so they were full of running and confidence and aggression, determined not to be pushed around by the big boys from the Premier League.

The game started off at a frantic pace, but even after the first few minutes, we had so much possession that it felt as if we had already established control. We were comfortable. I was revelling in playing centre midfield for the first time in my West Ham career. I was at the heart of things again.

About ten minutes in, I got the ball just inside the Bristol Rovers half, out towards the right touchline. Joe Jacobson was with me but I used my low centre of gravity to turn away from him and set off on a run.

Jacobson was a decent footballer who played out his career in the lower leagues, but as I twisted away from him and started to get away into open space, he decided to bring me down and take one for the team. He knew there was no way he was getting the ball by that stage. He knew, too, that there was no way he would ever catch me.

I was turning away from him, moving to my left and he lost his balance and started to fall to his right. As he fell, he kicked out at my right leg with his left boot. It was clumsy and he wanted to bring me down, but

I don't think he meant to hurt me. It wasn't like he went in two-footed or lunged at me over the ball, or took me out knee-high or anything like that. It is often the innocuous tackles that do the damage.

Look at the way Alan Smith, the former Leeds United player, broke his leg when he was playing for Manchester United against Liverpool at Anfield. He was just charging down a free-kick, but because of a particular set of circumstances, his leg buckled underneath him and took all his weight and he suffered a terrible injury.

It was a little bit the same with me. Jacobson just tried to trip me, but my right leg was planted in the ground with my studs, and when he kicked down on my leg, there was nowhere for it to go and that was why my injury, too, was catastrophic.

I felt the kick on my leg and I heard a pop. I thought my shinpad had snapped, because you just don't think your leg could make that noise. It's not something that's a part of your frame of reference.

I didn't feel any pain initially. Because I was running at full pace and he hit me from behind, I rolled a few times and as I rolled, I could feel that my leg was floppy. It was as if there was nothing supporting it. The bottom half of my leg and my ankle were wobbling as I was rolling. I was aware of that.

When I came to a stop, I put my hand up. I started shouting. 'I've broken my leg,' I screamed. 'I've broken my leg.'

Lee Bowyer was the first there. 'F***ing hell,' he said. 'Did you hear your shinpad?'

'I've broken my leg,' I said. I wasn't in pain. I was more scared than anything.

Anton Ferdinand came over, too. 'Who dunnit?' he said. 'I'll give them beats.'

Even in the state I was in, it kind of made me laugh. Then Anton asked me to hold his hand and squeeze it as hard as I could. He was trying to be considerate, but it was funny.

Then George, the West Ham physio, arrived and rolled me over. I just kept repeating: 'I've broken my leg, I've broken my leg, I've broken my leg,' as if it was some kind of mantra.

No one said my leg was broken. They could see it, I suppose. To them, it would have just been stating the obvious. They were just trying to keep it straight as possible, and after they had done that, they put me on the stretcher.

West Ham had a doctor called Jez, who was massive. He must have weighed about 20 stone. As I was getting stretchered off, all the Bristol Rovers fans were singing '*you fat bastard*' at the doc.

I know it sounds weird now, but that made me laugh, too. 'They don't like you much,' I said as I stared up at him from the stretcher.

For a little while, I started to wonder if I hadn't broken my leg after all. And you know what my overriding emotion was? It wasn't hope. It wasn't even relief. It was embarrassment. How embarrassing it would be if I was getting carried off and all it had been was a kick on the leg.

Maybe I was imagining it was worse than it actually was. The stretcher-bearers put me in the back of the ambulance with Jez and then the medics said they were going to cut my sock off, take the shinpad away and try and take my boot off. As they were taking away the shinpad, I looked forward and I could see the tibia bone trying to push through the skin.

That's when the pain kicked in. I just said 'gas and air' and suddenly the pain was ridiculous. They took me straight to a Bristol hospital and X-rayed me. I had a double break. Both the tibia and fibula were broken. I had been at West Ham for 12 days.

Curbs was upset about the tackle and was openly critical of Jacobson in the post-match press conference. I think he apologised later. Jacobson's teammate, Richard Walker, expressed his sympathy for me and said I 'must be the unluckiest man in football'.

A few days later, Jacobson sent me a card in hospital apologising for the tackle. It was a decent gesture, but I didn't reply to it. I didn't think he had hurt me deliberately, but I wasn't quite ready to absolve him of all blame. It was too early for that and I was still trying to come to terms with what happened. I don't hold any grudges about it now. It was an accident.

I went straight into the operating theatre at the hospital in Bristol that night to straighten the bones because they were so severely displaced. I woke up feeling groggy and the first person I saw was Craig. He had scored two that night – we won 2–1 – and he had come straight to the hospital from the ground with all my belongings. My agent David Manasseh was also there.

The next day, I was transferred by ambulance to Holly House Hospital in east London, not far from the West Ham training ground. I had been told by then that I was looking at nine months out of the game. The M4 and the M25 were at a standstill in places so they put the sirens on and we went down the hard shoulder.

It was a bit bumpy and every little jolt sent stabs of pain through my leg, but I still enjoyed the ride. I had always tried to imagine what it would be like to be in an ambulance when it was hurtling through traffic with its lights flashing. It was small consolation for a double leg fracture.

## THE BIG LIMP

# 24

It was a bad injury but it should not have been the death-rattle for my career. I was only 28. I was coming into my prime. I should still have had five or six good years ahead of me, particularly now that I had finally wised up and was starting to take care of myself. When I got over this, I was going to continue being a good pro. That was what I kept telling myself.

Other players had suffered similar injuries and had come back fine. I wasn't kidding myself. I knew it wasn't going to be quick and I knew it would take a lot of hard graft. But Aaron Ramsey, the Arsenal midfielder, and Luke Shaw, the Manchester United full-back, would later come back from similar leg fractures after nine months. Henrik Larsson, the Sweden forward, hadn't even taken that long.

West Ham chose the surgeon who was going to do the operation to pin my leg. He wasn't a leader in the field and I wasn't sure about that. Usually, you get whatever specialist you need to deal with each type of footballer's injuries. So a club would usually choose Andy Williams to operate on a knee injury, James Calder for an ankle or a foot injury and Steven Corbett for a shoulder issue.

That's what I'd tell any young footballer now: make sure you have a say in who is going to treat you and do not be shy about saying you want to go to the best man or woman for the job when it comes to repairing broken bones or shattered joints. It's your career and it's not a long one. Get the best person available to look after you.

West Ham didn't feel it was necessary to do that with this injury. Don't ask me why. I mentioned it to John Green, the private physio who diagnosed my hamstring problem, when he came to visit me and he seemed to think that was OK. He said it was a straightforward operation. So I went into surgery and they inserted a rod through the knee, down the length of the bone, and screwed the top of it to my knee and the bottom of it to my ankle. Job done.

Except it wasn't. It wasn't job done at all. Instead, it was the beginning of a long, debilitating, dispiriting process that killed my career. It was the start of a process that led to the West Ham hierarchy trying to shame me, because I had been able to play so few games for the club. It was the start of a process of rehabilitation and relapse that is every footballer's purgatory.

When you see that a footballer is going to be out for longer than was originally thought, you don't really think beyond the headline news. When you read that a footballer has broken down during his comeback, you don't really think about the effect that must have on the player. You don't think about the mental torture as well as the physical pain.

That's partly because to get any deeper into it is boring. To most of us, it's dull hearing about the minutiae of a recovery and the things that make an operation a success or a failure. We just want to see the player back on the pitch. We don't want to know about how unlucky he might be or how an operation hasn't gone to plan.

I could go on and on about what happened to me at West Ham. Believe me, I could. By the end of my football career, I knew so much about the human body and its frailties that I felt like I could have done the operations to fix me myself. I could tell you about everything that could go wrong when you are trying to enable someone to play again and how to avoid it.

I wish I'd known then what I know now. I wish that somehow I'd had the wherewithal to take a bit more control. I wish I'd stuck up for myself a bit more and insisted on who I wanted to do the operation. But I was new at West Ham and a player's default mechanism is to trust his club. And that's what I did.

My initial operation didn't work. Because the bone was screwed at the top and the bottom, it didn't stimulate any compression so it took forever for the bone to heal. I was paying for my own physio work with John Green, but after a few months I was still in constant pain.

John Green had spoken to Stuart Evans, who was a fracture specialist, to try to figure out what was going wrong. Every time your foot hits the floor and you bounce, you have got some kind of compression. But if you have got a screw at the top and the bottom and it is rigid, how are you going to get that compression?

This is where other human frailties like embarrassment had an effect: I didn't want to piss off the surgeon who West Ham had used by saying that in my opinion the operation hadn't been a success. I was trying to run, but I was running in pain. So we said the screw in my ankle was causing me discomfort and left it at that.

I should have been honest with the surgeon who carried out the operation and told him straight that I wasn't getting any compression, and asked him to take out one of the screws. But I didn't do that. So when I woke up from the follow-up operation, I had a bandage on the bottom of my leg and a bandage on the top of my leg. He had removed both the screws, from the top and the bottom of my leg.

A few months later, things still weren't right. The bone was healing better but every time I got up to three-quarter pace, I was getting shooting pains in my knee. I had been out for about nine months already by this point. It was starting to look as if I would miss the start of the 2008–09 season, which had been my initial comeback target.

We went to see Andy Williams and I had X-rays and MRIs and everyone was baffled. I learned to recognise that look. It was the look of bafflement. It must be one of the worst sights someone who is recuperating from an injury or an illness can see. It's the 'we don't know why you're not getting better' look.

I took a couple of weeks off completely, but when I came back and started again I was still getting pain. We went back to see Andy Williams. The next theory was that maybe because I had the screws taken off at the bottom and the top, every time I had compression, the rod was pushing into my knee and that was why I was getting the shooting pain.

They said one set of screws should have been kept in just to fix the bone in place and then I wouldn't have the stabbing sensation in my knee. So I had to have another operation.

I wish I could have got to that point a lot earlier. I don't know if I would have come back the same player, but I would have been a hell of a lot better than the specimen they spat out at the end of my medical odyssey.

So I had four operations for a relatively straightforward injury that should have kept me out for nine months. I didn't come back until 18 months after the original incident against Bristol Rovers.

The thing that hurts most is that you kind of get used to being out with injury. What you can't get used to is putting your trust and faith in medical experts, listening to them, doing everything they say meticulously, working hard day in and day out without ever kicking a ball and yet it still doesn't work. You still lose the playing time that is the most precious thing in your career.

You're trying to do your best to get back, you're hating being away from the game, and you're starting to hate yourself because you can't get back to doing the thing you love – and you are getting slammed by the press, the owners and the fans. After I'd left West Ham, David Gold put something out on Twitter saying I'd cost the club £16 million in fees and wages. That was a classy touch.

As an injured footballer, you can't tell your side of the story, because if you do, you will be hammering physios or doctors and that doesn't come across well. No one likes a footballer criticising the medical profession. We're kind of at opposite ends of the spectrum when it comes to respectability.

I still bear the physical scars, of course. And when I go through security at airports, the scanners go into overdrive. There are so many pieces of metal in me that I used to take X-rays of my legs with me to try and ease the process of getting through the airport.

When I finally made my comeback, it was against Barnsley in an FA Cup third-round tie at Upton Park on 3 January 2009. I came off the bench in the 70th minute as a replacement for Jack Collison and the ovation I got from the West Ham fans was incredible. We won the game 3–0, I hit the bar and nearly scored with a curler that was heading for the top corner until the keeper saved it.

Much had changed at the club by then. Alan Curbishley had been sacked. He never had a chance really, because of the rash of injuries that struck the club. Gianfranco Zola was the boss now and Steve Clarke, who I knew well from Newcastle, was his assistant. Clarke was very generous about me after the Barnsley match.

'It was good to have him back because he's had a dreadful time with injury,' he told the press. 'We all feel for him and he's been working ever so hard just to get back on the pitch again. He showed some good touches but he's not near match-fitness. We can work on that – he could be like a new signing.'

That was what I hoped, too. We had Newcastle at St James' Park the following weekend and I thought I had every chance of being involved. I knew that would have meant getting booed by 52,000 people, but by that point I really didn't care. I was just desperate to play as much as possible and make up for lost time.

I wasn't included in the squad. Steve Clarke asked me if I wanted to go on loan to a Championship club to get some match fitness, but I was already experiencing a few physical issues because I had been out for so long.

I was in full training but because I'd had such an extended absence, I was starting to get the cramping sensations again that I had with compartment syndrome when I was younger. Everything had shrunk in my leg and the casing around my calves had shrivelled again. I had to have another operation on both of my shins. That was another six to eight weeks out. It was carnage.

I had just had the excitement of coming back and the fans giving me an ovation and then I got hit with another setback. I felt so low. I had finally overcome all the problems associated with my broken leg, but now there was something else. Football feels cruel at times like that.

I worked my way back to fitness again before the end of the season. I came on as a sub for a few minutes in a match against Blackburn at Ewood Park in late March and got another ten minutes or so against Sunderland a fortnight later. I was taking baby steps.

I was on the bench for the last game of the season against Middlesbrough at Upton Park and I came on for Mark Noble eight minutes after the interval. We won 2–1, which sent Middlesbrough down, and I played well for the half an hour I was on the pitch. I was probably the last thing Gareth Southgate and his struggling team needed: an opposition player with a point to prove.

When we got back to the changing rooms, Zola and Steve Clarke said they had been so impressed by my cameo that it had convinced them to give me a starting role the following season. That filled me with hope and optimism. I'd played without pain and felt as strong as I'd ever been. I thought that maybe I was starting to turn the corner.

We played in the Asia Cup before the start of the 2009–10 season and it became apparent that Zola wanted to play a midfield diamond that campaign with me at the top of it, Noble and Collison behind and Scott Parker at the base. I liked the idea and I thought it would suit me.

I played in all of pre-season and I was feeling good. The week before the opening game of the campaign against Wolves at Molineux, I was flying. I felt unplayable. No one could get near me. On Friday, we had a passing drill and then training was over. I thought I'd have a couple of penalties to finish off and with my last kick of the day, I felt my thigh pop.

My heart sank. I was in pain but that was nothing compared to the dread and the disappointment and the embarrassment that was flooding over me. I couldn't tell the physio what had happened. I went to see him and said my thigh was tight, but I knew I had pulled it.

I started trying to convince myself it was only a bit of tightness, too. On the morning of the Wolves game, we did a fitness test in the corridor of the hotel we were staying in. I was sprinting up and down the corridor, but every stride I took sent stabbing pains shooting through my thigh.

I still didn't tell anyone I'd pulled it. Somehow, I passed the fitness test and made the starting line-up. So I played the first game of our season with a grade-one tear in my thigh. I was in agony but we won 2–0 and Mark Noble scored a great goal. Once we'd got the first game out of the way, I plucked up the courage to tell the physio about the extent of the injury.

It took me a long time to get over that thigh pull. Perhaps it was just age or the accumulation of injuries. I would play the odd game and then be out injured for another six weeks with another muscle injury of one type or another. I'd train and then break down, train and break down. I shed a few tears that season. I felt like chucking it in.

In January 2010, David Gold and David Sullivan bought the club and it wasn't long before one of them did an interview in which he talked about the extraordinary wages West Ham were paying and how one player who had barely played ought to have the decency to retire. The arrow was pointing right at me.

When you're an owner of a football club, you're entitled to think what you want. It didn't bother me, because he didn't know how many times I had gone into that physio's room at West Ham saying I wanted to pack it in. In some ways, we were singing from the same hymn sheet.

After the last game of the season, Karren Brady, the West Ham chief executive, asked me to go up to the boardroom to meet the owners. I had one more year left on my contract, so I was bracing myself for them saying I needed to retire. Brady, Sullivan and Gold were all there in one of the corporate suites and they were outwardly very nice but the situation turned a bit odd.

They kept dropping stuff into the conversation that seemed to be designed to let me know they were watching me. 'How's that nightclub in your house?' one of them asked. I explained it wasn't really a nightclub, it was just an outbuilding where I'd put some decks in so I could have family and friends round now and again.

Then they mentioned the name of a restaurant I'd been to the previous night and started talking about how good it was. There was no real resolution to the conversation. When it was over, I came out thinking: 'What just happened there?' It was bizarre. It was just the way they worked.

I got on really well with Karren Brady, actually. I think she's very good at what she does. She's a very tough negotiator, but I liked her. For a woman to be in that industry and to be so successful, I really admired that because it is so heavily male-dominated. I wouldn't necessarily be quite as generous about Gold and Sullivan, but they put the money in. It's up to them how they behave.

Zola was sacked at the end of the 2009–10 season, after we finished 17th in the league, and the owners replaced him with Avram Grant. I wasn't even in the 20-man squad for the first game of the new season, away at Aston Villa, which we lost 3–0. I played a reserve game the next Monday and then Avram asked me if I could play left-wing against Bolton Wanderers the following Saturday.

I played for 77 minutes and got through the game fine, but we lost 3–1. I started the next game, away at Manchester United, too, and hit the post in another heavy defeat, but I could feel that my thigh problem was starting to flare up again. By the time we played Chelsea in the next game, I was in a lot of pain. I couldn't play through it any more.

I slipped back into the same frustrating, sad pattern of playing one game and missing three or four with a niggle of one kind or another. I probably would have jacked it in, if the owners hadn't done that article in which, to me, they were seemingly trying to force me into retirement. It was that stubborn streak in me again.

If you ask West Ham fans now, they would say what a waste of money I was, and they have got every right to say that. I didn't even score a goal for West Ham in four years. I didn't play four or five games on the trot, ever. But you know what? Every time I went out there, they were brilliant with me and I will always remember that.

After all the grief I got from the fans at Newcastle, there were these supporters at West Ham for whom I did nothing and they never turned on me when I was on the pitch. That's a special kind of fan. They were very knowledgeable supporters. On the odd occasion I could drag myself on to the pitch fully fit, it was a privilege to play in front of them.

Sometimes in football, someone will try a 50-yard killer pass and an opposition player intercepts it and you will hear a groan. And then someone runs 50 yards and does a sliding tackle and they get a huge cheer. But if someone tried something ambitious at West Ham and it didn't quite work, they would give you a round of applause. I loved that about those fans. It kills me that they didn't even see a fraction of what I once was. It pains me.

As the 2010–11 season was winding down and I was still struggling with the thigh problem, Karren Brady rang me on a Friday morning and said Ipswich Town wanted me on loan. I thought about it. They were my home-town club, I still lived there. I thought I might as well give it a go. There was also the fact that my youngest son, Kody, was due to be born that week and I desperately wanted to be around for that.

Paul Jewell, who was the Ipswich manager then, rang me a few minutes later and told me that training started at 10.30am and that he wanted me to come in. They were away at Leeds the next day and he said he would like me to be involved. I didn't have my boots but I borrowed Paul Jewell's Copa Americas and joined the rest of the lads for training.

We did a box and some keep-ball and then we went into a game. It was the last ten minutes of training when I felt my thigh go again. I was so embarrassed. There was no way I was saying anything. I told them it was a bit tight and travelled up to Leeds on the coach with the rest of the lads.

I played 75 minutes with a grade-one tear in my thigh. I still didn't say anything. We had a warm-down on Sunday because we had a home match against Watford on the Tuesday. The next day at training, I was struggling to move. Paul Jewell must have looked at me and thought I was some gnarled old pro who just didn't care any more. But I really did care.

I was in constant pain, but I didn't know what to do to spare myself any more embarrassment. Ipswich had made a big fuss in the media about the local boy coming back to his roots for the game against Watford at Portman Road and Jewell was really keen for me to play.

I started making excuses. I said I'd like to start on the bench. I said I wasn't used to playing three games a week because of all my injuries. Jewell was fuming with me and he had every right to be. I knew what he was thinking: 'This guy hasn't played for two years, his home-town fans are desperate to see him play and he can't be arsed.'

In the end, I persuaded him not to start me. We were playing badly, so I came on early in the second half. I was still in a lot of pain, but I got on the ball as much I could. It didn't do any good and we lost heavily. I could see that Jewell was livid. He wasn't happy we'd lost, for a start, but he also thought he'd just signed a player who'd rather be on the bench than on the pitch.

We had Scunthorpe at home a few days later and I was pencilled in to start. In training the day before, the ball bounced off me as I was trying to control it and then after I ran to retrieve it, I gave it away with a sloppy pass. My thigh was killing me and I thought to hell with this and walked off.

I could hear Paul Jewell shouting and yelling but I kept walking. I told Matt, the Ipswich physio, a little bit of my long injury history, and he suggested a programme of neural stretching. I tried it out, missed a couple of games for Ipswich and then played at Burnley and at home to

Palace. My thigh suddenly felt a lot better. The new stretching technique was a revelation

I went back to West Ham full of confidence .

I didn't know it at the time, but my last game for the club had been the second leg of the Carling Cup semi-final against Birmingham at St Andrew's back at the end of January. I was picked on the bench. We were protecting a 2–1 lead from the first leg and Carlton Cole put us further ahead in the first half.

They got one back through my old sparring partner Lee Bowyer in the second half and then I was brought on for Zavon Hines with 19 minutes to go. About the first thing that happened to me was that I got smashed in the face by someone's forearm and broke my nose. A few minutes after that, Birmingham got another goal to take the tie to extra-time.

They went into the lead on aggregate early in extra-time, but we still knew we only needed one more goal to go through on away goals. I thought I was going to score it, too. The ball fell to me on the volley and I only had Ben Foster to beat from a few yards out but somehow I put the ball over the bar.

I had pulled on a West Ham shirt for the last time, the team that should have seen the best of me but in the end saw very little of anything at all except a sad, dejected man limping to touchline after touchline.

## THE LAST SHOT

The logical thing to do when I left West Ham would have been to retire. It wasn't as if I hadn't been thinking about it from time to time over the last couple of years as I staggered from one injury blow to another. But when my time at Upton Park came to an end, the thoughts of quitting had disappeared and I wanted to find another club.

There were several things that were pushing me that way. The new stretching routine that had been recommended to me at Ipswich had made a big difference and I felt that my thigh problems were behind me. I felt in much better shape physically. I'd been training with West Ham reserves in my last couple of months there and I felt sharp and enthusiastic again.

Psychologically, I wasn't ready to retire, either. I'd worked so hard to get back from so many injuries that I had this irrational idea that my luck was bound to change. I thought that maybe my career was about to enter an Indian summer. I still had ambitions. I thought that if a Premier League club signed me, I might still regain my place in the England squad.

I loved the game, too. That was the main thing. I'd always loved the game but I'd only realised in the last couple of years quite how much I loved it. Maybe that's always the way. You don't know what you've got until it's gone and all that. I was doing everything possible to look after myself now and live like a model pro. I thought surely that would give me another couple of years.

I had this chequered past and I wanted to put that behind me. I wanted to put it behind me by achieving more things on the pitch. I wanted people to talk about me as a player again. If I hadn't broken my leg, I feel sure that would have happened and now I wanted another chance.

You look at some of our great players like Frank Lampard, Jamie Carragher and Steven Gerrard: they all had wild moments in their youth but they matured and their careers flourished through their hard work and talent, and everyone forgot about what they had done when they were kids. Maybe I wanted a bit of that, too.

I didn't want to be known as the bling boy or the brat any more. I just wanted to get my head down and play and lose some of the negativity that infected people's views of me. I'd brought a lot of that on myself, I know, and now I wanted to try to undo some of it.

There was a guy who lived next door to my mum in Ipswich called Ronnie Mauge and he had played for Neil Warnock when he was manager of Plymouth Argyle. Warnock had just got QPR promoted to the Premier League and Ronnie told me that Warnock wanted to speak to me about joining them.

I went to meet Warnock at his house in Richmond and got on with him really well. He told me all about his plans for the season ahead and as soon as I got back in my car, I rang David Manasseh and said I didn't want him to talk to any other clubs and that I wanted to join QPR.

I signed a one-year deal on £20k a week. I was acutely aware of my injury history and I wanted to be fair to Warnock and QPR, so I suggested that we insert a clause in the contract that said that if they weren't happy with me when it came to January that season, then they could terminate my contract. Dave was against it but I was grateful they were giving me another chance, and I insisted on putting it in.

The set-up at QPR was a bit different to what I was used to. Warnock had this pre-season routine that he never strayed from whichever club he was at. He took the lads for some friendly matches in Cornwall. We stayed in a kind of hostel and it was pretty basic. I roomed with Jay Bothroyd and tried to keep my head down.

A lot of the lads had come up from lower league clubs and I wanted to try to make sure no one thought I was behaving like a Billy Big-Time. Maybe they thought I'd be agitating to go out and get wasted every night. That wasn't me any more.

The lads organised a couple of nights out, but I made excuses and stayed in. I didn't want any grief. I didn't want even to put myself in a position where I could attract any trouble. I wanted to come in under the radar and concentrate wholly on the football.

After one of these nights out, Jay came back to the room and left the door open. I was trying to get to sleep but I was aware that the QPR keeper, Paddy Kenny, had wandered in and he started being a pest. I told him to get out and go to his own room, but he wouldn't.

He asked me who I thought I was, refusing to go out with the rest of the lads. He said I was a Big-Time Charlie. He said I obviously thought I was too good for the rest of them because I'd played for England, and on and on. I told him he was talking rubbish.

So he jumped up on my bed and started throwing haymakers at me while I was lying there. Now Paddy Kenny's a big lump, and I'm not saying I could beat him in a straight fight, but one thing I have learned over the years is that someone who is sober and has got their wits about them can smash someone who's so pissed they can hardly stand

So I got him in a headlock and threw him on the floor. He was wedged between the bed and the radiator and I was strangling him, and Jay Bothroyd was laughing because I was nearly choking him out.

'Calm down, you f***ing prick,' I kept saying to him but he still wanted to fight, so I kept him in the headlock. He started gurgling then and Jay was laughing and laughing. I didn't throw any punches or anything because he was helpless. The last thing I wanted was for it to escalate into a full-blown fight.

I didn't want to get into trouble for a scrap, for God's sake, but I had to defend myself when he was on my bed punching me. In the end, I let him go and he leapt up and said 'outside now'. I told him to get out of my room.

When I got up in the morning and went to get breakfast, he was waiting outside like he was some sort of hard man. I asked him what he wanted to do and before he could reply, Fitz Hall appeared and told Paddy to zip it and marched him off. I was cursing my luck. A week into pre-season and I was already making friends.

It was around that time that Tony Fernandes was being heavily linked with buying the club from Flavio Briatore and Bernie Ecclestone, and suddenly it seemed as though QPR might soon have money to burn. Warnock asked me to ring Scott Parker and Craig Bellamy because he wanted to sign them both.

Neither worked out. Scottie was impressed with what QPR were offering but he was happy at Spurs, and Craig was at Liverpool being managed by Kenny Dalglish, so he was in no hurry to move either. So we ended up buying Joey Barton, Shaun Wright-Phillips and Luke Young, all good signings.

I had been playing right-back throughout pre-season and Warnock picked me there for our opening game of the Premier League season, against Bolton Wanderers at Loftus Road. Five minutes in, my studs got caught in the turf and I felt a shooting pain in my right foot. 'Not again,' I thought. 'Please, not again.' I tried to run it off, but I couldn't.

I didn't want to walk off. I was too embarrassed to do that. Warnock could see what was happening and he was shouting at me to go down. So I lay on the turf and a stretcher came on to carry me away. My debut had lasted six minutes, although I think that might have included the time it took to cart me off.

I had an X-ray and they said I had a little chip in my foot. A few weeks later, I went to see James Calder and he said it was what they call a Lisfranc injury, which is a displacement of the bone and is very hard to detect on scans and X-rays.

Mr Calder said I could do three months in rehab or have an operation. It would take longer to come back from the operation, but at least that way, I would know it was fixed. I said I wanted the operation, but Mr Calder was reluctant. He said surgery should always be the last option.

I knew how cursed I was. I knew deep down that if I didn't have the operation, the problem would still be there. But I understood the medical logic about how surgery should be a last resort and so I agreed to do the rehab.

Fairly soon after that, Tony Fernandes bought the club and Phil Beard came in as his chief executive. They were both great people, but some of their working practices didn't sit easily with me. They had a habit of asking players how they thought things were going. Now, I know players and if something's going wrong, it's never their fault. It's very easy to point the finger at someone else.

We had a players' committee, which was Clint Hill, Joey Barton,

Shaun Derry and me. Phil Beard came to see us and asked us what we thought about the club, the training ground, the coaching staff and the management.

Joey is someone who is brutally honest. He said training was rubbish, he had a go at Keith Curle, who was Warnock's assistant, he was saying this was being done badly and that was amateurish. He ripped the whole set-up to shreds.

He was just being honest, but I didn't think that should be happening. That could be costing people's jobs, and however forthright and articulate Joey was, it was just one opinion.

It was around that time that Joey recommended that Peter Kay should come in and offer counselling to anyone who wanted it. That was when I finally began to talk about what had happened to me in my childhood and I will always be grateful to Joey for organising that in the first place.

The rehab on my ligament injury was going well and I was feeling fitter and sharper. We had a game against Liverpool at Anfield before Christmas and I sat on the bench with the substitutes to watch the game. Craig was on the bench for Liverpool that day and when the game started, he pointed at Joey and shouted over: 'F***king hell, how bad is your mate.'

When Craig got on the pitch, he made a beeline for Joey and wound him right up by telling him he was shit. That was standard for Craig. After the whistle, I wandered on to the pitch and Joey walked past me and said: 'Your friend's getting smashed.' When Bellers walked past, I told him to be careful when he got to the tunnel.

By the time I got there, all hell was breaking loose. When I got into the changing room, Joey wanted to take it out on me. 'It's always you and your f***ing friends,' he said. We had our Christmas party in Liverpool that night. It was one of the few footballers' parties that passed off without incident.

The following Wednesday, I played in a friendly against Tottenham's Under-23s at the QPR training ground at Harlington. The game was only a few minutes old when I went to receive a throw-in and let it run across my body. As I pushed off, I felt my big toe give way, so I knew my Lisfranc injury had re-occurred.

I didn't even signal to anyone. I just put my head in my hands and started crying. I hobbled away to the physio's room, weeping, and Sangita, who was the deputy physio, came running off the pitch into the room and asked what was wrong. I was inconsolable. All I could think of was that I should have had the operation.

Then Warnock dashed in. He had been watching the game. There were a few other players in the room and he kicked them all out so it was just me, him and Sangy. I was distraught and he was so upset for me that he started crying, too. I think that says a lot about the kind of man he is.

We went back to see Mr Calder and he looked at the scan and said that they would have to operate on it now. I gave him a dirty look, but he stood by his original decision. 'Kieron,' he said, 'if twenty more players came to see me with the exact same symptoms, I would always err on the side of caution. You might think you are cursed, but I would do the same again and again.'

It softened the blow a bit. I had the operation and I went back to the training ground in the first week in January. The clause in my contract said that the club had until 31 January to terminate it and Warnock had already let me know the executives weren't going to keep me on.

Neil said that he had arranged a role for me as a QPR ambassador for the remainder of the season, which would at least mean I could do my rehab at the training ground and then we would see how things were going in the build-up to the following season. A few days later, Warnock was sacked.

Mark Hughes was appointed and I waited for the official confirmation that my contract had been terminated. And I waited. It got to 31 January and I still hadn't heard anything, so I went to training as usual. I passed Phil Beard a couple of times in the corridor and we swapped pleasantries and nothing else was said. I thought maybe they were going to give me another chance after all.

I went home at the end of the day and had one missed call from a withheld number. At training the next day, Mark Hughes called me in. He said he knew the club had terminated my contract but that I was still welcome to come in and use the facilities. I told him that, actually, they hadn't terminated the contract. He seemed surprised.

Then Phil Beard came to see me. He said they had been trying to contact me to terminate the contract. A couple of days later, I got a letter through the post and the date on the letter was sometime in January but the stamp on the envelope was 1 February.

I spoke to Gordon Taylor at the PFA and he said I was entitled to all my money. So I went to Phil Beard and proposed a deal to him. I suggested from now until the end of the season, I'd be on two grand a week.

After that, I asked them to give me the chance of being named in Mark Hughes's 25-man squad on 1 September and if I made it, then my wages would go back up to £20k a week. If I didn't make it, they could just get rid of me.

I was saving them half a million quid, effectively. They agreed to the deal. Some QPR fans thought I was signing a year extension and weren't too happy. I didn't blame them, even though it wasn't accurate, but I did well enough in pre-season to make the 25-man squad at the start of the 2012–13 season.

Things were fairly tempestuous at QPR at that time, though, and Mark Hughes was sacked in November 2012 and replaced by Harry Redknapp.

I was a bit disappointed with Harry. I always thought he would be like Sir Bobby Robson and that everyone would love him. I thought he would be a master of man-management and that he'd be putting his arm around everybody, but he wasn't really like that. I got on fine with him, but at QPR half the dressing room loved him and half didn't and he would publically hammer some players like José Bosingwa.

I played right-wing against Manchester United at Old Trafford in late November when Harry was watching from the stands before he officially took over. I made a goal for Jamie Mackie but we lost the game 3–1 and I didn't even travel to the next game. As the season wore on, most people got a chance but Harry left me on the sidelines.

We drew West Brom in the FA Cup third round and the week before the game, I went to Harry's office. 'Look,' I said, 'you might think I'm a shit player or a crock or whatever, but every player in the 25-man squad has been given a start. Just give me a start.' Harry said he'd take it on board.

He was as good as his word. I played right-back in the Cup game and then switched to left-back, and with about ten minutes to go, I misplaced a pass to Jay Bothroyd. It was intercepted and West Brom went up the other end and scored.

Two minutes into injury time, I came haring up from left-back, went on the overlap and scored the equaliser with a left-foot shot across the keeper. I was buzzing. It was my first goal since I'd left Newcastle. I'd finally been given a chance, I'd done well, the physios were happy for me and all the hard work had paid off.

We came into training the following Monday. I was sitting in the physio's room getting some treatment and I got a message to say Harry wanted to see me in his office. I had just scored and I knew he was having problems with Bosingwa at right-back. I went in thinking he was going to ask me to play the following Saturday.

He could hardly look me in the eye. I wasn't overly concerned because he's like that most of the time. And then he blurted it straight out: 'Kieron, I'm going to have to let you go.'

It was a shock. It was my first start for two months and I'd done well. It was like someone had given me a punch to the gut and winded me when I wasn't expecting it. He said he wanted to bring in Loïc Rémy and free up some wages.

I told him he didn't need to make excuses about money. I said if he didn't fancy me as a player, that was fine. Football's about opinions. I asked for a game and he gave me a game and now he wanted rid of me. I wasn't expecting it and I was hurt but it was OK. It was his choice.

I think Harry was expecting a confrontation, but there wasn't one. It seemed to be a recurring theme of my later years in the game, but I felt more embarrassed than anything else. I went to sign some sort of official release form with Caroline in the office and then I headed out to my car. I didn't even change out of my kit. I didn't want to have to talk to anyone.

Jay Bothroyd saw me and asked where I was going. I told him I was going to get something from my car. I didn't tell him the truth. I got in the car. I rang up David Manasseh and told him they had terminated my contract. Sangi rang and I told her what had happened and that I'd been too embarrassed to tell her to her face. Then I drove away.

# 26

## THE RELEASE

After QPR, I knew it was over. I wasn't the player I once was. Players like Paul Scholes could have played until they were 40 because it's all in their brain. Their speed is in their mind. With me, it was all about pace and power, and once the pace and power were gone, I was a shadow of a player.

I was still quick. I'm still quick now. But there was a time when I could do a 100m sprint and then do another one a few seconds later. By the time I left QPR, that was gone. I needed more recovery time. The power in my legs was going, too. I didn't have the strength.

Sir Bobby Robson used to say I had two hearts because I had so much energy, but he wouldn't have said that about the player who drove away from the QPR training ground that day. When your game is based on pace and energy and they start to diminish, it is time to face up to the end.

When the news got out that QPR had let me go, Tony Mowbray rang me. He was the manager at Middlesbrough by now but I had played alongside him when I was a kid at Ipswich. I was the raw right-back and he was the experienced centre-half who would guide me through matches and make sure none of the opposition picked on me. He was always a guy you wanted in your corner.

He asked me if I'd come and play for him at Middlesbrough and I thought I might as well. I had a lot of time for Mogga and maybe I was still stinging a bit from the shock of being released by QPR. Maybe I was just annoyed at myself for being surprised in the first place. I should have seen it coming, but I didn't.

I gave Mogga my word that I'd join him at Middlesbrough on 1 February, and for the next couple of weeks, I thought I'd train at Ipswich with the youth team to keep myself fit. The first week, I trained with the youth team on Monday and Tuesday, had Wednesday off and then came in on Thursday. When I got there, I was told Mick McCarthy, the Ipswich boss, wanted me to go to train with the first team.

I enjoyed it and we had a quick match at the end. I got one-on-one with Aaron Cresswell, who was a promising young full-back there at the time. I had my back to him and he tried to pressure me. I did a stepover one way and then went the other and sent him to the High Street. I went past him and slid Eddie McGoldrick in and he scored.

All the other players were laughing and making fun of Cresswell for what I did to him. After training, Mick called me into the office and said they'd like me to sign on until the end of the season.

I would have loved to have one last shot at playing for Ipswich. There would have been a nice symmetry to ending my career where it had begun, but I had promised Mogga I would sign for Middlesbrough so I had to turn Mick down.

I'd had so many injuries and so much wear and tear over the years that I couldn't train fully any more, so I had an agreement with Mogga that if I played a midweek game, I wouldn't play the following weekend.

We also had an agreement that if I was due to play in a Saturday game, I wouldn't come up to Middlesbrough until the Wednesday before.

I wouldn't say I had a transformative effect on Middlesbrough. Not in a good way, anyway. The first game, inevitably, was away to Ipswich at Portman Road. We lost 4–0. We played 16 games in my time at the club and won three of them. There had been hopes of a play-off place when I joined. We finished the season in 16th.

At least I was playing football. I played in nine games while I was there. I scored a couple. I had the odd niggle, but I was OK. They were a good set of lads, too, and I loved playing for Mogga. He loved football and he loved trying different formations. We were just a team lacking in confidence.

The Championship seemed harder to me than the Premier League, but it was probably just that I was older. It's like being a runner in a marathon and following a pace guy who keeps a steady speed all the way around. Late in the marathon, you think the guy's speeding up. But he isn't. It's just that you're slowing down.

I didn't have the pace or the power any more. I couldn't get away from people like I used to. I knew by then that it was definitely my last season as a professional footballer.

I'd agreed a deal with Middlesbrough that meant I was on £15k a week but if I played in less than half their games in a month, it went down to £2,000 a week. With my first week's wage, I paid for the Ipswich Under-14s to go to Catalonia to play Barcelona's Under-14s.

There were six games in April. I missed a couple but I played against Bolton Wanderers at the Reebok on 20 April 2013. I scored in a 2–1 defeat. It meant that our last mathematical chance of a play-off place had gone.

Mogga said he was going to put me in the squad for the following week's game against Charlton Athletic. That meant I'd play in three of the six games in April. I pointed out to Mogga that that meant the club would have to pay me £60k that month instead of £8,000 if he left me out.

I didn't want to take the piss out of him or the club. That £50k difference could mean a new training pitch or a new youth coach, something that would properly benefit Middlesbrough, rather than me playing one last meaningless game at the end of my career.

Mogga shook my hand and thanked me for the gesture. And that was it. I'd played my last game at Bolton and I hadn't even realised it. But I knew the end had been coming. It wasn't as if it was a shock.

I wasn't sad when I stopped. People ask me if I miss playing football and the answer is that I don't. Not because I didn't love the game, but because in the last five years of my football career, I was never fit and I was always doing rehab. It was miserable.

I got used to missing football. It's not like I played 300 games in those last five years and then it all came to a sudden stop. I was delighted that I didn't have to feel embarrassed in front of my family any more. I was relieved I didn't have to feel embarrassed about myself in front of the fans any more. I was delighted I wouldn't be embarrassed in front of the physios any more.

I'd had enough of letting people down. I didn't want to come in from training again and say I'd done my thigh. When people pour scorn on people like Darren Anderton, Michael Owen and Daniel Sturridge because of their injury record, I don't think they realise how much embarrassment there is when you injure yourself.

I've tried to articulate it already but I've lost count of the amount of times I injured myself, and I didn't want my number to come up and do that walk of shame to the touchline. Somehow, I'd always manage to get to half-time so I didn't have to do that walk.

I have a few regrets about my career. I wish I had looked after myself more when I was younger. I had a great time, but it cost me. I was regarded as one of the outstanding talents of my generation when I was a young player, but I didn't have the career that men like Steven Gerrard, Frank Lampard and Rio Ferdinand did. Not even close.

I was smart too late. There is never a truer word spoken than that. By the time I realised that I needed to look after myself better, the damage had been done to my body. So even though I became the model professional in my late twenties, the sins of my previous existence, and their ally, a bit of bad luck, chased me down and made me pay.

But I still count myself lucky. Sure, I didn't have the career that Steve or Frank or Rio had, but I still had a damned good career. I played for my home-town club, Ipswich Town, I played for a great club like Newcastle United, I played for great football men like Sir Bobby Robson and Graeme Souness and I played for my country at a World Cup.

Sometimes, I see documentaries on television or read articles in newspapers that are the sad stories of men or women whose lives have been ruined by being the victims of sexual predators in their youth. They have been unable to recover from what happened to them. They have turned to crime or to drugs and they have slipped away to another life, far from the one they might have had.

That didn't happen to me. I kept my secret for a long time, but I unburdened myself of it in the end. It damaged me and it affected relationships and friendships, but I did not let it ruin my career. Actually, I think it was probably football that saved me.

Every time I crossed that white line and ran on to a football pitch, that was my escape. That was the time when I could forget about what happened to me in that front room on the Poets' Estate. That was when I could lose myself in the game and push away the bad thoughts.

Football, and football people, saved me. I will always be thankful for that.

# 27

Many years ago, I was in a bar in Ipswich and I saw a girl across the room and I thought how beautiful she was. I caught her eye and smiled at her and she stared back at me like I was some sort of leering wretch. It was such a withering look, it made an impression on me. Let's just say I wasn't meant to take any encouragement from it.

Some years later, around the time I had joined QPR and had finally brought myself to talk about the episode of sexual abuse that had had such a big impact on my life up to that point, I pulled up at some traffic lights in the town and a car drew up next to me.

I looked over and it was the same girl. I tried to get her attention, but if she was aware of the man in the car alongside gesticulating at her, she didn't show it. She kept her eyes in front and when the lights changed to green, she drove off and I lost track of her again.

I did at least know her name by then and I texted Titus Bramble's brother, Tes, and asked him if he could message Hollie on Facebook and ask her if I could have her number. So I got her number and I called her and now we are married and now I am happy.

It feels like it was fate, really. Until I started pouring everything out to Peter Kay, I wasn't really much of a partner to anybody anyway. When I was with the mother of my three boys, we were in the same house but I might as well have been in the house on my own.

I was aloof. I was distant. I must have been an absolute nightmare to live with. It was just who I was and I didn't realise I was doing anything wrong, but I must have been unbearable. She would start ranting and I would look at her and think: 'You are living in a nice house, so what are you moaning about?' That was the way I was then.

People talk about finding 'the one' and I never really used to believe that that happened. Now I have found 'the one' and I know that I got lucky. We met each other at just the right time, when I was finally coming to terms with what had happened to me and opening myself up a bit more to the people around me.

I knew she was the one after we had been together for a couple of months. Maybe it was even earlier than that. Every time I saw her, I got butterflies in my belly. It was like an adrenaline rush. After two months, I was gone, hook, line and sinker.

I thought it couldn't get any better than that, but then it did. She introduced me to her two daughters, Marlee and Meeya, and I introduced her to my kids, Kie, Lexi, Kaden and Kody, and it took our relationship to a whole different level.

If she'd smiled back at me in that bar all those years ago, maybe it wouldn't have worked because I wouldn't have been ready for it. So I think it was fate that kept us apart and fate that brought us back together.

I'm not saying I've been the perfect partner. We got married in August 2014 and I had tried to do the sensible thing by going on a quiet stag trip to Dubai with my cousin Emma's fiancé, Ben, and my mate, Nev. We did all the water parks and soaked up some sun so I'd look fit and healthy for the big day. We had a great time and it passed off very uneventfully.

When I got back, though, some of my friends in Ipswich insisted that a big crew of us went to Newmarket races the weekend before the wedding. They hired a coach and 40 of us piled on to it. I should have known better. I should have seen it coming.

I really hadn't been drinking much at all for the previous few years. I maybe had a glass of wine on special occasions, that kind of thing. But when we got there, they started pumping drinks down my throat and I played along with it all. I guess I couldn't quite let the Brat Pack days go without one last flourish.

My mate Conrad pointed at the bar and said I had to do the top shelf of optics all in one drink. It was brandy, tequila, whisky, whatever. DJ Spoony was there and he was going mad at them and telling me not to do it, but like the prat I am, I yielded to the peer pressure and necked it down.

Then Conrad pointed to the bottom shelf of optics and said I had to down all of them in one hit, too. Spoony and Simon Milton told me not to do it, but again, I was too stupid and too proud to listen to them. I tried to neck that one, too, but I spilled it when I was about halfway through it. I probably drank 12 shots in five minutes.

That's pretty much all I remembered for a while. They tell me I passed out about five minutes after that, amid the throngs at the racecourse. I was violently sick and they had to drag me into a toilet. I was sick some more and then they dragged me to a taxi. I was reeling around so much I knocked the wing mirror off the taxi as they were trying to push me into it. I bet that driver was happy to see me in his cab.

They managed to get me back to my house outside Ipswich. Hollie was away in Marbella having a last break before the wedding, so they called my mum and asked her if she could come and look after me. They laid me on the bed when they got me home and I was sick all over that, too.

Ben stayed in the house that night just to make sure I survived it, I think. I got up the next morning because I was playing in a golf tournament at my local club. I had a shocking headache, but I thought if I drank a lot of water and shovelled down a couple of tablets, it might take the edge off it and I'd be able to play.

I realised my heart was beating fast. I could feel it thumping in my chest. I mentioned it to Ben. He's got loads of techie stuff and he put this exercise monitor on me and it said my heart was going at 200 beats per minute. I got my golf gear on, but I started to feel a bit weird.

So we jumped into Ben's car and he drove like a maniac to get me to the Ipswich Hospital on Heath Road. I was starting to feel really weird now, although that probably wasn't helped by the way he was driving. We overtook an ambulance that had its sirens on at one point.

When we got into reception, I keeled over. The next time I opened my eyes, I was lying in a hospital bed and I had loads of wires attached to me. They said that because I hadn't really been drinking too much in the past couple of years, my body had gone into toxic shock with all the shots I'd poured down my throat. It didn't know what hit it, basically, and this was its response.

I was in hospital for two days. Hollie flew straight back from Marbella. We thought the wedding was going to be called off. It was a huge upset. I made it, fortunately, but I wasn't in the best shape. There was certainly no question of me joining in the champagne toasts on the big day. It made me feel queasy just to look at alcohol.

Hollie wasn't too sure about me doing *I'm a Celebrity . . . Get Me Out of Here!* either. I was offered the chance to do it in the autumn of 2015 and I was tempted. It was must-watch television in our household when it was on and my kids loved it. I wanted to do it for them really.

When I say I did it for my kids, I suppose I did it for me, too. Apart from Kie, they weren't old enough to remember their dad playing football. All they knew was someone who said he was a football player but spent five years limping around, trying to get over injuries. I thought that probably didn't make me much of anything in their eyes. I wanted to do something that would make them proud of me.

Whenever we watched *I'm a Celeb*, I was always banging on about how I could do the bushtucker trials easily and the kids always said there was no way. They knew I was petrified of spiders and snakes, for a start.

If there's a spider in the house and the kids are screaming and yelling, I'd love to be able to say that I slide a piece of paper under it and take it out into the back garden and place it lovingly on a window sill. But what actually happens is that I get a towel and whack the crap out of it.

As for snakes, I'd rather fight a lion than come face to face with a cobra. I told the producers of the show that when I met them. They seemed quite pleased. They asked how I was when I was hungry. I said I'd never been hungry. When I feel like I need food, I eat food. I'm not being flippant. I've been lucky, I know that.

Hollie was a bit apprehensive about it because she knew it would bring the spotlight on us. She'd never had to deal with that really, because we got together when I was playing for Middlesbrough and my career was nearly over. She didn't like the idea of even a brief glimpse of fame, but she knew I wanted to do it for the kids and that the kids would love it, and so she gave me the OK.

She was the only one who knew. The producers are fanatical about you keeping it a secret, so I didn't tell my mum or the kids. I flew into Brisbane and was taken to a hotel on the Gold Coast. They took my mobile phone away and allocated me a chaperone who made sure I had no more contact with the outside world. He was a decent bloke. He bought me a load of box-sets and got me addicted to *Narcos*, the US TV crime series about the drug trade.

Dr Bob, the show's medic, came in at one point and brought out a sheet of paper that tells you all about the snakes and spiders and tics that are around you when you're in camp in the jungle. I wasn't sure how seriously to take that. I'd always told myself that if it's on TV, there can't be anything that really hurts you. Now I started to wonder a little bit.

I met up with all the other contestants. There was Jorgie Porter, the former *Hollyoaks* actress, the *Dragons' Den* guy, Duncan Bannatyne, the *Geordie Shore* star, Vicky Pattison, a pop star, George Shelley, Ferne McCann, from *The Only Way is Essex*, Tony Hadley, from Spandau Ballet, the boxer, Chris Eubank, and Lady Colin Campbell, the socialite we all knew as Lady C.

Lady C asked me straightaway if I was a footballer. She said she used to go out with an American footballer. 'When you climb Mount Everest,' she said, 'you never want to go back down.' She wasn't shy.

I got along with everybody on the show really. I liked Lady C and Chris Eubank in particular. I'm a huge boxing fan and Chris had always intrigued me. They say it's best not to meet your heroes, but Chris was one of mine and he was everything I thought he would be.

A lot of people were surprised that Lady C and I hit it off, but I'm close to my mum and even though she had a vicious tongue, Lady C was a motherly figure. Duncan and Tony took a dislike to her and that made me want to stick up for her even more, which soon became a source of conflict in the camp.

I didn't find the lack of food difficult. The worst thing for me was boredom. If you didn't do a bushtucker trial, you were in the camp all day with nothing to do. I found it hard not knowing what was going on in the outside world. I'm a child of the smartphone generation and I wanted to know the football results.

The only time I even got a hint of anything that was going on was when I saw Ant and Dec. They're both big Newcastle fans and I knew Ant reasonably well before I went on the show. So when I asked them how the Toon had got on, they'd give me the thumbs up or, more often, the thumbs down.

I did quite a few of the bushtucker trials. They were a lot of fun, a great adrenaline rush. I liked the pressure of having to get stars for your teammates. On one trial, there were snakes in a box and I had to unscrew a star with my teeth with a snake staring straight at me. I knew my kids would be watching, so not doing it wasn't an option.

The only one I found marginally scary was when I had to try to grab a star from round an emu's neck. Just before I went into that room, Dr Bob had said that I mustn't run in there so I knew there was something slightly dangerous. That emu was massive. You know that the spiders and the snakes aren't going to bite you, but the emu was a big bird. It looked like it could do you some serious damage.

The tension between Lady C and Tony and Duncan started to become a big problem. One day, Duncan was trying to get to sleep and Lady C was chewing my ear about what bastards they were and I was trying to tell her to chill out a bit. Duncan had a go at me and said I was making it worse.

I didn't want to disrespect Duncan. He was an older man and I had made my mind up that I was going to do my best to be respectful and kind in the camp, whatever happened. I wanted to do what was right for the camp, but the angst in there was starting to get to me and it didn't seem like fun any more.

I broke down and said I wanted to leave. I thought it was wrong that people were ganging up on Lady C. They were sending someone to come and get me out when I woke Chris up to say goodbye. Chris said I was doing the wrong thing. He reminded me that I'd always said I was doing this to make my kids proud and asked me what message it would send to them if they saw me quitting like this.

He was right. I decided to stick around. I thought I might be voted out early anyway when the public began to make their choices. To tell the truth, I thought I'd be hated. I thought the viewers would rush to get rid of me. I had a reputation as a spoilt brat, there had been all those stupid rumours about me burning money in nightclubs when I was younger and I was the one who was blamed for the fall of Sir Bobby Robson. I didn't think people would exactly take to me.

I was surprised when Chris was voted out. I thought he was pure entertainment. Sometimes, it's just the way the show's edited. That's one of the things you have to consent to when you sign up for the show: they can edit it how they want. You're at their mercy, really. That's fine. Those are the rules and you play by them.

I got to the penultimate day. By that stage, I'd begun to wonder if I was actually going to win, so I was a bit gutted. But I finished fourth and I'd stayed in far longer than I ever thought I would. The disappointment didn't last anyway. It disappeared as soon as I saw my wife again.

I turned my phone on and I had hundreds of messages from friends and family saying how well I'd done and how well I'd handled myself. There was one from Jonathan Woodgate. 'My friends were convinced you were a twat,' he had written, 'but now they can't believe what a good fella you are.'

In its own way, that was pretty nice. I felt pleased that there must be more people out there who had once thought I was a brash idiot who now had a more balanced, more positive view of what I was really like. Whoever you are, it's nice if people think you're a decent person.

I went to get weighed and I'd lost more than a stone. There's not a lot of meat on me anyway so you can imagine how I must have appeared. Bear in mind we hadn't seen each other for a month, but when I took my clothes off to get in the shower, my missus said: 'I don't want to be rude, but could you put your clothes back on, you look like Skeletor.'

The kids were happy when I got back. They'd loved it. That was all I'd wanted out of it, so that made me feel good. I had a lot of offers to do other television work, but I wasn't interested. A lot of people go on that show to revive their careers, but that didn't apply to me. I just wanted to go back to being happily retired.

And that's what I am. I'm not a footballer any longer and I still don't miss it. I'm lucky that I'm still involved in the game. I work with the Under-16s at Ipswich Town and I'm studying for my Uefa A Licence. The club have been great with me. There's a pathway mapped out for me if I do well, so we'll see.

Craig Bellamy and I are still great mates. If he gets a manager's job, maybe I'll go and be his assistant. I'll be the good cop to his great dictator. Can you imagine the pair of us telling players how to behave? We could certainly tell them that we know the pitfalls.

I might have got smart too late in my football career, but I wised up just in time in real life. I've got four great kids and Hollie has got two lovely daughters, and every other weekend, we're one big family of eight and every other weekend, it's just the two of us.

Actually, I'm getting carried away a bit there. Every other weekend, we're one big family of seven. Kie is 17 now, so he is too cool to be rocking around with us. It's true what they say about time moving on fast.

Sometimes, I think back to the way I used to be when I was with a partner. It was never enough. If we were on holiday, I'd want to go and meet up with other people or just go out by myself or with the lads. I could never go away with anyone for longer than a week.

Now, if people ring me up when I'm with Hollie and ask me if I want to join them, it's different. 'No,' I say, 'I'm staying here. I'm happy where I am.'

## ACKNOWLEDGEMENTS

I'd like to say a few thank yous.

To David and Jonathan – you are the best agents in the world but I never classed you as my agents, just two of my best friends.

To Bryan Klug – I have had a lot of coaches in my life, right through from the age of 10 to when I played the last game of my career at Middlesbrough, but you were the best and the most important coach I ever had and you were a major reason why I became the player I was.

To Oliver Holt – you were one of the few journalists who used to give me a fair shake and I always appreciated that. I'm so glad you have helped me tell this story.

To Nev, Milo and Leechie – you are my brothers from another mother.

To Spoony – we became really close twelve years ago and you were the first friend who wasn't afraid to lay down the law to me and not care about my status. It was no coincidence I started to mature as a person from that point. Why couldn't we have been close a few years before that?

To Craig – what a rollercoaster ride we had as players. I know your ride is still going. You're going to be a great manager one day.

To the mother of my three boys – I want to respect your wish not to be named in my book but I also want to thank you for giving me the great gift of our three boys. You have been a truly amazing mother and that is reflected in the people our sons have become.

To Zoe – you are the strongest and most determined person I have ever come across. You inspire me and I hope our princess turns out just like you.

To Kirsha – you have turned your life around and I'm so proud of you for that.

To Marlee and Meeya – I'm lucky that your mum brought you into my life. You have completed my family.

To Mum – you are my hero. No amount of words will ever quite do justice to what you have done for me but hopefully my actions have shown you.

To Hollie – you came into my life when it was at its lowest point and I am now happier than I have ever been. That is all because of you. I'm the luckiest guy in the world to have you in my life.

# INDEX

Getty Images: p. 3, below right (Martyn Harrison/AFP), p. 4, above left (Matthew Lewis), p. 4, above right & centre (Laurence Griffiths), p. 4, below (Alex Livesey), p. 5, centre (Michael Steele), p. 5, below (Stu Forster), p. 6, above left (Laurence Griffiths), p. 6, centre (Ben Radford/Allsport), p. 6, below right (Gary M. Prior/Allsport), p. 7, centre (David Cannon), p. 7, below (Ross Kinnaird)

PA Images: p. 2, centre right (Neal Simpson/EMPICS Sport), p. 2, centre left & below (Steve Mitchell/EMPICS Sport), p. 3, above left (John Giles/ PA Archive), p. 3, above right (Jon Buckle/EMPICS Sport), p. 3, below left (Chris Ison/PA Archive), p. 5, above (Nick Potts/PA Archive), p. 7, above (Owen Humphreys/PA Archive)

REX/Shutterstock: p. 8, above right (Nigel Wright/ITV)

All other photographs from author's personal collection.

ROI KILL O' IHEGRANGE9712  RECORD 7516

12/08/22     11:02

A0000000031010
VISA DEBIT
****1660

CASH EUR 200.00

YOUR BALANCE IS EUR 50,829.63